T0004363

Macron Unveiled

The Prototype for a New Generation of World Leaders

Alain Lefebvre

Macron Unveiled

The Prototype for a New Generation of World Leaders

With a preface by Michael Pembroke

GAUDIUM

Gaudium Publishing

Las Vegas ◊ Chicago ◊ Palm Beach

Published in the United States of America by
Histria Books
7181 N. Hualapai Way, Ste. 130-86
Las Vegas, NV 89166 U.S.A
HistriaBooks.com

Gaudium Publishing is an imprint of Histria Books. Titles published under the imprints of Histria Books are distributed worldwide.

Library of Congress Control Number: 2021953218

ISBN 978-1-59211-145-9 (hardcover)
ISBN 978-1-59211-211-1 (softbound)
ISBN 978-1-59211-260-9 (eBook)

Contents

Introduction

Emmanuel Macron knows that the world of the twenty-first century is changing with unforeseen rapidity. From the start of his presidency, Macron's strategic independence was evident. The first head of state that he invited to France for an official visit was President Putin. And Europe is central to Macron's vision of an effective multilateral world order. In this respect, he exhibits similarities to Charles de Gaulle, who challenged American hegemony within NATO and strived to make France an independent European power. Macron is more diplomatic, more nuanced, and more modern, but like de Gaulle, he aspires to make France an independent, humanist, European power; one that is a global force for good within the limits of its ability and influence, without unrealistic objectives, without overreach, without making the mistake of trying to solve all the world's problems.

The United States' recent ignominious withdrawal from Afghanistan — after 20 years and almost $3 trillion in expenditure — was a watershed moment in history, one that will not be lost on Emmanuel Macron. The American failure in Afghanistan serves to reinforce the overwhelming lesson of the past 75 years since World War II, that military solutions are rarely if ever a successful long-term answer to political conflicts, even when there is short-term success. The use of military means to make other sovereign regimes, foreign cultures, and different civilizations conform to a particular world view — whether under the guise of spreading democracy or dressed up as nation-building or masquerading as a force for common good — never was, and never could be justified. Macron knows that too.

Shortly after his election, he took an early and emphatic stand on the U.S.-led offensives against Iraq and Libya, stating that: "Democracy is not built from the outside without the support of the people. France did not participate in the war in Iraq, and it was right. And it was wrong to wage war in this way in Libya."

Few would now doubt the wisdom of Macron's position on the conflicts in Iraq and Syria. Democracy may be the most desirable form of government but it cannot be 'imposed' from the outside, let alone by military force. And it is not necessarily practicable or appropriate for every country. The variety and diversity of the world's cultures, political systems, and civilizations defy ready categorization, let alone simplistic ones. Many political systems and forms of government may not meet our approval. Some are positively distasteful; others egregious; a few iniquitous. And many forms of folly and malevolence masquerade as democracies; while many authoritarian regimes are benign and others far less so. There are no simple solutions. Emmanuel Macron understands that.

After decades of American unilateralism culminating with President Trump's 'America First' mantra, France and Germany, guided by President Macron and Chancellor Merkel respectively, have been active in promoting the return of a multilateral world order, based on a framework of international cooperation underpinned by strong and effective institutions, in which Europe plays a key role. In Macron's vision of a future world order, the best guarantee of global security and prosperity is a multilateral rules-based order, not exclusively a U.S.-led rules based order. For Macron, one consequence of the diminution of the power, prestige, and authority of the United States is the need for a strengthening of international institutions and increased global cooperation. In the new and unfolding world after Afghanistan,

American power and influence will remain significant, although not as pervasive or pre-eminent as it has been, while the European Union, Russia, China, and the United Nations Security Council will also be important cornerstones of a multilateral world order. The European Union, China, and Russia are all working, for example, on ways of challenging the primacy of the U.S. dollar as the world's dominant reserve currency, including, in the cases of China and Russia, on the adoption of new financial instruments and digital currencies.

The recent diplomatic contribution of France in the war-ravaged Middle East, provides another insight into how the future might look when there is a lighter American footprint. As the United States military presence in Afghanistan, Iraq, and Syria ends or is reduced, diplomacy is returning. The recent Baghdad Conference for Cooperation & Partnership hosted by Iraq — which Macron was instrumental in organizing — was a remarkable historic victory in itself. America was not invited to the table. The conference brought together friends and foes: Iran and its sometime enemy Saudi Arabia; Qatar and its recent adversaries the UAE, Egypt and Kuwait; as well as Turkey and Jordan. All participants agreed to support Iraq in preserving security, reconstruction, and economic reform and stressed the necessity for regional cooperation in dealing with common challenges. King Abdullah of Jordan noted that Iraq was the priority of all participants. The conference — for which Macron can take much credit — was a significant step for Iraq towards a post-American era in the region.

Similarly, European Union diplomacy, especially from France and Germany, has been instrumental in maintaining engagement with Iran — despite Washington's vilification of Iran, the painful provocation caused by the unilateral withdrawal of the United States from the nuclear deal, its re-imposition of sanctions, and its assassination of Iranian General Qasem Suleimani. On this issue as well, Macron has placed France at the center of the negotiations. The European efforts are providing a bridge for U.S.-Iranian re-engagement, which may regrettably still come to nothing given the bitterness of some hardliners in the Iranian regime. But the prospect of normalized economic relations with Europe provides an incentive for Iran to commit to some form of reconstituted deal limiting its nuclear weapons aspirations. France is playing an indispensable role.

In relations with China also, Macron has shown pragmatic leadership in contrast to the binary and often antagonistic approach of the United States. Europe has its disputes with China — currently reflected in subsisting mutual sanctions — but France and Germany in particular are careful to avoid demonizing China. President Macron has warned that 'ganging up on China' would be 'counterproductive' and that it is necessary to 'find the right way to engage'. The ratification of the China-E.U. trade treaty is currently on hold but each is the other's largest trading partner and analysts believe that the agreement will eventually come into force. An economic resolution between China and Europe seems more likely than any resolution with America.

When necessary, Macron is realistic and firm with China. He is not afraid to criticize Beijing but he avoids unnecessary confrontation. His forceful response to the constant clamor for action over the treatment of Uighurs in Xinjiang, was icily direct: "I am not going to start a war with China on this subject." The Uighur issue is a troubling domestic question, unique to China, that arises inside a sovereign country. Macron knows that there are other ways of attempting to influence China's behavior. He also knows that it is a mistake to conflate moral issues with strategic concerns; and that human rights abuses and moral objections to them do not provide a legitimate basis for invasion and war.

In the Indo-Pacific, Macron has grand ambitions. France was once a colonial power in the region and Macron clearly aspires to increase its strategic presence there in the future. In fact, France was the first

European Union country to embrace the 'Indo-Pacific' concept in 2018. By 2021, the French Navy's operational activity in the region had become particularly intense. Macron wants France to be a mediating, inclusive, and stabilizing Indo-Pacific power, striking an equilibrium between the importance of balancing against China with the need to avoid an escalatory posture towards Beijing; promoting a stable, law-based, multipolar order in the region, and not one solely focused on America's perceived security interests. France's Indo-Pacific stretches from Djibouti on the Horn of Africa to Polynesia in the South Pacific and covers a larger area than that over which the United States seeks to extend its influence. Through France's extensive territorial presence, its growing naval projection capabilities, and its active diplomatic engagement, Macron seeks to make France a committed regional actor and a moderating force that serves as a bridge to Europe.

Diplomatic engagement is key. In France's relations with the major powers, it seeks balance, not uncritical ideological alignment with anyone. Under Macron, France is a friend and ally of the United States but will not allow itself to be systematically aligned with Washington on all issues regardless of the subject matter. Macron is however on good terms with President Biden and shares much of his outlook. His preference is to deal with all parties rather than to slavishly support one of them. In general, Emmanuel Macron's personal disposition is towards accommodation over confrontation, negotiated solutions to ultimatums, and diplomacy to war. He does not have that cast of mind that defines international reality as basically military and which tends to discount the likelihood of finding a solution except through military means. Yet when the circumstances require it, he has acted, and has shown he will act, firmly. His stated choice is to enforce red lines when they are set, which occurred when France joined the coalition airstrikes directed at Syria's clandestine chemical arsenal.

Emmanuel Macron is nothing if not clear-eyed. Fundamentally, he is a pragmatist — a non-ideological political leader, influenced by the values of the Enlightenment, who eschews a binary approach to international relations. Americans tend to hunger for a simple storyline with heroes and villains. But such thinking — good (us) versus evil (them) — is the antithesis of Macron's way of dealing with foreign states and leaders. He understands better than Washington has historically demonstrated, the need for consensus, the importance of pragmatism and the desirability of being willing to compromise. Macron's language is that of diplomacy and negotiated solutions in preference to military responses. And he adds a certain idealism to his realistic pragmatism, reflecting to some extent the romanticism of Charles de Gaulle, who famously said that France's vocation since 1789 has been "to serve the cause of man, the cause of freedom, the cause of human dignity." It is a refreshing change.

Macron's younger, more modern, more independent, perspective is evident in other ways as well. He has positioned France to be a global champion in the fight against climate change. And he has opened the Palace of Versailles, which has traditionally been used for the most important state visits by the kings, popes, emperors and tsars of yesteryear, to a cavalcade of business leaders from the world's most significant Asian, American, and European companies. The CEOs of Coca-Cola, Netflix, Google, Hyundai, Samsung, Toyota, Cooper Pharma, Rolls Royce, and many others have all been welcomed. Perhaps partly as a result, France was the most attractive European country for investors in both 2019 and 2020.

In the domestic arena, Emmanuel Macron has made no secret of his admiration for the Swedish model as a means of achieving both economic prosperity and social justice. Success has been harder to achieve in practice given the nature of French politics and the disruption caused by the Covid-19 pandemic, but during his presidential campaign, references to Sweden and the Nordic model were a recurrent theme in Macron's speeches. He was in good company. Franklin Delano Roosevelt often cited Sweden as a model to be admired — "a royal family, a socialist government and a capitalist system all working side by side" in a system that maintains a well-functioning market economy and private ownership while ensuring an equitable redistribution of wealth.

A key feature of the Nordic model is pragmatism, combined with transparency and a certain tough-mindedness. Through his policies and actions, Macron has exhibited similar characteristics. They have helped to contribute to his position as the first French political leader who is independent of the policies and ideologies of both the left and the conservative side of politics. In fact, Macron's pragmatism is his main argument, his most important weapon, and his greatest distinguishing feature. It is a mark of his independence from the entrenched and dogmatic left/right divide in France and it is the reason for his independence — where necessary — from Washington and London in international relations.

Emmanuel Macron is a lesson for the rest of the world. He is a student of philosophy who believes in the importance of pragmatism in dealing with conflicts, especially in international relations. Pragmatism, as a philosophical concept, is the antithesis of an ideological approach to the resolution of conflicts. An ideological approach lies behind the ascendant American attitude to China — advocating that the United States and its allies engage in a great Manichean struggle with China that will define the next century. Former Secretary of State, Mike Pompeo, described it as a conflict "between tyranny and freedom." President Biden sees it as a struggle between authoritarianism and democracy. It should be nothing of the sort. Macron understands that.

After Afghanistan, America's next crisis is China. A pragmatic approach to China involves recognition that the satisfactory resolution of the disputes and differences with China requires a mutual accommodation that permits all affected parties to coexist in relative peace and prosperity, despite those differences. Conflict with China is not a zero-sum game. Unlike the former Soviet Union, China does not threaten to attack or invade the American homeland. Nor does it seek to export its ideology or system of government — Taiwan being a notable historical exception. Many, perhaps most, differences with China will never be resolved. But there are many areas that are ripe for cooperation between China and the United States, and many areas where their economic and technological competition can only advance the interests of humanity. President Macron's pragmatism provides a model. If he is re-elected for a further five-year term in 2022, Macron's friendship and influence might just steer President Biden in the right direction. The world wants accommodation between China and the United States, not confrontation. Macron's story is fascinating. He is a man of the times.

Michael Pembroke

Author of *America in Retreat* (2021) and
Korea-Where the American Century Began (2018)

Chapter 1
Seduction

On the 2nd of June, 2017, a young French president, sworn in several days before, released a video criticizing and mocking Donald Trump, the president of the United States of America. In this video, he explained why the U.S.'s decision to withdraw from the United Nations' Paris Agreement on climate change was a mistake and finished with "Let's make the planet great again." It was a parody of Donald Trump's campaign slogan, "Make America Great Again," and certainly not the best way to initiate a friendly relationship with the American president.

To European viewers, this video triggered memories of another parody targeting President Trump's motto, "America First." Humorists from The Netherlands' *Zondag Met Lubach* late-night show launched the "Who wants to be second?" video campaign in January 2017. The satirical promotional video mockingly appealed to Mr. Trump, urging him to declare the Netherlands second, after America. Soon after, an online group called "Every Second Counts" invited satirists worldwide to produce similar videos proving their countries deserved second place. The campaign went viral — hundreds of videos were made, some of them seen by more than 215 million viewers.

So when Emmanuel Jean-Michel Frédéric Macron used another of Trump's slogans to attack the American president's decision to withdraw from the Paris Agreement, it was a bold and dangerous move from a beginner without any experience in international relations, even if it improved Macron's reputation with green activists.

Things were already bad between Macron and Trump. Just days before, at the G7 Summit, White House pool reporter Philip Rucker described their handshake as a tense affair, writing, "Each president gripped the other's hand with considerable intensity, their knuckles turning white and their jaws clenching and their faces tightening." It was a moment during which everyone present felt awkward — until Trump loosened his fingers. Trump, known for a bizarrely long and domineering handshaking style, had already trapped Japan's prime minister, Shinzo Abe, in a marathon nineteen-second handshake but was not the winner in his encounter with Macron.

There were other incidents of tension between the two men during that summit, for instance, when Trump allegedly tried to prevent Macron from bypassing him to say hello first to German Chancellor Angela Merkel.

It may not have been notable, except that Macron spoke about the handshake in the French press, explaining that "My handshake with him is not innocent, it was... a moment of truth. We must show that we will not make small concessions." It did not go over well with Donald Trump. According to the *Washington Post*, who quoted unnamed White House aides, Macron's words "irritated and bewildered" the U.S. president.

Relations between the men seemed to go from bad to worse when Arnold Schwarzenegger posted a short video on Twitter where he, along with Macron, took jabs at President Trump, again using the slogan, "Let's make the planet great again." The ten-second clip runs for its entire duration with the caption: "With President Macron, a great leader!" something that certainly did not make the American president happy.

Yet, less than three weeks later, on the 14th of July, a miracle happened. Donald Trump accepted Macron's invitation to participate in the French National Day Parade to commemorate the centenary of the United States' entry into the First World War. On the first day, a smiling Donald Trump declared that Paris was "one of the most beautiful cities in the world" and intended to return there. He added, with Macron smiling near him, "Everything will be all right, your president is tough, and he is not someone who will be let down or be tolerant of outlaws." At the event, Trump was beaming, frequently on his feet and applauding the French troops, tanks, and fighter jets. White House observers stated that it was the happiest they had seen the American president in months.

At the end of the visit, the BBC reported that an unlikely friendship had been born. This friendship was communicated through speeches — after all, the two are politicians — and physical gestures. Trump often put his hand on Macron's shoulder. Another time, Macron placed his hand on Trump's back. The two men shook hands frequently during the visit. At a press conference, the American president declared: "France is America's first and oldest ally. Many people don't know that [...] It was a long time ago, but we are together. And I think together, perhaps, more so than ever. The relationship is particularly good."

For Emmanuel Macron, it was a big win, even though Donald Trump was not popular with the French people. Macron was the first ally Trump found among the foremost European leaders. The American president did not seem very interested in a "special relationship" with the United Kingdom, and his relationship with German Chancellor Angela Merkel was tense.

This explains why Emmanuel Macron was the first head of state invited to the U.S. for a state visit — a visit where, according to NBC News, "President Donald Trump and his French counterpart Emmanuel Macron put their warm bromance on full public display...

engaging in frequent personal displays of affection at the White House that revealed how friendly they had grown since a tense meeting last spring."

After this peak of what journalists called a "honeymoon," the same scenario played out repeatedly: everybody expected a clash between the two presidents before they met, but only positive meetings and exchanges followed.

For example, in November 2018, Macron pushed for creating a European army. Mistaken by a bad transcription of an interview, Donald Trump (who was en route to Paris) posted the following tweet: "Emmanuel Macron suggests building its own army to protect Europe against the U.S., China, and Russia. But it was Germany in World Wars One & Two — How did that work out for France? They were starting to learn German in Paris before the U.S. came along. Pay for NATO or not!"

The two presidents then met in Paris, where Macron explained that his declaration was a push to increase Europe's participation in the continent's defense. A happy Trump tweeted: "I appreciate what you are saying about burden-sharing." The relationship was saved until the next tweet.

A more serious incident happened toward the end of 2019. During the previous months, Macron blocked the E.U.'s expansion into the Western Balkans, proposed stricter rules for participating in the E.U., and tried to develop the dialogue between Iran and the U.S. In an interview with the *Economist* in November 2019, he warned European countries that they could no longer rely on America to defend NATO allies, adding, "What we are currently experiencing is the brain death of NATO." He stressed what he saw as a waning commitment from its biggest guarantor — the U.S. — and criticized the U.S. for not consulting NATO before pulling forces out of northern Syria. He explained that Europe stands on "the edge of a precipice" and should start thinking strategically as a geopolitical power, or it would no longer be in control of its destiny.

These comments did not go over well with Donald Trump.

During NATO's seventieth anniversary summit, held in London at the beginning of December, President Trump complained that the French leader had been "very disrespectful" to other alliance members. He added, "It is a very, very nasty statement. I think they have a very high unemployment rate in France. France is not doing well economically at all... It is a very tough statement to make when you have such difficulty in France when you look at what is going on. They have had a very rough year. You just can't go around making statements like that about NATO. It is very disrespectful."

The situation worsened when Paris approved a levy on up to 3 percent of revenues earned by digital technology companies in France. International efforts had failed to find a new model for taxing revenues earned through online sales and advertising. Technological companies often paid little tax in countries where they have no physical presence, even though they generate significant income. Washington said the tax singled out U.S. companies such as Google, Apple, Facebook, Amazon, and Netflix and threatened retaliatory import duties of up to 100 percent on French cheeses, yogurt, sparkling wine, handbags, and cosmetic products.

According to journalists, President Trump arrived at the NATO summit in London in a fighting mood, and his target was President Macron. Journalists prepared for the clash of the year.

And here are the first words of President Trump when meeting the press after twenty-five minutes with Macron: "It's great to be with President Macron of France. And we have had a fairly long relationship and a very good one... And we will be talking about a lot of things, including NATO, and including trade. We do a lot of trade with France, and we have a minor dispute. I think we will probably be able to work it out. But we have a big trade relationship, and I am sure that, within a short period of time, things will be looking very rosy, we hope. And that is usually the case with the two of us. We get it worked out. We have had a lot of good — a lot of good things. We have done a lot of good things together, as partners."

It was not the expected bloodbath, and Trump was right: even though there are still unresolved problems, the men agreed to make changes to NATO.

If we look at the long-term relationship between the two men, President Trump summarized it quite well in the summer of 2019: "We've been friends for a long time. And every once in a while, we go at it just a little bit — not very much. But we get along very well. We have a very good relationship — sort of, I think I can say, a special relationship."

But how does that working relationship — and some element of a friendship — characterize the relationship between two leaders who are so different? And what does it say about Emmanuel Macron?

Some theorized that the leaders bonded because they were dark horses — elected against all odds. That may be correct. One year before the election, nobody took either of them seriously. In the U.S., Chris Cillizza from the *Washington Post* ranked the top ten Republican candidates for the nomination on the 10th of May, 2015, without mentioning Donald Trump. When Donald Trump announced his candidacy on the 16th of June, almost nobody believed he would actually run, and the idea of him winning seemed laughable. Nearly everyone thought it was a publicity stunt.

The same goes for Macron. On the 16th of November, 2016, six months before the election, Emmanuel Macron was thirty-nine years old, had never been elected before, and yet was a candidate to become the next French president. Contrary to his predecessors, Macron was neither a leader nor a member of any of the main political parties. A leader of the Socialist Party said in *Le Monde*[1] something that everybody thought in France: "Macron will learn that, in this old country called France, one cannot be elected President of the Republic without a strong political apparatus, or important support in the regions." Macron, though popular, was lagging in the polls in the third or fourth positions during the first round of the election. It seemed unlikely he'd have any chance to go to the second and last round, where only the first two candidates could participate. He also made several mistakes during his campaign.

Yet, he won.

When Macron met Trump for the first time, there was no sign that the fact that Trump and Macron were, as some American media put it, "two political mavericks" could compensate for their differences. Donald Trump supported Macron's populist rival, Marine Le Pen, and Macron received last-minute endorsements from former U.S. President Barrack Obama.

Trump and Macron were so different that nobody had expected anything like friendship, let alone "bromance." How did it happen? Why did Emmanuel Macron — a man of culture, a philosopher who wrote his doctoral dissertation on the German philosopher Hegel, a modern leader fighting for human rights — push to develop a closer relationship than was strictly necessary with Donald Trump, a man who supported his opponent, was negatively perceived by 82 percent of the French, and seemed more interested in business than in philosophy and culture?

Macron is not the first French president to try to earn a privileged relationship with their American counterpart. The U.S. is considered the world leader, so it is expected (and strategically advantageous) that the president of an allied country attempts to befriend U.S. leadership.

Previous French presidents — Nicolas Sarkozy and François Hollande — had tried to develop good personal relationships with their American colleagues, but they were unsuccessful.

From the 2nd to the 18th of August, 2007, just weeks after his election, Nicolas Sarkozy decided to take a vacation in Wolfeboro, New Hampshire. He pushed to get an invitation from President George W. Bush, whose family's summer residence was in Kennebunkport, Maine, just a hundred kilometers from Wolfeboro. The American president agreed to invite the new French president and his family to an informal family picnic at his retreat. Sarkozy arrived forty-five minutes late, and his wife was unexpectedly absent, blaming a severe throat ailment that prevented her from making the one-hour trip from the Sarkozy's' rented villa. However, she was seen the days before and after the picnic shopping with friends. It was not the best way for a French President to develop a personal relationship with his American counterpart. Even at a professional level, President Sarkozy, who was not a born diplomat, has not been successful: at the 34th G8 summit held in Japan in July 2008, the two presidents had a fierce dispute that began a period of strained relations between France and the United States.

Later, the relationship between President Obama and President Hollande was initially good, but without the apparent warmth between Trump and Macron. However, when a disagreement arose about the military intervention against the Syrian president, Bashar al-Assad, that personal relationship could not bridge the gap. Bitter, President Hollande even declared in 2014: "The Americans, whatever they do, are arrogant. Always. Even in their mistakes, finally."[2] Like Sarkozy, he was not the perfect diplomat.

Macron's interest in fostering positive relationships with U.S. leadership was about more than demonstrating that he's among the world's leaders. His objective seemed to be securing Trump's participation; getting the U.S. back into the Paris Agreement, and perhaps changing Trump's negative opinions about multilateralism. It was also about love — a 250-year-long love story between France and the United States of America.

Such a statement seems exaggerated. After all, depending on circumstances and leaders, there have been variations in the opinions of French people about U.S. politics. It is fair to say relations haven't always been positive between two countries: in September 2018, only 44 percent of the French surveyed considered the U.S. a reliable ally, a significant drop from the last survey taken during the Obama administration (77 percent), just above that of India (41 percent), and surprisingly, not much above China (32 percent).[3] Only 20 percent of the French people surveyed approved of U.S. policy. But, at the same time, 73 percent of respondents said they still have friendly feelings toward Americans, and 82 percent declared that it is important that France maintains a strong relationship with the U.S. French people may have disapproved of Trump's policies and disliked him personally, but they still appreciated the United States and its citizens.

Where does this appreciation come from? Historians on both sides of the Atlantic have tried to analyze the evolution of the relationship between old France and young America. On the French side, as stated by the American historian Durand Echeverria, "...whenever the American image could serve as a symbol for a policy which visibly contrasted with that of the French regime in power, it aroused a vogue of Americanism among members of opposition parties. But, when the contrast between the French and the American regimes was reduced to a minimum, or when this contrast was not clear, this situation gave rise to anti-Americanism. What is more, these political attitudes had, as a side effect, the power to distort, for good or bad, the idea that the French had of American society and culture."[4]

That is the historical analysis, but one cannot understand France's relationship without knowing the life and deeds of Franco-American hero Marquis de Lafayette. He is undoubtedly considered a hero in the U.S., but French people also know about him and his role in the American Revolution.

It is also true for French Presidents. At his picnic with George W. Bush, Sarkozy declared, "I just finished reading a biography of Lafayette, and I wanted to tell President Bush about that. The U.S. and France have been allies and friends for 250 years. At the birth of the United States, France chose the side of the U.S."

It is also not a surprise that, at his first official visit in Washington as the new president of France, Francois Hollande emphasized during the press conference that, "We were allies in the time of Jefferson and Lafayette, we are indeed still allies today. We were friends in the time of Jefferson and Lafayette, and we will remain friends forever."

In the French version of Wikipedia, the article about Lafayette is much longer than the one about French president de Gaulle, France's hero. And video gamers have discovered Lafayette as one of the main characters of the popular title *Assassin's Creed III*. History lives.

The story of Lafayette, the American Revolution, and the French Revolution was the first building block for the special relationship between France and the United States and is certainly known by Macron, a keen reader of political history. Lafayette, a French aristocrat and a military officer, fought in the American Revolutionary War. He is a romantic figure: officer of the musketeers at age thirteen, a general in the U.S. at age nineteen, and a friend of George Washington, commanding both French and American troops in several victories, including decisive battles for American independence.

For a French mind, the Marquis de Lafayette is fascinating. He lost his father at age two, his mother at twelve, and married at age sixteen. He was bored at the king's court, where he was not particularly popular because, according to his own words, he was too awkward "to bend to the graces of the court or the charms of a supper in the capital." After hearing of the American Revolution, he bought a ship, and against the king's official orders, went to America where George Washington saw his potential, adopted him as a surrogate son, and gave him significant responsibilities in the American army.

The description of Lafayette in *Washington: A Life* by Ron Chernow could also apply to Emmanuel Macron: "florid language," "poetic effusion," "transparent ambition," "panting for glory," "canine appetite for popularity and fame," "amiable, polite, affable," "very conciliatory temper" ... Lafayette "was a master of flattery and liked to hug people in the French manner."[5] The resemblances with Macron are striking, but they stop there — Macron does not seem to share in Lafayette's "uncommon military talent" described by George Washington.

The story continues with France supporting Lafayette's ideas, sending weapons and an army to support the American Revolution, and helping to create the United States of America. As is usual in politics, the reality is that France did not exactly support the Americans in the Revolutionary War out of pure, altruistic kindness, even if there was an element of idealism.

Since the sixteenth century, the French monarchy had been involved closely in colonizing the North American continent. Colonization efforts began with Quebec and Louisiana; in the eighteenth century, French settlements were created in Florida, Michigan, and along the Mississippi River. The development of the French colonial empire in America, called Nouvelle-France, ended with the Treaty of Paris in 1763 after being defeated by the British. Nouvelle-France disappeared.

Revenge against the British was undoubtedly a leading element in the French decision to support America, but it was not just about revenge. Before the start of the French Revolution in 1789, the French felt sympathy for what was happening to America. Additionally, French economists, philosophers, and revolutionaries believed that

America could be (to use French economist and politician Turgot's words) "the hope of mankind."[6] They theorized that the nation could serve as a laboratory for experimenting with social programs that Europe could later implement.

That is ultimately why the French government decided to support the American Revolution, with the false accounts disseminated about America's military prowess and readiness for the war. Benjamin Franklin, then the U.S. Ambassador in Paris, was primarily responsible for the false reports that the American army was strong enough to crush the British alone, and that it was well-equipped. In reality, the American military was not strong enough to defeat the British, and it lacked weapons, ammunition, and even basic supplies. France's involvement cost a fortune and ruined its economy, leading to the French Revolution in 1789.

Aside from Lafayette's and France's roles in the American Revolution, a singular fact may partly explain the special relationship between the nations: even if the two countries have been rivals, they have never been adversaries in a war. There were tensions during the reign of Emperor Napoleon III, who favored the Confederacy. But the French emperor was removed in 1870 after the Franco-Prussian War. The small local American community led by the U.S. Ambassador to France provided such successful medical, humanitarian, and diplomatic support to Paris' people during the troubles in France that America gained much credit. World Wars I and II have reinforced the French affection toward the U.S. The image of U.S. soldiers distributing chocolate bars to French children while traversing France in 1944 is still now part of French folklore, films, and history books.

When Emmanuel Macron invited Donald Trump to Paris, he likely had this shared history in mind. He almost certainly had America's contributions to the culture and the arts in mind — an important topic for a president who declared, "There is nothing I love more than literature."[7] After all, France and the United States of America have more Nobel prize-winning writers than any other nation. It may have had more of an impact on Macron than the economic and military might of the United States.

However, Macron "invested significant amounts of time and political capital in trying to establish a relationship with Trump since coming to power in Paris in May 2017."[8] He probably thought he could develop a working relationship with Donald Trump because of his exceptional gift of achieve his objectives by charming and seducing anybody in a face-to-face meeting. Macron has a reputation for using his charisma to develop his career, befriend influential people, and promote his ideas. Anne Fulda, a French journalist and Macron's biographer, devoted an entire chapter to Macron's seductive abilities.[9] She details how Macron built his career by developing relations with French leaders in business and politics, and used their influence to emerge as a leader in the French political landscape without having ever been elected.

Emmanuel Macron can charm almost anybody. The French writer Emmanuel Carrère spent a week following the new president in September 2017, a few months after his election, during an official visit to the island of Saint Martin, a French territory in the Caribbean that had been devastated a few days earlier by Hurricane Irma. In an article written for the *Guardian*,[10] Carrère describes Macron's technique: "Every interaction with Macron follows the same protocol. He turns his penetrating blue eyes on you and does not look away. As for your hand, he shakes it in two stages: first a normal grip, and then, as if to show that this was no ordinary, routine handshake, he increases the pressure while at the same time intensifying his gaze [...] Then, with his other hand, he clasps your arm or shoulder, and when the time comes to move on, he relaxes his grip while lingering almost regretfully, as if pained to cut short an encounter that meant so much to him. This technique works wonders with his admirers, but it is even more spectacular with his enemies."

On the 14th of July, 2020, Macron demonstrated his exceptional ability to charm his opponents.[11] After the traditional French National Day parade and his solemn interview on French television, Macron took a walk with his wife and a small group of security officers in a part of Paris where the main events of the French Revolution happened. A party of Yellow Jackets, members of a French protest movement, were also there. They began to chant "Here we are" — the rallying cry of the Yellow Jackets — along with "Macron resignation" and "you're going to be fired." As the president and his wife tried to walk away, the protestors followed him, continuing their noisy chants.

Another president would have called for security to remove the protesters or escaped in the presidential car. Instead, Macron went to talk face-to-face with his opponents, telling them: "It's our national day. I'm going for a walk with my wife, and you disturb us. Be cool," he added, smiling. The tense atmosphere relaxed. Macron and the Yellow Jackets discussed their protests, and at the end, Macron's main opponent in the group was not convinced but concluded: "I cannot even hate him."[12] Macron answered, "That's for the best," and the presidential promenade continued without further interruption.

In addition to seduction, Macron is persistent and seldom takes "no" for an answer. It showed even during his early years when he studied piano. When he failed the entrance examination to a state academy of music because of one teacher, he insisted on having his test with the same teacher the following year. He has difficulties accepting that he cannot convince other people. From a psychological point of view, it may come from high self-esteem, which reinforces his power of seduction and makes him highly persuasive,

Has Macron been successful in developing beneficial relations with President Trump? Superficially, it certainly seems so, as the American president has treated France better than Germany, Canada, or the U.K. Macron was the first Head of State invited for an official visit to the U.S. The 2019 G7 meeting held in Biarritz, France went well, which had not been the case for the previous one in Canada. Macron and Trump have discussed without drama their occasional differences. But these positive results cannot hide the fact that there are limits to Macron's power of seduction. Despite Macron's best efforts to convince Donald Trump to do otherwise, the U.S. ultimately left the Paris Climate Accord and the Iran nuclear deal.

It worked better with President Vladimir Putin of Russia.

***

Macron invited President Putin to Paris for a first state visit in May, 2017, some weeks after his election, to show his respect for Russia and its president. It was also a high stakes visit for Putin, as he did not get many invitations to Western capitals. Just a year prior, French president Francois Hollande had refused Putin's visit to Paris to inaugurate the Russian Orthodox cathedral and the new Russian cultural center as a sanction against Putin's aggression toward Ukraine. Macron behaved with the Russian president differently, dramatizing the Kremlin's visit under the gold of the Palace of Versailles, where Russian tsars have been visiting French kings during the last centuries, winning Putin's approval.

But Macron has also been able to speak plainly to Putin; for instance, he recalled "the importance of subjects that affect our values and our public opinions, respect for all minorities and all sensitivities," stressing "the case of LGBT people in Chechnya as well as certain NGOs [...] For my part, I will be vigilant on these points which correspond to our values." Putin looked frustrated and lost, but he took it, and one year later, Macron's charm paid off: Putin invited Macron for a state visit to

Russia, including participation in the Petersburg International Economic Forum.

In 2019, before the G7 meeting in France, Macron invited Putin for a visit at the summer residence of French presidents, the Fort of Brégançon. The French newspaper, *Le Parisien*, described the pleasant and relaxed atmosphere between the two leaders: "It is 5:00 p.m., Vladimir Putin shows up at Fort de Brégançon, a bouquet in hand. Emmanuel and Brigitte Macron are waiting for him in the courtyard. Warm smiles, kisses, and handshakes... If it weren't for these hosts and their special guest, the place — the summer residence of French presidents — or the imposing security system (frigate offshore, filter barrages on the road), one would think that we are witnessing a reunion with friends. With an unusual smile on the lips, the Russian president congratulates the Macrons for 'their superb complexion,' and raves: 'It's a beautiful place!' The president reserves the highlight, the 360-degree sea view, for the bilateral meeting: a tour of the fort, between pines, oleanders, and olive trees, with a stopover at the belvedere, before a dinner in the garden, prepared by the head of the Elysée Palace. And as a gift, an original edition (signed by the author) of Turgenev's *New Muscovites!*"

That was a real surprise. In 2017, Putin had supported Macron's rival, populist Marine Le Pen, employing all the power of disinformation from different pro-Kremlin media operating in France for her, including what could have been a damaging story about his alleged homosexuality. In addition, state-funded *Russia Today* and *Sputnik* attacked Macron's marriage, writing that at the age of fifteen, he "was sexually abused by his teacher, who at the time was thirty-nine years old." and is now his wife, Brigitte. The same woman received Putin with a large smile some months later. And when Macron was elected, readers of the pro-Kremlin *Komsomolskaya Pravda* reported that France had elected "a psychopath." Two weeks later, Putin was in Paris when the French president declared: *"Russia Today* and *Sputnik* have been organs of influence and propaganda," and announced that they would be banned from any official accreditation by the French authorities. Yet, Macron was able to charm the Russian president, and the two seemed to develop good personal relations.

Macron's ability to connect with others has also impacted the European Union, creating unlikely alliances. Victor Orban, the Hungarian populist leader, announced a political tug-of-war on the sidelines, telling Macron that Europe's destiny would play out between the two of them, "the populist and the European." In October 2019, when the leaders met in Paris, there were clear signs of a good relationship between the men: Orban, obviously happy about the meeting, declared that Macron was "highly respected" in Hungary because he had "brought back the intellectual strength of debates about visions into European politics." Macron's charm prevailed again.

In December of the same year, Macron and Orban's alliance allowed them to shake the status quo during the E.U. election nominations, allowing Macron to impose practically all his choices. As explained by Daniel Hegedus, a fellow at the German Marshall Fund in Berlin, in *Star and Stripes* magazine on 11th of January 2020: "Orban and Macron come from very different places, but both seek to disrupt the status quo. There's now talk of an Orban-Macron axis in Europe."

Charisma is a strong asset for a president, and it can be advantageous, but is it dangerous to yield to Macron's charm?

People debate whether Macron's charm has an element of genuine empathy or is simply a tool he uses to manipulate others. In France, opponents explain how Emmanuel Macron uses seduction to develop his networks and reach objectives that oppose the French people's interests. And sometimes, it seems to include some egoistic objectives: his biographers explain how he approached his teachers as a child, an adolescent, and a university student to discuss their teaching after hours and how they were charmed. Later, he also developed a network of people happy to help him navigate in Paris' networks, and his enemies have said that, once Macron reached his goals or no longer needed their influence, he let the relationships fade away.

But it would be a mistake to consider Macron self-serving. Macron has undoubtedly charmed influential people, but he is genuinely enthusiastic about having interesting intellectual exchanges, allowing others to confront his ideas, and understanding the logic and philosophies of those different from him. Moreover, Macron does not target influential people exclusively. In his book, *L'ambigu M. Macron* [translated: *The Ambiguous Mr. Macron*], the journalist Marc Endeweld recounts a story told by one of Macron's school friends: "He wanted to be loved by everyone, with permanent empathy, but it was not calculated, he was sincere."[13] His empathy was not reserved for the other students: "he took the time to shake hands with the school caretaker, or to kiss on the cheek the cleaning lady."[14]

When asked about Macron's time in the private sector, the bank owner David de Rothschild, who employed him, declared: "There is something undoubtedly endearing in his personality... In everyday life, he does what is normal and that many people do not care to do: he says hello to the secretaries, asks how they are, hugs them. When you talk to him, he can show kindness, empathy."[15]

It is a trait that President Macron may share with President Barrack Obama, who said that empathy "is at the heart of my moral code, and it is how I understand the Golden Rule — not simply as a call to sympathy or charity, but as something more demanding, a call to stand in somebody else's shoes and see through their eyes."[16] But Emmanuel Macron could learn from the former U.S. president how to show this empathy in public appearances, not only in face-to-face meetings, as seems to be the case.

However, the most revealing story about Macron's game of seduction is his relationship with Michel Rocard, a French political icon who has helped Macron in his career. Michel Rocard had a strong influence on French politics. He was the French Prime Minister from 1988 to 1991 and previously served as a minister, a senator, and a member of the Parliament.

Rocard was an interesting member of the Socialist party, an internal opponent to President Mitterrand, leading the party's progressive and innovative right-wing, called in France "the Second Left." He strongly opposed the Communist party and was one of the few French politicians with international experience. He had been regularly visiting the U.S. after having met and impressed in 1970 Robert Sargent Shriver Jr., American Ambassador to France, who recommended that the U.S. keep close contact with the brilliant French politician.

Macron met Michel Rocard at an event organized by businessman and political activist Henry Herman, who had met young Macron at the end of his studies and introduced Macron to his colleagues. Emmanuel and Michel discovered that they had a lot to talk about and frequently met for dinner with their wives. In an interview, Rocard explained how Macron charmed him: "He is of exquisite courtesy and rare kindness. In addition to a strong intelligence, he can be attentive to the other, which is extremely rare."[17] The men were close; Rocard was present at Macron's wedding in 2007 and had even participated in its preparation. No other politician was invited. Rocard also played an essential role in Macron's decision to go into politics. When Macron became deputy Chief of Staff of President Francois Hollande, he discussed it with Rocard beforehand.

There has been a lot written about how they differed and what they had in common. However, they shared the same diagnosis about France, according to Rocard, "a cursed country, resulting from a marriage of Marxism and Jacobinism, and heir to the centralization driven by Kings Henri the 4th and Louis the 14th."[18] They were two moderates wanting to open France to the market economy.

Macron's enemies tell this story to show how Macron, a young ambitious, had used an influential French politician for his interest and let go of the relationship when it was no more needed. The truth is different. Rocard stated that, because he was not very popular, he did not want to embarrass Macron in his political journey and avoided meeting him and supporting him publicly after he declared for the presidential election. They remained in contact privately. Michel Rocard's wife describes in a book published in 2020: when Rocard had a pulmonary embolism in June 2016, the Macrons went to his bedside.[19] Macron is, therefore, the last politician who saw Michel Rocard alive.

That is unlikely to be the behavior of a cynical upstart. Though Macron has an extraordinary capacity to befriend everybody, there is an element of honesty and candor in his relationships. That may even be the very reason they are charmed.

In his impressive book *Adults in the Room*, Yannis Varoufakis, who had been the Greek minister of finance, explained the gory mechanics of the Eurozone management of a possible Greek default in 2007.[20] He explains how all E.U. commissioners and country leaders — including Presidents, Prime Ministers, Ministers of Finance, and Ministers of Economic — refused to help the Greek government and systematically broke their promises. All but one. According to Varoufakis, Macron has been the only one standing for Greece. Varoufakis explains: "Perhaps because Macron did not emerge from the test tube of social-democratic party politics, he was the only minister of the Franco-German axis to risk his political capital by coming to Greece's aid. [...] Macron understood that what the Eurozone finance ministers and the troika were doing to our government and, more importantly, to our people, was detrimental to the interests of France and of the European Union."[21] It should be mentioned that politically, Yannis Varoufakis is far on

Macron's left — not a political ally — which makes his testimony credible.

However, Macron isn't always nice and charming, as proven by the tensions with Recep Tayyip Erdoğan, the Turkish president who asserts himself as a global defender of Sunni Islam and oppressed Muslims — or, as some people refer to him — the "new Ottoman emperor." Erdoğan intervened in Syria against the Kurds (allies of the U.S. and their allies in the fight against the terrorist organization Islamic State), in Egypt against the rebellion opposed to the Sunni government, and in Nagorno-Karabakh to support Azerbaijan against Armenia. The discovery of large deposits of natural gas in the eastern Mediterranean led him to launch a naval prospecting operation supported by Turkey's naval forces in Greece's waters.

When Erdoğan met the newcomer Macron in 2017, he seemed happy to meet a young president who appeared eager to please him and the European leader most keen on developing relations with Turkey. But in 2019 and 2020, the charming French president became Erdoğan's primary opponent, criticizing his moves, obliging him to withdraw his fleet from Greece's waters by sending the French fleet, and asking for NATO's and European Union's sanctions against Turkey. It could have ruined the Turkish economy. Still more disturbing for Erdoğan, Macron sought to strengthen the control of Muslim places of worship on French soil and end the sending of foreign imams and preachers to France, particularly those sent and paid for by the Turkish government.

Macron may have a dazzling smile, but he also has sharp teeth.

Time passed, and American leadership has changed with the newly elected president, Joe Biden. According to a YouGov poll performed in September 2020 for the French news website *L'internaute*, 84 percent of French people wanted a Biden victory. Macron likely wished for Biden's success also, fearing that Trump's reelection might encourage his far-right opponent, Marine Le Pen, in her bid for the next presidential election.

The first meetings between the two men took place at the G7 in Cornwall in June 2021, and it was clear that Macron was looking for a "special relationship" with the newcomer.

The *Wall Street Journal* wrote, "President Biden and French President Emmanuel Macron threw their arms around each other as they walked on the beach. Later the two men shared a tête-à-tête as aides looked on. At one point, Mr. Biden asked Mr. Macron to answer a reporter's question for him. At the summit of the Group of Seven leaders in Cornwall this weekend, the two presidents embraced each other, sometimes literally, as allies on a host of issues — from multilateralism to fighting climate change — after years of volatility between Mr. Macron and former President Donald Trump."[22]

Macron's charm met Biden's empathy. But this time, German Chancellor Angela Merkel was the first European leader invited for an official visit to the White House.

Chapter 2
The Shapeshifter

"Shapeshifters have a purpose and an ambition that is beyond their own success. They care about the impact they have upon their communities and the people within them."[1]

— Debbie Seunarayan

On the 10th of December, 2016, a crowd gathered at the Parc des Expositions, a convention center in Paris. There were more than 10,000 people, rare for a political meeting in France, and an incredible turnout for a young candidate with no experience. At 4:45 p.m., Emmanuel Macron entered the room. Enthusiastic attendees reluctantly gave way to their hero, this polite and calm young man, invariably well-dressed in tailored suits. The candidate climbed on the platform and began a rather classic and technocratic speech about his program.

Macron was passionate but calm, as usual, but he changed over the course of the speech. He shapeshifted. His voice became louder. The transformation is startling. He put his arms in the shape of a cross, and he shouted to the point that his voice broke: "For those who were afraid that En Marche! was a lonely adventure, tonight you reassured them. This project, together, we are going to implement it. You have given me a lot since April. I will carry it to the end. You are going to win it."[2] His eyes face heaven, a position reminiscent of Christ on the cross.

A shapeshifting political star was born.

Shapeshifting is the human ability "to physically transform through an inherently superhuman ability, divine intervention, demonic manipulation, sorcery, spells or having inherited the ability."[3] In popular mythology, shapeshifters are creatures capable of changing their physical form. To be a natural shapeshifter, you need to transform willingly. (A werewolf, which automatically transforms when the moon rises, does not qualify as a shapeshifter.) And the shapeshifter must maintain their human consciousness, even when in animal form.

Stories of shapeshifters exist on all continents. In British mythology, some fairies, witches, and wizards could transform themselves into animals, some only capable of giving the impression of shapeshifting — a limited power to deceive the eye, called a "glamour." In Greek and Roman mythology, Jupiter, the King of Gods, saw Europa, the beautiful daughter of Agenor, the Phoenician King of Tyre, picking flowers by the sea. Jupiter fell in love with her instantly and transformed himself into a magnificent white bull. He convinced her to climb on his back and swam with her to the Mediterranean island of Crete, where he revealed his identity, shapeshifted back, and they lived happily together and had three sons. Europa became the first queen of Crete. This is especially interesting considering that Europe is at the heart of Macron's program, and he has been given the nickname "Jupiter."

Generally, shapeshifters are up to no good. According to Irish and Celtic mythology, creatures called *púca* can take the appearance of different animals. They can bring good fortune to those who meet them, but they bestow bad luck more frequently. Luckily, one could recognize *púcas* because, even in human form, they retain an animal feature, such as a paw or tail. Though some stories tell of *púcas* helping people, there are considered malevolent, and children were threatened with them if they misbehaved.

On the American continent, Native American folklore also generally considers shapeshifters evil. For example, in the Navajo culture, skin-walkers are secret witches (mostly male, some female) who emerge at night, taking the form of swift-moving animals like the wolf and the coyote. They are said to gather in foreboding places to work dark magic against their victims and engage in various taboo rituals. However, according to Anthropologist David Zimmerman of the Navajo Nation Historic Preservation Department, "Like humans, they do kill, and like humans, they have motivations for those acts of aggression. Power and revenge fuel their murderous intent, but such things cannot occupy the brain of a rational creature all the time, and Skin-walkers do not make murder part of their daily routine."[4] In the Indian Hopi culture, some shapeshifters are more protective of their people, such as the "Snake People" shapeshifters, who can take the form of snakes and humans. Legends tell that a female shapeshifter married a Hopi and brought the Hopi people medicines and the gift for making rain.[5]

In modern societies, the shapeshifter legend persists, most notably in the form of the "Lizard People" conspiracy, a theory that the world is secretly ruled by "interstellar lizards," or reptilians in "human suits." According to believers, these reptilians run the U.S. and occupy key positions all over the world.[6] They are believed to have modified human DNA to achieve their nefarious objectives. The British writer and conspiracy theorist David Icke is the most known supporter of this theory with his book, *The Biggest Secret*, published in 1998, which includes interviews with two Brits who claim that members of the British royal family are nothing more than reptiles with crowns. According to him, our reptilian masters are "stopping humanity from realizing its true potential." Those who believe in this theory have accused many prominent people of being part of this lizard race, including George H.W. Bush, Henry Kissinger, Bill and Hillary Clinton,

Barrack Obama, Joe Biden, Mitt Romney, Newt Gingrich, Donald Rumsfeld, and even Bob Hope.

Politicians often leverage this folklore to their benefit. For example, when Republican J.D. Hayworth opposed John McCain during the 2010 Arizona Senate primary, he declared: "What we are seeing is that John McCain sadly has lost whatever character he had. Instead of being a senior statesman, who should be revered and, quite frankly, should be voluntarily retiring [...], he is a cynical, political shapeshifter." Jennifer Rubin wrote in the *Washington Post*, "Hillary Clinton, expert shapeshifter," accusing the then-presidential candidate of changing her mind about the war in Iraq: first supporting it firmly, then voting against the Surge to gain the support of the far left, then she presented herself again as a hawk for her presidential bid to win over moderates. Rubin's conclusion: "What is Clinton's real view on Iran or Iraq? Gong! Irrelevant. She is only interested in what position will help her current political aims."[7]

In this case, the French do not speak of shapeshifting and instead employ other names for politicians who change their minds: weathervanes, windmills, chameleons, opportunists, or yellows. None of them are positive. In a book devoted to these turncoats, French historian Bruno Fuligny separates those who have changed sides for getting material advantages (venal weathervanes) from those who do it for intellectual reasons (cerebral weathervanes).[8] But, as stated by Ralph Waldo Emerson, "A foolish consistency is the hobgoblin of little minds, adored by little statesmen and philosophers and divines."[9] French writer Victor Hugo would agree; he went from monarchism to socialism and declared that it is normal to change your mind when "the facts lead you to change your thinking." The French neoclassical painter Jacques-Louis David is another example of a turncoat: he was protected by King Louis the 16th, who bestowed advantages such as an apartment in Le

Louvre, but became a revolutionary and voted for the execution of the King, and then became an admirer of Napoleon Bonaparte.

Contrary to his predecessors and many French politicians, Emmanuel Macron has seldom been called *une girouette*, the French term for a weathervane. However, he has been accused of attracting them, as people working with him generally come from other traditional French political parties from the right and the left and are considered traitors by their ex-colleagues. Macron himself seldom changes his mind, even if he may change some details of his plans to adapt to the reactions of the French people or his entourage. But people were impressed by his ability to transform and empower the crowd during his presidential campaign. It was then that his opponents and the media began to believe Macron might win the election.

Macron's rise surprised the French because he has a very classical background for a French politician. As a student, he was mainly interested in literature, even if he was in a scientific section during his secondary studies. He considered becoming a writer, but instead studied philosophy at the University of Paris-Ouest Nanterre La Défense, obtaining a master's degree with a thesis on Machiavelli and Hegel. Then he worked as an assistant to Paul Ricoeur, a French philosopher. When he decided that literature and philosophy were not his paths, he studied political science. He obtained a master's degree in public affairs from Paris School of Political Affairs, majoring in public affairs and economy before training for a senior civil service career at the selective and prestigious École Nationale d'Administration (ENA).

These last choices would be a typical career path for an ambitious and brilliant student, but after four years, Macron changed: he decided to leave public service and work as a private banker at the Rothschild & Cie Banque. He was highly successful there. Despite a considerable loss in his income, he moved on to take a political position, working as the deputy chief of staff for President Hollande for two years before becoming the Minister of Economy. But he changed again: he left the government to begin his presidential campaign.

During the campaign, Macron addressed various topics, depending on the group being targeted or the people in the room. Politicians all do that, but his high level of education in various domains made it easy to exchange with specialists: in addition to traditional political interviews and requests to speak or write about philosophy, economy, or literature, the highly-educated politician was interviewed about the French history in the magazine *L'Histoire* and participated in a panel about science with five high-level scientists in the scientific magazine *Science et Avenir*.[10] It was impressive.

Macron has often shown his capacity for adaptation in any situation. When he launched his presidential campaign, he was considered a young and polite minister. This soft-spoken and reasonable technocrat knew how to persuade the financial world and big companies. During his campaign rallies, he morphed into a preacher with Christ-like attitudes for his supporters. During his debate with far-right representative Marine Le Pen, he was quiet and almost humble, which emphasized his opponent's aggressiveness. At his inauguration, he was a solemn and impressive figure. In 2019, he abandoned his tailored suits from his Parisian tailor and was photographed in New York with a hoodie and a three-day beard. Later, he was seen at night in a turtleneck sweater, talking with homeless people in the streets of Paris.

Macron can be very approachable and then publicly scold a teenager for calling him "Manu." One day, Macron seems to be a typical conservative. He complains that France puts a "crazy amount of money in social subsidies" or insists that an unemployed gardener should cross the street to find a job in a bar or a restaurant.[11] The day after, he may show empathy and increase the subsidies for disabled or older adults living below the poverty line.

Different moments, different publics, different styles, and different messages.

These variations do not mean that he is changing his goals: it is an essential difference between a shapeshifter and a weathervane. A weathervane may suddenly change direction, following the wind, without having an objective; a shapeshifter like Macron retains their objective but changes their appearance and their behavior to achieve their goals. According to Macron's entourage, when he meets somebody, he listens carefully and adapts his behavior and his argumentation without losing track of his position. It may give the impression that there are several different Macrons.

In 2015, when he was the French minister of economy, Macron presented and defended the law for "growth, activity and equal economic opportunities," which later became known as Macron's Law. It was a challenge; Macron was facing a hostile Socialist Parliament, which didn't favor the market economy and opposed limiting social benefits. Macron had hardly convinced President Hollande, a Socialist, to present the law: it was a pro-business law aiming at deregulating the economy by ending the monopoly of the French national railway company, reducing barriers to entry for certain professions, capping redundancy payments, allowing the state to sell shares of public companies, offering the possibility of transferring the ownership of military armaments to private commercial companies, and more.

Macron's colleagues and French political leaders expected that defending the law in the French Parliament would not be possible for the inexperienced newcomer and that it would be the end of Macron's political career. Additionally, nobody in the government wanted to openly support the law, even Prime Minister Manuel Valls, who shared some of Macron's opinions on the need to deregulate the French economy but was beginning to see Macron as a rival.

Macron started his petition with a poorly considered argument, declaring that the law was needed because "some young French people want to become billionaires because the Net economy is for Superstars."[12] *Les Echos*, a French financial newspaper, placed Macron's portrait on the front page with the headline, "Young French people must want to be billionaires."[13] In a country where equality is an essential value, this opinion did not go over well. According to the media, sending Macron to defend the law meant that it was doomed.

Generally, ministers defending a draft law presented by the government use their majority in the Parliament to reject opposition proposals without discussion. In Macron's case, even the majority was partly against him. However, he used a different approach: he spent his nights and days in the Parliament, even eating in the Parliament's restaurants and bars to increase his contact with Parliament's members. Denys Robiliard, a socialist member of the Parliament, explained: "Throughout the committee's meetings, he stayed all the time, eighty-four hours of discussion. We never saw that before. He has great listening skills."[14]

The young liberal minister in a left-leaning government adapted his approach and his arguments to the different groups in the Parliament, including the most opposed to the project. He listened carefully and respectfully, changing the draft law to satisfy the left and the right. He accepted thousands of amendments coming from all sides. He multiplied bilateral meetings to better understand why people were opposing some articles of the law. As explained by Gilles Finchelstein, a French leftist spin-doctor (not a political ally for Macron), "He bewitched parliamentarians! His choice to go completely, to accept to take the arguments for what they are, and not where they come from, and to spend an incredible amount of time in Parliament has convinced all other politicians."[15]

Macron succeeded, proving himself to be a flexible negotiator, capable of convincing a majority to support his law without changing any of the law's core elements.

Shapeshifting can be useful in political life. Michael Saward, an Australian and British professor of politics and international studies, claims that it may be a key quality for politicians. In his article "Shapeshifting Representation," he provides a good explanation of Macron's success. According to Saward, political representatives often need to be, or at least to appear to be, different things to different people. How they appear to others may be a choice; a shapeshifting representative "attends to how he appears in different spaces and different times, and to modes of mediation of his style and persona, with an eye to strategic advantage for himself, and perhaps his party, faction, sponsors and constituents. He is, arguably, the quintessential twenty-first-century political representative."[16]

It ties up with most modern management theories that argue modern managers need to be highly adaptive shapeshifters because organizations, companies, and the business landscape in general are more prone to rapid and disruptive change.[17] It appears to be our new normal and is unlikely to change any time soon.

This shapeshifting leadership theory can be applied to the world of national politics. Becoming a resilient country in a chaotic world is easier said than done. The reality is that most countries are functioning routinely, and politicians are part of that. There are often, at least in western countries, two dominant parties, one more conservative and one more progressive, and the power shifts between them. Parties differ in their approach to how they spend taxpayer dollars. Conservatives prefer privatization and keeping government expenses to a minimum. They aim to improve the economy by reducing taxes. Liberals would prefer taxpayer money be redistributed and invested in social problems that benefit the country's citizens. Other parties have a tough time surviving because citizens expect peace and civility inside the country, and disruptive politicians generally don't fare well.

It is the same for companies. As explained by Daina Middleton, CEO of Ansira and author of Grace Meets Grit: How to Bring Out the Remarkable, Courageous Leader Within, "most companies are accustomed to a more stayed approach to operating their businesses. This is the way businesses have operated for decades, and it worked in the old economic model. Economists teach us that businesses grow to the point where returns to scale diminish. Consistency and repetition are important during this growth in order to achieve scale. The industrial machine age was born on this concept. Repeatable, linear models drove efficiency and effectiveness."[18]

It was adequate in a world where communications were slow, information scarce, and events happening abroad didn't immediately impact the country and its companies. Citizens did not get the information before their governments as it is now: authorities had time to analyze a situation and decide.

The Wall Street Crash of 1929 happened on the 4th of October. The crisis arrived in Europe through two channels. First, American banks, which participated in many European banks and stock exchanges, urgently repatriated their assets to the United States, making the financial crisis spread gradually throughout Europe. At the same time, international economic exchanges suffered the full brunt of the slowdown, then the negative effect of protectionist reactions made the situation worse. But it took around eighteen months before Europe was fully impacted.

But when the Great Recession began in the U.S. after a financial crisis in the Fall of 2008, it took only three months for the first E.U. countries (Estonia, Lithuania, and Ireland) to enter into a recession, then all of Europe followed. And when the coronavirus crisis began in Wuhan, China at the end of December 2019, it struck Europe at the beginning of

March 2020, and the U.S. a few weeks later: European and American governments had only some weeks to face an unexpected crisis. In such a case, these world leaders had to be flexible, which would not have been a necessity fifty years or a hundred years ago.

Also, the world has massively changed since the beginning of the twenty-first century. Products and services can be accessed and delivered instantaneously and virtually. This new environment contributes to rapid cycles of impulsive growth. These cycles are expected to continue to accelerate, diffuse, and disappear at a perpetually dizzying pace. It puts a heavy burden on governments, which cannot continue to act in traditional ways. For example, between the moment when parliamentarians create a committee to reflect on specific topics and initiate a report's production, there are good chances that a disruptive event or a scientific discovery will render the committee's report obsolete.

So new leaders are needed, according to Daina Middleton: "For years, leaders have focused on speed and agility alone. But they are no longer enough. Globalization, technology and social-political changes, as well as fast-moving cycles, are prompting leaders to prepare in advance for shapeshifting their organization to respond to the complex [...] challenges. To adopt a more adaptive approach to leadership, they need to be agile and resilient as individuals. Resilient leaders are adaptive, emotionally intelligent people able to absorb complex change and help others move forward to achieve success."[19]

Macron's shapeshifting abilities, which have been a political asset for him, have also benefitted the international community because he can quickly grasp challenges and find creative solutions. His adeptness does not necessarily guarantee success. Shapeshifters in political environments face two challenges: people have little confidence in politicians who present different faces, and the political and administrative systems, built in older times, slow the decision process and cancel the advantage of shapeshifting leadership.

French people love new ideas in politics, but they do not like changes; their ideal world is stable and anchored in the past, which is probably the inheritance of slower urbanization than in other countries.[20] More than half of French citizens live in towns with fewer than 200,000 inhabitants. It has impacted the way people face change. If you show them a new proposition, a new idea, they will rush to it and adore it — but as soon as they realize that the implementation of this novelty could change something for them, they balk. Suddenly, they are reluctant to enter the twenty-first century and fear, more than other peoples, the new forms of the economy. They are even afraid of Europe.

This is where Macron's major challenge lies: what is the point of electing a shapeshifter when the majority of French people dislike change? Macron may react rapidly, but it has been challenging for French people to follow him. France is excellent at preparing big projects and implementing them slowly and steadily. Consider the successes of fast trains like the French TGV, advances in aviation with the Airbus, and space with Ariane Rockets. But shapeshifting has not been a French strength — until now.

In France, the President and the government should be able to act fast. The French administration is very efficient and led by senior civil servants educated at the famous École Nationale d'Administration (ENA), an exclusive public graduate school. President Charles de Gaulle created it in 1945 to democratize access to the higher ranks of the French civil service. Standardizing the training required for senior public servants worked so well that after de Gaulle's presidency, four out of six French presidents were ENA alumni: Presidents Giscard d'Estaing, Chirac, Hollande, and Macron. These French senior civil servants are motivated, have the education and experience necessary to implement changes, make decisions, and execute strategies fast and carefully.

But people have long been troubled by the collective power the network of ENA alumni wields. Pierre Bourdieu, a French sociologist, anthropologist, and philosopher, wrote in 1964 that ENA, like other French schools, was monopolized by the "heirs of the dominant culture" before inventing the term "State nobility." This group of powerful civil servants "functions a bit like a big family [...], in the manner of the ancient Chinese clans which extended their branches as their members passed the exams giving access to public jobs."[21] They tend to be reluctant to implement changes that they have not prepared. They have a robust network system, and they can be seen as a power behind the throne. They oppose all measures that could reduce their power.

Since being elected, Macron has complained that his policies are implemented slowly by reluctant civil servants who sometimes oppose them. Having all the levers for implementing political decisions, the ENA's alumni can block or stall reforms, rendering Macron's shapeshifting skills utterly useless, including in times of crisis (such as the coronavirus pandemic). In 1995, during the French presidential campaign, Alain Madelin, a pro-U.S. classical liberal who had been a minister of industry, economy, and finances in conservative governments, even declared, "Ireland has the IRA,[22] Spain has the ETA,[23] Italy the mafia, and France has the ENA." To tackle this problem, Macron announced a reform of the ENA and of the recruitment and the management of senior civil servants, giving more flexibility and allowing for the recruitment of managers from the private sector.

***

Macron's ability to shapeshift is an asset for France and the world. We could use more politicians with this ability. But how do you find or educate them? His youth can provide some answers to this question.

Macron spent most of his youth in Amiens, a small French town with little more than 100,000 inhabitants, 160 kilometers north of Paris. He lived with his parents, both doctors, in a relatively modest house. He occasionally went to play at the local tennis club and the swimming pool, and he took piano lessons at the local conservatory. Holidays meant going skiing or visiting other parts of Europe with his parents and extended stays in a small town known for their hot springs in the Pyrenees mountains where he stayed with his grandparents, indulging in the joys of pétanque,[24] ping-pong, or fishing with his grandfather. Macron's life, by all accounts, was very stable, easy, and protected.

Growing up, Macron turned to intellectual challenges. His father wanted to become an archeologist, but chose to follow his parents' advice and pursue medicine instead. He was a voracious reader and would discuss history, politics, philosophy, and literature with young Emmanuel.

Macron's maternal grandmother, who lived near the family in Amiens, took young Emmanuel in as her protégé. She became a great influence on him. Having been a teacher, she pushed him to discover literature and to study. He saw her during the week and went on vacations with her to Bagnères de Bigorre, where they spent their days fishing, playing, practicing piano, discussing philosophy, and analyzing books.

Young Macron lived in a quiet town with a loving family and had all the time and support he needed to focus on his main passion: books. At age sixteen, he wanted to be a writer. He had already written three books, including a complex novel, *Babylon, Babylon*. It tells the story of

Hernán Cortès, the Spanish Conquistador, who led the expedition that caused the fall of the Aztec Empire and brought large portions of what is now mainland Mexico under the rule of the King of Castile in the early sixteenth century. Apparently no one has read it except Brigitte Macron and the publisher who refused it.[25]

Reading is known to have a strong impact on the brain. In an article written by Christine Seifert and published by the *Harvard Business Review*, reading fiction "predicts increased social acuity and a sharper ability to comprehend other people's motivations."[26] Seifert explains that "reading literary fiction is an effective way to enhance the brain's ability to keep an open mind while processing information, a necessary skill for effective decision-making." Experiments have also proven that reading literary fiction leads to a better capacity for understanding others' mental states, a crucial skill for a politician.[27]

Macron explained that literature occupies a central place in his life because "literature is not separated from life." He adds: "Literature sheds light on each of the situations we encounter. It gives substance to our lives. But books, of course, are not only guides to life. They lead us on paths we never knew. They open up horizons that we never suspected."[28] The French President, who is often perceived to be wiser than his years, has acquired a unique personality thanks to the hundreds of books he has read. It has enabled him to mirror different personas, depending on what he feels is needed in the moment. That may be the explanation of his abilities, the kryptonite that can, according to his supporters, transform him into Superman when it is necessary to save France, Europe, or even the world.

Yes, it is an asset, but it is also a curse. It is challenging for French people and Macron's international counterparts to guess who the real Macron is. Christophe Barbier, a well-known French political journalist, wrote a book about Emmanuel Macron with the title *Macron Sous Les*

Masques (Translation: Macron Under the Masks). On the back cover of the book, one can read, "Hidden under the masks, what authentic Macron can we find? A seer or a blind man? We know the spectacular ascent of the young president. By bringing him to power, the French chose renewal and progressivism. But thirty months later, we still know little about the intellectual and political development of Emmanuel Macron." The book does not offer an answer to that question. How could it? Macron shapeshifts when needed and is practiced in the art of theater since he met the woman who became his wife.

Chapter 3
Brigitte

"I have been, no doubt, really persistent... But I must say that the real courage is hers. She was the one showing generous and patient determination."

— President Macron

Love stories sometimes end badly. France was shocked at the end of the sixties by the suicide of a thirty-one-year-old teacher, Gabrielle Russier, who killed herself after being condemned to one year in prison for having a relationship with a sixteen-year-old student. Books were written, famous French singers such as Charles Aznavour composed successful and compassionate songs, and a film about the story by director René Cayatte became a success. And the French public opinion on this difficult topic became more tolerant.

This is probably why few have reacted negatively to the Macrons' love story. According to Maëlle Brun, her biographer, in 1993, Brigitte Auziere, a married, 39-year-old teacher who ran an after-school theater club, met Emmanuel Macron, a brilliant young student of approximately fifteen or sixteen years old (the details are not public). Emmanuel Macron, while playing the role of a scarecrow, impressed Brigitte in the play she produced. At the beginning of the next school year, Emmanuel came with a proposal for a new play, the "Art of Comedy," written by the Italian author and actor Eduardo De Filippo. It was a play written for five or six actors, but Emmanuel asked Brigitte to help him rewrite the play to provide a part for each of the seventeen students participating in the theater club.

Working together day after day, they fell in love. Later, as planned by his parents and in agreement with Brigitte, Emmanuel went to Paris to study in a well-known high school, living independently. He would meet Brigitte on the weekends in Paris or Amiens, their hometown.[1] Before leaving Amiens, he had declared: "You are not going to get rid of me! I will come back, and I will marry you." Two years after Emmanuel left for Paris, Brigitte's husband left her. They finalized their divorce, and in October of 2007, Emmanuel and Brigitte married. Ten years later, Emmanuel became the youngest French president ever, and Brigitte was by his side.

This story caused a lot of pain to Brigitte's husband and children at the time. But today, Emmanuel Macron has her children's full support. He quickly developed a strong relationship with them and even declared he loves them as his own children — which is interesting, considering that Brigitte's son, Sebastien, is six years older than Macron, and Brigitte's daughter, Laurence, was in the same class as Macron at school. All of Brigitte's children supported Macron during his bid for president: Sebastien, a statistician, oversaw social media management for Macron's campaign, and Tiphaine Auzière, Brigitte's youngest child, was a candidate for his party. During the campaign, Macron, then thirty-nine, declared, "And then I have seven grandchildren," referring to Brigitte's grandchildren.

It is a remarkable story, and certainly an interesting one, as it reveals several specific traits of the French president and of the French First Lady.

Nobody should underestimate Macron's capacity to be persistent and to be sincere. Macron had to face the opposition of his parents, who were not at all supportive when their son fell for a married woman twenty years his senior. They tried different approaches to end the romance but didn't want to provoke a crisis with their son. They met Brigitte to ask her to break off the relationship, but she refused to promise that they would not continue to meet. When Emmanuel decided to go and study in Paris, his parents were thrilled, expecting that it would lead to the affair's end, but their son did everything he could to see Brigitte. Much to their chagrin, Macron kept his promise and persisted.

There is a saying in France, attributed to Napoléon: "*Impossible n'est pas Français.*" Essentially, the meaning is: "In France, there's no such word as 'can't.'" Nobody would have bet a cent on Macron marrying Brigitte Auziere, but he did it. The same applies to his election: nobody considered Macron a serious contender. When Macron first spoke about developing a program and a center for Europe's defense, nobody was supportive, and it looked like a dead-end, but it exists now. And after the coronavirus crisis, Angela Merkel and her government supported Macron's idea to have Europe distribute subsidies instead of loans to the European countries who have most suffered economically, even though it went against Germany's doctrine.

Impossible is not one of Macron's words.

In France, as in many other countries, people tend to think that their politicians lie and hide secrets. In Macron's case, this suspicion seems stronger than normal. That may be that he is perceived as "too polite to be honest" (as the French saying goes), but in this love story, Macron proves that he is capable of deep sincerity. There was no hidden agenda, and that has certainly attracted supporters for the French president, primarily among women. The fact that he married a woman more than twenty years his senior has been important for his image; during his campaign, Macron's typical supporter was young, female, and educated. Some people have mocked him and his wife, but it has not played well in a country where sexism is today unacceptable.

According to Macron himself, Brigitte has taken on more risk and has shown the strongest personality. She was married when she met Macron. She had three children, a nice life with a supportive husband, and a comfortable teaching position at a school in a small, traditional French town where her family was well-known. What made her risk everything for the love of a sixteen-year-old? If one wants to understand it and know what kind of First Lady she is, her life before Emmanuel Macron may provide insight.

***

Brigitte Trogneux (her maiden name) was born into a wealthy family in the town of Amiens in 1953. The family story started in 1872 with a simple confectionery and chocolate factory near the cathedral of Amiens, founded by Jean-Baptiste Trogneux. Originally, Jean-Baptiste sold soufflés and savory puddings, but then made a fortune selling a special type of macaroon created by his son, Jean. Today, the recipe is the official macaroon of Amiens.[2] The fifth generation of the family still runs the successful company, which expanded to seven shops in the north of France.

When Brigitte Macron was young, her family lived in an apartment above the family shop. The last of six children, she was born twenty-two years after her oldest sibling. Her brothers and sisters knew the hardships of war, including the bombing of the shop, but she arrived in the family when life was easy. In addition to the apartment, her parents owned a comfortable villa in Le Touquet, a trendy seaside resort on the coast, with lovely beaches, casinos, and golf courses for the French and British bourgeoisie, where the family spent their summers.

Brigitte was described as a happy, active, and funny young girl. Her father, extremely strict with his other children, was very fond of and very flexible with his youngest, and they had a special relationship. He admired and encouraged her, which certainly boosted her self-confidence.

In an interview with *Elle*, the French magazine, she reflected on her family's values and her childhood, emphasizing the importance her parents placed on showing respect to others. "I could do anything, even bring back bad grades, but they were extremely strict about respecting each other. I was not a very wise girl. I was often punished to impertinence. Because at the Sacré-Coeur school in Amiens I never showed submission, never. [...] I had a critical mind early on."[3] Despite her punishments (on at least one occasion, Brigitte was required to clean the school's windows). She was quite spoiled, easily getting gifts for her successes at school or on special occasions. She got an Italian moped, a Piaggio Ciao, for her junior school certificate, an unusually extravagant gift at the time in France.

Brigitte enjoyed a lot of freedom and often went dancing with friends of similar backgrounds on Saturday evenings. The blonde beauty was considered the leader of her group of friends, going skating every week and organizing parties. She is described as very popular, always positive, and smiling, joyful, even playful. According to Maëlle Brun, she hid the boys' normal clothes during gymnastics and didn't return them until later that afternoon, after the end of the classes.[4] She was a good friend to her classmates, providing advice on how to dress and how to deal with boys and delivering love letters for her friends who wanted to hide their romances from their families.

Brigitte also has a secret side. As her husband has beautifully written in his campaign book, *Revolution*, "Behind the decided spirit, there is a sensitive continent to which only the fragile people have access and where they can find themselves."[5] The French First Lady is not only a strong and loved person, she also experienced serious trauma during her youth. She lost her big sister when she was eight years old and a six-year-old niece the following year. In a discussion with the French writer Philippe Besson in September 2016, Brigitte explained: "I was very spoiled. Emotionally, socially, I had everything, I couldn't complain about anything, and yet I was a teenager in pain."[6]

Brigitte also had a rather strict education. From age six to seventeen, she attended private religious schools in Amiens. In France, children usually attend public school, which generally provides a solid education. Less than 17 percent of French children study in the private sector. Even if Le Sacré Coeur received students from poor backgrounds, it was a place where affluent families send their children. In Brigitte Trogneux's times, children had uniforms and, as it was a Catholic school, students had to go to mass every day and confess their sins twice a week. Brigitte was rebellious and said to Philippe Besson about this period: "I was brought up in religion, therefore in fear. The fear stayed."

Brigitte Trogneux received a baccalaureate with the highest honors. This was a special event for her family, as few people in their lineage had earned a diploma. When a typical move would have been to work for the family business, Brigitte decided to study literature and obtained a master's degree with a thesis on courtly love in the Middle Ages. At twenty-one, she married a twenty-three-year-old banker. For her family and friends, the marriage was not a total surprise, as they knew that Brigitte wanted children, but the personality of her husband (an introvert and reasonable young man who was nice but not very talkative) surprised her close friends. However, Brigitte seemed happy, organized a successful social life, and showed her capacity to develop close relationships with people.

When Brigitte was thirty-one, she had the opportunity to work as a teacher in the private school system. This was a life-changing event for her and the students she taught. One of them, Thomas Martin, said about her in 2019, "She was pretty cool, charismatic, dynamic, entertaining, and dramatic in the way she behaved and ran the classes, and that made the classes a little more exciting." He added, "It was thanks to her that I tried hard and improved my spelling. She made us read a lot, so I started reading. She knew how to make things interesting, even exciting."[7]

Brigitte had found her calling and was an extremely popular teacher. Again, the best description of this success comes from Emmanuel Macron: "I have always admired her commitment and her courage. As a teacher of French and Latin, in the first place. She has never ceased to practice, with a supportive strength, this profession discovered at the age of thirty and which she loves more than anything."[8]

Brigitte and Emmanuel met and fell in love. Among the ingredients of the story, there was a shared love of literature. In an *Elle* magazine interview, Brigitte said, "I have a boundless passion for Flaubert[9] . It's unthinkable to me that someone might not have read *Madame Bovary*."[10] According to her confident Philippe Besson, a successful French writer who followed the Macrons during the campaign, "she thought *Madame Bovary* was a masterpiece, that she loved Flaubert's style, his power and the fact that from the first line you are at the heart of the story... I believe she identifies absolutely with Bovary."[11]

Madame Bovary is the story of a rich farmer's daughter, Emma Rouault, who married Charles Bovary, a doctor. Raised in a convent, Emma would have liked to live in the dream world described in romance novels, but the discrepancy between her dreams and her own life triggered a nervous illness. Her loving and quiet husband then decides to settle in another village where she meets local personalities, in particular a notary's clerk and a country gentleman, who become her lovers. In the end, after spending a fortune that she cannot repay, Emma commits suicide. It is not Brigitte Macron's story, but when she met Emmanuel, she was married to a medical practitioner and had raised her children, and, like Emma Bovary, she was perhaps ready for a new and more adventurous life. It could explain the romance.

Emmanuel Macron liked Flaubert, but admired another famous French writer, Marie-Henri Beyle, known as Stendhal. On the official portrait taken when he took office as the new French president, the portrait that now hangs in all French public buildings, everybody can see two books. One of them is a masterpiece written by Stendhal, *The Red and the Black*, whose hero is Julien Sorel, a moving young man who tried to satisfy his heroic ambition through his pride and talent in the post-Napoleon times in France and fails.[12] Macron may also identify a bit with Julien Sorel: a young mind, sincere and passionate, who has heroic ambitions and moves to Paris to satisfy them. There are similarities, but Macron has no intention to fail in his objectives.

Others have remarked on the relation between Macron and Julien Sorel. British cultural and political magazine *Standpoint* published an excellent article, "The Modern Julien Sorel," in which an interesting argument is presented: "Much of the narrative of the novel centers on Sorel's melodramatic love affair with the wife of the mayor of the provincial town where his big break occurs, Madame de Rênal. She is, for a country boy, a sophisticated and dazzling catch [...] Sorel is transformed by her from the shy tutor imported into the grand household into the fearless lover who cuckolds the most important man in town — albeit with some crass and ridiculous exploits along the way."[13] Unlike Julien Sorel, who betrayed and almost killed Madame de Rênal, Macron "showed breathtaking courage, conviction and self-belief to take as his partner a woman twenty-two years older than himself. He deserted his own family to lead a life as independent, single-minded and focused as it was unorthodox and unprecedented."[14] Ruthless and romantic.

***

So, it looks like an improved Julien Sorel has met and fallen for a modern and more realistic Emma Bovary, creating an extremely solid couple. Brigitte Macron has played a key role in her husband's success, and she continues to support him as France's First Lady.

Originally, the term "First Lady" referred to the first woman in the UK's monarchical order of protocol (the mother of the sovereign or the empress, for example).[15] At the end of the eighteenth century, the term was borrowed from the British monarchy by the drafters of the White House protocol to describe the American president's wife. In 1978, a law entered into force under the presidency of Jimmy Carter which allows the president's wife to have a staff of around twelve people.

In France, the Constitution does not touch on the issue of the first lady, and there is no law giving her a specific role or a staff. In practice, however, she is part of the institutional protocol, particularly for official visits and dinners. Now, the French First Lady has a customary role. She receives requests and complaints from ordinary citizens and investigates and answers them, which has obliged her to have some staff support from the president's office.

President Giscard d'Estaing's wife assisted him at specific activities during his campaign, and he presented his presidential greeting for the New Year on December 31, 1975, with her by his side. (This was part of a strategy borrowed from his role model in the matter, the President of the United States, John F. Kennedy, and his wife, Jackie Kennedy.) But it was his successor's wife, Danielle Mitterrand, who shook the status quo. When her husband Francois Mitterrand was elected in 1981, the couple was on the brink of divorce. The president had been living part-time with another woman with whom he had a child. At the time, a divorce would have been a scandal and would have ruined his political life. Though she was stuck with him, his wife decided to be active, declaring, "I am not a useless vase." She created an autonomous third-world political engagement, with political and humanitarian positions deeply rooted on the left, whether regarding Fidel Castro, Salvadoran guerrillas, or Mexican Zapatistas. She supported the Palestinian cause, even though she had links with Israel after her son went to work in a kibbutz. Her husband was not always happy with her interference with French foreign affairs, but she paved the way for French first ladies, who are now more visible and more politically active.

During his campaign, Macron announced his intent to clarify the role of the first lady, who appeared at dinners and state visits but remained in obscurity the rest of the time. Once elected, he proposed a law, inspired by similar American legislation. Parliamentarians rejected the proposal, accusing Macron of hypocrisy: at the same time, Macron had proposed a law prohibiting parliamentarians from hiring family members as staffers. Negative campaigns beset the presidential couple. There were personal attacks and a national petition against the recognition of Brigitte Macron's official role. Several fake news posts circulated on social media, including one about a possible salary for the First Lady, but this was never even considered.

Macron was not able to pass the law, but he is persistent. He decided to publish a transparency charter, formalizing his wife's status as the head of state's spouse, and recognizing a "representative role" of France alongside the president, especially at international meetings. The

French First Lady does not have the same staff or budget as her American counterpart, but her role is now extended. She supervises official receptions and sponsor events, responds to "requests" from foreign personalities or French citizens wishing to meet her, and may also take part in national and international actions implemented with other spouses of heads of state, "in particular to fight against climate change or violence against women and children." She also maintains a continuous link and relationships with civil society actors "in the fields of disability, education, health, culture, child protection, and equality."[16] The French First Lady may also "perform missions and make proposals" entrusted to her by the president. This last part recognizes that the French First Lady, like her American counterpart, has a political role.

But strong first ladies have always played a political role, even before the American law was voted in 1978, as a law or an absence of law cannot change the impact of a couple's relationship on their activities and their mutual influence. Florence Harding, American President Warren Harding's wife until he died in 1923, was a strong woman and a divorcee.[17] She was so deeply involved in her husband's political campaign that when he was elected, she asked him: "Well, Warren, I have got you the Presidency, what are you going to do with it?" (He replied: "May God help me, for I need it.") Florence influenced Harding's choices of cabinet members and openly took political positions. She was also the first presidential spouse to send responses to the many letters received.

American presidents have been promoted, supported, and sometimes driven by their wives throughout the country's history. Mary Todd Lincoln (wife of President Abraham Lincoln) fought for emancipation, provided intelligence and advice to the president and military staff, and toured Union Army camps. Numerous abolitionists attested to her strong values and her influence on Abraham. She considered the Emancipation Proclamation of 1863 to be a personal victory.

Edith Wilson, who lived in the White House with her husband Woodrow Wilson from 1915 to 1921, played a presidential role herself when her bedridden husband entrusted her rather than resigning or letting the vice president step in. For months, Edith was the real power behind the throne.

Eleanor Roosevelt (wife of U.S. President Franklin D. Roosevelt) was an extremely active Democrat. She pushed for progressive policies at the national level with progressive women's groups, such as the Women's Trade Unions League, The League of Women Voters, and the World Peace Movement. She also taught, but Roosevelt was more known for her career as a famous writer, lecturer, freelance journalist, and radio broadcaster. She was afraid of losing her independence when she became First Lady in March of 1933, but she did not. Eleanor began to have her own press conferences, wrote regular newspaper and magazine columns, and kept her radio show. In 1940, Eleanor became the first presidential spouse to deliver a speech at the Democratic National Convention, when she urged attendees to accept Roosevelt's vice-presidential pick, Henry A. Wallace. She was also directly involved in the president's policies and decisions, even if she frequently downplayed her role in political matters.

After World War II, how large or small of a role the first ladies played depended on their preferences and personalities, but the emergence of modern media obliged them to be more active in their husband's campaigns. First ladies humanize presidential candidates, making them seem more relatable and down-to-earth. They have been very involved in their husbands' presidential campaigns, often campaigning separately. They have generally denied any influence on their husband's administration policy (except Hillary Clinton, a politician herself). However, all of them had unquestionably influenced their spouses: Lady Bird Johnson worked with her husband's cabinet, briefing the president before they visited foreign countries; Pat Nixon was the first incumbent first lady to endorse the Equal Rights Amendment and the first to disclose her pro-choice view on abortion; and Nancy Reagan, who advocated for drug education and prevention programs for children and young adults, was involved in the selection of candidates for major positions and participated in the dismissal of Donald Regan, who was chief of staff at the time.

Brigitte Macron, who refuses to be called the "First Lady," has more in common with the most influential American first ladies than with her French predecessors. Even the strongest ones, such as Danielle Mitterrand or Bernadette Chirac, did not appear to influence their husband or French politics.

Brigitte has a strong personality, with an exceptional mix of simplicity, honesty, intelligence, culture, and dynamism. She pushes for more, reaching the moon, but she is also a realist: when Emmanuel wanted to become a writer, she urged him to choose another profession ("or you will be called a gigolo," she declared).[18]

Brigitte campaigned with and for her husband, a new concept in France. Usually, French would-be presidents present their spouses officially at one or two events, and that's all, but Brigitte was visible even before the campaign. From the time Emmanuel was appointed as France's minister of economy in 2014, the couple became media darlings, mastering their communication with the support of Michèle Marchand, a French specialist of tabloids. At the time, any magazine with Emmanuel and Brigitte on the cover sold a lot more than usual, a substantial advantage for a future presidential candidate.

Brigitte was also a member of the campaign's strategic team. It is reported that at the first meeting to prepare the future campaign, Emmanuel Macron reserved the seat near him for her: "Everyone looks for their place, elbows to sit as close as possible to the future candidate. But an armchair to his right is ostensibly forbidden to them. Upon arriving, Emmanuel Macron immediately puts his jacket on the back of the seat. Signifying by this simple gesture, the political weight of his wife."[19]

During the campaign, with the multiplication of advisers and the development of En Marche (the political party created by Emmanuel Macron), Brigitte's role has been officially limited and even questioned by people from Macron's entourage, who worry that her presence could harm his political profile. But when her husband faced difficulties, she has been asked to intervene publicly because polls showed that French voters considered her accessible, generous, and more aware of the problems they face in their daily lives.

The couple preferred to campaign together (or in the same areas) to be together in the evenings. Every day, they exchanged many phone calls and messages, keeping a permanent communication channel open. It was no surprise that she influenced the campaign to the point that some people were using her to send him messages and ideas they felt were important.

In the last months of the campaign, when the victory was more than a faraway dream, Brigitte read all of the first ladies' biographies. From Nancy Reagan, she may have borrowed the will to focus on creating a home from the presidential palace, where Macron's predecessors have never really lived. The Elysée Palace, which has never been organized for families and children, began to feel like a home after the Macrons moved in. Its decorations have been modernized, and the heavy drapes have been taken away from the windows to allow daylight in.

As Brigitte has said repeatedly, "I am not the French First Lady. I am just Brigitte Macron and I am the wife of the president." It could be considered a sign of modesty and prudence, but it seems more like a rebellion against the fate that has put her, an independent woman who values her autonomy, in a position where her freedom is somewhat limited.

Brigitte does not attend the official meetings of the French government, and she does not participate in her husband's activities when her presence is not officially required, but, as Emmanuel Macron declared in 2017 during the campaign: "She will have the role she has always had with me, she will not be hidden, because she shares my life, because her opinion is important, and because the presidential function carries something that has a personal dimension."[20] He declared to the writer Philippe Besson about Brigitte's role "Brigitte, she is me. And I am her. That's all."[21] Every evening, except when he is (seldom) traveling without her, she is the last to see him and talk to him, and in this intensely close couple, that means that she has political influence.

Brigitte played a role in the choice of certain ministers of Macron's government. She learned of Jean-Michel Blanquer, a specialist of education, when he participated in a radio program to talk about his book, *The School of Tomorrow*. She loved what he said, bought the book, prepared reading notes for her husband (as she does with interesting books), and told him that he should meet with Blanquer. Macron did and chose him as minister of education. More recently, during the government change in July 2020, it was revealed that Eric Dupond-Moretti, a French criminal defense lawyer, famous for his record number of acquittals and surprisingly chosen to be the French minister of justice, was appreciated by Brigitte, who had previously invited him to meet her at the Elysée Palace.

Brigitte established close links with some ministers, and she receives them in her office in l'Aile Madame (the French equivalent of the East Wing in the White House). In addition, she frequently participates in confidential dinners several times a month with the leaders of the political groups supporting her husband. She generally does not intervene in these meetings, but when the participants ask her opinion, she gives it with her well-known straightforwardness and frankness. One participant noted: "We all know that if she has something to tell him, she will tell him. She gives him her opinion on many subjects. She is not stupid. Quite dangerous to think that she is stupid... She totally knows our world; she knows us all."[22]

Unfortunately, Brigitte's role is seldom mentioned in the international press or by world leaders. People prefer to focus on her looks, like President Trump telling her in 2017, "You are in such good physical shape!" During her official visits with her husband, more pages are written about her outfits than about her visits and appointments, (as is often the case with other First Ladies.) With a new leader such as Emmanuel Macron and with them having a very unique love story, it would be much more revealing to investigate her interests as they are often shared by her husband.

It does not appear that international players have recognized her importance and her influence yet. She has not pushed for recognition, even though she has developed a global network in the field of education, including UNESCO leaders.

Brigitte Macron is not a decorative object in the shadow of her husband; she is his strength, his adviser, his love, and she matters more to him than anyone else.

Chapter 4
Populism

"I'm a great believer in luck, and I find the harder I work, the more I have of it."

— President Thomas Jefferson

When French Emperor Napoléon appointed a new general for his army, he used to ask after studying their files and assessing their merits: "Very well, but is he lucky?" It appeared as a sign that the Emperor did not rely on pure rationalism to pilot his armies, but it was a very rational attitude considering that luck can generally be associated with several essential qualities: to be lucky, you have to be at the right place at the right moment, you have to believe in your luck, and then you have to be able to rely on your intuition and understanding of people to act efficiently.

And Macron's success in the 2017 presidential election was a very lucky one, considering the organization and the tradition of the French democracy. There are generally two institutions in old Europe: a king or a president, whose role is usually very formal and quite limited, and a prime minister, who is the chief executive. The United Kingdom, the Netherlands, Sweden, Denmark, Norway, and Spain all have a queen or king, formally the head of state. Germany, Italy, Greece, or Finland, for example, have a president as the head of state. But these queens, kings, or presidents have a representative role performing various official, ceremonial, diplomatic, and representational duties. They symbolize the country's unity, and one or two of them are theoretically in charge of ensuring that the government respects the constitution, but they generally avoid intervening in politics.

If Prince Charles of England makes a speech to support the fight against climate change (he has several times), people start questioning the need for England to keep a monarchy. For them, the royal family is not supposed to intervene in political affairs, and should stay a symbol and a marketing tool. In some countries, it may even backfire: when the Grand Duke of Luxemburg, head of state, a symbol of the country's unity and guarantor of national independence, exercised his executive power under the constitution and refused to sign a law legalizing euthanasia in 2008, there was immediately a constitutional change so that laws would no longer require the Grand Duke's formal assent (implying "approval"), but his task of promulgating them as chief executive remained.

Let's not exaggerate. Some of these institutions can be extremely useful in times of crisis. During the summer of 2019, Italian President Sergio Mattarella, who has only the formal role of appointing the prime minister chosen by a majority in the parliament, played a decisive role in obliging political parties to join a coalition. Typically, the president is not active in the formation of the government, but he instead multiplied the number of meetings with political leaders and used the media to apply pressure until he found a majority. In a more dramatic move, Haakon VII, the King of Norway since 1905, was key to Norwegian resistance against German invaders during World War II. He refused to bend to German invaders and escaped heroically with his family, like-minded diplomats, and members of the Parliament through the Norwegian mountains and forests in the Nordic winter. He made his way to London, where he organized the strong Norwegian resistance movement.

But these are exceptions, and queens, kings, grand-duke, or presidents are generally powerless. The prime minister, as chosen by a majority in the parliament, has the real power.

But France is different. It began in 1958: there was a major political crisis, after more than ten years of government instability, a painful defeat in Vietnam, and an uprising for independence in what was then French Algeria, followed by a military coup d'état by military leaders to impose a change of policies in favor of the right-wing partisans of French Algeria. The government, under pressure, resigned, and the French president, seeing that the nation was on the brink of civil war, appealed to General de Gaulle, "the most illustrious of the French... The man who, in the darkest hours of our history, was our leader for the reconquest of freedom and who, having achieved around him national unanimity, refused the dictatorship and established the Republic."[1] De Gaulle accepted the proposal under the precondition that a new constitution would be introduced, creating a powerful presidency with a sole executive. It was unique in Europe, but Parliament voted for it, even though some feared a dictatorship.

France then became the only European country with a strong president, directly elected by the people, as it is in the U.S. French presidents select and dismiss prime ministers who are formally the head of the government and responsible in front of parliament. But as stated by President Sarkozy about his prime minister, François Fillon: "The prime minister is subordinate; I am the boss."[2] It means that the French president does not really share the power with his prime minister, and some even suggest merging the two functions, following the U.S.'s example.

France also has a parliament with a Senate, elected locally by local representatives, and a National Assembly, elected by direct universal suffrage with a two-round system by constituency. These constituencies are somewhat similar to U.S. Congressional districts. They each have approximately 100,000 inhabitants and elect a single representative.

When the National Assembly, which has powers comparable to those of the Senate in the U.S., is dominated by opponents to the president, the prime minister becomes dominant, and the president has a more formal role, except in defense and foreign affairs. It has happened three times since 1958. From 1986 to 1988, President Mitterrand's socialist party lost the elections, and Mitterrand was obliged to choose Jacques Chirac, his conservative opponent, as prime minister. There was a second episode from 1993 to 1995 when President Mitterrand shared power with opponent prime minister Edouard Balladur. The last cohabitation happened from 1997 to 2002 when President Chirac was obliged to choose a socialist prime minister, Lionel Jospin.

Interestingly, these couplings under the same yoke functioned quite well. The presidents were active in foreign affairs and defense, where they imposed their ministerial picks on the prime ministers and left the daily management of other issues to the prime minister.

The striking difference between the French and the U.S. systems is the absence in France of the States and the country's extreme centralization, reflected in the electoral system. For example, in the U.S., the president is not directly elected by citizens, but by an electoral college where each state designates a certain number of members. This means the electoral college can elect a President who did not get the majority of votes. It happened already four times. This is impossible in France, where the president is elected directly by the French people with a two-round system. The French National Assembly, which holds the main elements of the legislative power, is elected locally. But the Constitution states that its members do not represent their region. The French Senate, whose members are supposed to represent the French territories, is a weak version of the U.S. Senate: French senators are elected by local politicians and not by the citizens, which means that political parties chose the senators, not the people.

However, since 1958, this organization has stabilized the French democracy and given clear majorities to lead the country. The election of the members of the National Assembly with a two-round system created, until recently, a two party dominant system with the social-democratic party called Parti Socialiste (Socialist Party) on the left, and a conservative alliance whose name changes regularly on the right.[3] For the presidential election, the situation is the same, aggravated by the fact that only the two candidates with the most votes are chosen for the second round if nobody gets a majority before then.

From 1958 to 2002, the second round of presidential elections each consisted of a battle between the candidate from the left and the one from the right, with the exception of the 1994 election when Valéry Giscard d'Estaing from a centrist party got elected. He garnered support from some conservatives against their official candidate. He chose conservative Jacques Chirac as his Prime Minister. In 2002, a third force emerged with the National Front, an extreme-right and anti-immigration party with a provocative stance: Jean-Marie Le Pen, its leader, denied the existence of the Shoah. It was the first sign that a minority of French people were tired of the main political parties. However, French presidents continued to come either from the left or the conservative right, and nobody expected any change. It was the same in the U.K., where the two main political parties, the Conservative Party and the Labour Party, have provided all the prime ministers, and in the U.S., where the Democratic Party and the Republican Party have won every United States presidential election since 1852, and most of the congressional and senate elections as well.

But then Emmanuel Macron came on the scene and announced that he was a candidate for the presidential election. He had previously been the deputy chief of staff for President Hollande, a Socialist Party leader, and had worked as a Minister of Economy in the socialist government led by Manuel Valls. But he refused to become a Socialist Party member. He declared his candidacy for president on the 16th of November 2016, before even President François Hollande, leader of the left and Macron's former employer, had announced his intentions! Had the president run for re-election, it likely would have ruined Macron's chances.

In addition, neither of the two major parties supported him. The conservatives would not back somebody who had been a minister in a socialist government. Born in 1977, Emmanuel Macron had grown up in a society where the fight for human rights have slowly replaced Karl Marx's class struggle. He was the poster boy for liberalism and the free market: the socialists did not want to support him. And in the early polls, it was clear that Macron was going to lose. But Lady Luck intervened.

First, President Hollande announced that he was not running again. This was undoubtedly due to his lack of popularity and the fact that he had asked that his four first years be judged based on his results in the fight against unemployment (they were not good). Nevertheless, Hollande hesitated. He wrote later in his book *Les leçons du pouvoir* (Translated: *Lessons from Power*) that he was tempted: the lack of popularity one year before an election had not prevented some of his predecessors from being reelected. But he was also under attack from his own party, the Socialist Party, where his opponents wanted to force him to go through a primary.[4]

He could have avoided this humiliation with some clever maneuvers. However, in the fall of 2016, two French journalists published a book of interviews with President Hollande whose title alone was an attack against him: *Un Président Ne Devrait Pas Dire Ça...* (Translated: *A President Should Not Say That...*).[5] It became a bestseller, and the president's reputation suffered greatly. Very bad polls, dirty secrets exposed, internal attacks from within his party, and Macron's "treason" prevented any possibility of his being elected again, and François Hollande did not run.

Later, Macron got lucky again. The primary on the left was devastating for his opponents. He had one main rival from the Socialist Party, Manuel Valls, who was President Hollande's prime minister, and had a political approach similar to Macron's: he was a social-liberal, with similarities to Tony Blair. As prime minister, he had more prestige than Macron and would have been supported by many left and moderate voters. But the Socialist Party organized a primary, and Manuel Valls was defeated by a pleasant but inexperienced leftist politician called Benoît Hamon, dubbed the "French Jeremy Corbyn" by *Politico*.[6] Hamon was a lame campaigner and easy prey for Emmanuel Macron: many Socialist Party voters supported Emmanuel Macron, who had been able to attract key members of the party during his campaign.

Then the Conservative Party organized its primary. Former Prime Minister François Fillon, a low-key politician, won against all odds after a brilliant campaign against former Prime Minister Alain Juppé and former President Nicolas Sarkozy. It was terrible news for Emmanuel Macron, as Fillon, a committed Catholic, could aggregate all the movements on the right, from the center-right to the more extreme anti-abortion and even anti-immigrant movement. Macron's task seemed impossible — he needed the center-right votes to have any hope of winning. Four months before the election, he lagged behind Marine Le Pen, the populist leader, and François Fillon. Then the Penelopegate happened.

On the 24th of January, the investigative magazine *Le Canard Enchaîné* revealed that Penelope Fillon, the Conservative candidate's quiet and discreet British wife, was paid for eight years as a parliamentary attaché for her husband (and for his deputy when he was a minister) and that she may have never really worked in the parliament.[7] It also seems that she had been paid by a magazine, the *Revue des Deux Mondes*, owned by a billionaire and a friend of her husband without any task justifying these wages. In the middle of the campaign for the presidential election, on the 14th of March, 2017, the financial prosecutor's office indicted François Fillon for embezzlement of public funds. Against all evidence, François Fillon denied any wrongdoing. As a result, staff left his campaign team and he dropped in the polls. However, he refused to withdraw and let someone else replace him as the Conservatives' candidate. From March, Macron harvested the center-right votes and rose in the polls: he appeared to be the preferred choice for all those moderates from the right and from the left who had no sympathy for a very leftist-Hamon or for the former prime minister indicted for embezzlement.

The cherry on the sundae arrived when one of his rivals, Francois Bayrou, the prominent Center Party leader, unexpectedly declared that he supported Emmanuel Macron. He is a respected politician, who received 18 percent and 9 percent of the votes during the two previous presidential elections. It was a logical move. His supporters were ready to vote for Macron, and Macron was more than happy to get the unexpected support from a respected heavyweight, if not ultimately successful, in French politics.

Even in such a favorable situation, with encouraging polls putting him at the top, it had not been easy for Emmanuel Macron. Marine Le Pen, the leader of the extreme-right, was extremely dangerous. She used the Fillon indictment to confirm her claim that politicians from other parties were a rotten bunch and that only her party could clean French politics, the French equivalent of President Trump's "draining the swamp." On the left, another politician was rising fast: Jean-Luc Mélenchon, a defector from the Socialist Party pushing for a more extreme socialist policy with the support of the Communist Party. He is a remarkable speaker and was harvesting more and more votes, threatening Macron and Le Pen in the polls.

Macron may have been at the right place at the right moment and believed in his luck, but that was not sufficient for a young politician to rise to the top. He had to prove his worth, and he did. He understood that he had to behave differently from traditional French politicians.

In France, political campaigns for presidential elections usually consist of a limited number of rallies, billboards, and radio and television spots. Another part of the campaign is local: every village and town organizes at least one farmers' market a week. Candidates' local teams distribute their leaflets and discuss their candidates with the people. There are two debates: the first one with all the candidates (ten to twenty of them in one or two evenings) before the first round of the election; the second debate, between the two winners of the first round, is the most important one. It is long and hard for the candidates, but it is also as popular in France as the finale of a soccer world cup. Except for this final debate, presidential campaigns can be pretty dull.

Unlike the U.S., there are additional constraints on French presidential campaigns. There is a ceiling of €17 million to the campaign's expenses for each candidate (less than $21 million). Also, donations from private persons cannot be anonymous and are limited to €4,600 (around $5,000) for each donor. Private companies cannot finance political campaigns. Candidates in the second round can spend an additional €5 million (less than $6 million). Those candidates who get more than 5 percent of the votes get back 47.5 percent of their expenses. So, despite the use of some modern tools as social media, French presidential campaigns were old-fashioned, and sometimes boring.

Macron's campaign was different.

In his campaign headquarters, Emmanuel Macron hung a giant poster of John F. Kennedy, and his entourage often presented him as the

French Kennedy. He did not hesitate to quote him at the French business association's summer school, where he declared, "Don't ask yourself what the country can do for you, but what you can do for your country." However, his campaign has been more inspired by Barack Obama's methods: the inspiration came from team members who had participated in or followed Obama's campaign. For example, journalist Laurence Haïm, twenty-three-years-old and a correspondent for French television to the White House, joined Macron's campaign early and strongly advised him to take inspiration from Barack Obama's campaign. Haïm declared, "Emmanuel Macron is the French Obama. Since I arrived [from the U.S.], all this really makes me think of the Barack Obama campaign that I covered. There is incredible energy here, it's like a start-up."[8]

Emily Schulteis, a German freelance journalist, wrote an interesting article in *The Atlantic* describing how Obama's campaign inspired Macron's team. She writes in particular: "An eloquent testimony of this inspiration is the unprecedented operation of supporters and campaign volunteers he's built, using U.S.-style mobilization techniques that, in some ways, mirror the organizational style of Barack Obama's campaigns. Today, En Marche has more than 3,900 local volunteer committees and hundreds of small events each day across the country.

What resulted was the *Grande Marche* (Translation: the Great Market), a nationwide door-to-door campaign that aimed not to secure votes but to function as a sort of listening tour across France. Macron's team wanted to know what French voters were thinking, which issues interested them most, and what they liked and didn't like about the country's politics."[9]

They used specific algorithms created by a team of supporting specialists "to identify precincts and neighborhoods that were representative of France as a whole. The Grande Marche was a way for Macron to introduce himself to voters indirectly and cast his movement as one that was coming from the people. Grande Marche volunteers knocked on roughly 300,000 doors through the spring and early summer, collecting more than 25,000 interviews with voters. While typical door-to-door interactions last usually only a few minutes, the volunteers spent an average of 14 minutes with each person who opened the doors to let them inside. The Grande Marche was unprecedented in France, both for its scope and for how long before Election Day it was conducted. The effort also benefited Macron's campaign because it served as a training ground for new volunteers, many of whom had never volunteered for a campaign before."[10]

Such a move has been beneficial for Macron's campaign. It made him popular. His team developed a database of thousands of quotes, searchable by issue and region, which the campaign communication team later used. They learned what the most important topics for the voters were. More importantly, around four thousand volunteers were trained for the campaign, which is a new concept in France. According to Emily Schulteis, La Grande Marche has the same grassroots volunteer structure as the one pioneered by the Obama campaign in 2008. The comments received were used by Emmanuel Macron to adjust his election program released progressively from early spring 2017, which was late in the campaign process.

The inspiration from Obama's campaign went further, with a young photographer, Soazig de la Moissonière, chosen to follow Macron's campaign. She became his official photographer in March 2017. Her work during the campaign has been compared to Pete Souza's, Obama's official photographer. The pictures covering Macron's public travels look like backstage candids, making the candidate appear human and approachable, in contrast with the usual French formal political campaign pictures with candidates trying to look as presidential and as official as possible.

According to François Durpaire, a French historian specializing in the United States, "Emmanuel Macron's campaign is a copy and paste of Obama's in 2008."[11] There are several elements: "first a kind of relaxed attitude in the campaign's atmosphere, but also a certain top-down decision system, with a strong decision-making pole at the top. It reminds me of how Obama used to behave."[12] Durpaire also refers to Macron's symbolic gesture when he puts his hand on his heart when the French national anthem La Marseillaise begins. It is unusual in France, but a common American tradition. Macron's meetings were also very different his opponents and predecessors: he stood and spoke without a desk or apparent notes (but with a teleprompter), wore a simple shirt or jacket on his back, did not hesitate to give the floor to the audience. He even employed a well-rehearsed strategy of planting the crowd — people carefully disseminated in the audience responsible for applauding at the right time. Again, an atypical strategy for France's political meetings, but a common American one.

Macron's team used an American product, Nation Builder, to target groups of possible supporters. Politicians use this political software to build their websites, manage email campaigns, and raise money. One of their more notable clients is President Donald Trump. Indeed, the company is making a massive impact on U.S. politics. But it is also now used by Europeans, and Macron's campaign is its most significant European success.

Such an interest in modern ways of dealing with politics and using the latest technology has been part of Macron's allure, especially among young voters. He had two iPhones and is a keen user of the Telegram application to communicate informally with his ministers. In May 2018, he invited sixty world leaders of technology companies such as Facebook, Uber, Microsoft, IBM, SAP, or Intel to promote France as a country for top technological experiments and developments. In October 2020, when dozens of elected officials from the Greens,

Socialists, and other leftist parties asked him to delay the rollout of the 5G technology until summer of 2021 due to uncertainties concerning its impact on health and environment, he declared: "France is the country of innovation... We are going to put to rest all false ideas. I hear many voices explaining that the complexity of contemporary problems should be addressed by going back to the oil lamp. I don't believe that the Amish model can solve the challenges of contemporary ecology."[13] In the eyes of French people, during and since the last presidential election, Emmanuel Macron has become the image of modernity, while other French politicians were older and outdated. It had an incontrovertible impact on his election.

That was new, but it may not have been sufficient. Macron's election was not only about being lucky, or able to seize opportunities, or even being able to use modern technologies to organize an Obama-style campaign with a geek-like image. The second-round debate between Macron and his extreme-right or populist rival Marine Le Pen showed another face of the young candidate.

As previously mentioned, the debates often make or break the French Presidential elections. Since 1981, they have been followed by 60 to 80 percent of the French adults, when in the U.S., for example, the debate between Donald Trump and Joe Biden has interested less than 30 percent of them. They are excellent moments of television, and everybody waits for one candidate to trap their opponent. Almost everybody who watched in 1988 remembers the thirty seconds of the debate between the sitting President, François Mitterrand, and his opponent Jacques Chirac, his Prime Minister. Chirac declared to Mitterrand: "Allow me to say that this evening, I am not the prime minister, and you are not the president of the Republic: we are two candidates... equals... who submit themselves to the judgment of the French... You will therefore allow me to call you Monsieur Mitterrand!" And Mitterrand, with his usual finesse, replied: "But you are perfectly correct, Monsieur le Premier Ministre!"[14] which was a way to elegantly refer to Chirac's inferior position and thus to humiliate him. Mitterrand won the debate in the eyes of the French, and was re-elected president, which was not expected before the campaign.

In 2017, Emmanuel Macron was in trouble before the debate with Marine Le Pen. In the first round of the election, Macron received more than 24 percent of the votes, and Le Pen 21.3 percent. The first polls after the first round gave Macron a strong lead, with 68 percent and 32 percent to his opponent. But mistakes were made. At the first round's evening party, Macron showed a lack of humility: he presented himself as a winner when he had less than a quarter of the people voting for him and still had a second round to face. He organized a party for his teams and for famous people in a well-known Paris restaurant, La Rotonde, to celebrate his "victory." People were shocked: they did not see a reason to celebrate when the extreme-right was in the second round for the second time in French history. As stated by Gerard Darmanin, a member of the conservative party, Les Republicains, who later became Macron's minister, "I found it quite indecent. Jacques Chirac did not party when Jean-Marie Le Pen [then the extreme-right leader] was in the second round. It's indecent to party when the extreme right is in the second round."[15]

Macron accumulated mistakes and blunders for one week. He had lost his magic touch and went down nine points in the polls, scoring under 60 percent of the votes. France and Europe were bracing for Marine Le Pen's comeback, an event that would have been as surprising as the Brexit vote in the United Kingdom or Trump's victory in the United States. Then came the second debate.

This debate may have changed the political future of the French extreme-right, at least in the short term. It took place on the 3rd of May, 2017, four days before the final round of the election. The preliminary briefings for Marine Le Pen were short since she was busy with public events and television appearances and was an excellent debater. Macron was not used to difficult political debates and was seen as fragile. Everybody was expecting an aggressive Le Pen to dominate the young and inexperienced Macron.

Le Pen and her team had defined a debate strategy: she would focus on ways to push Macron to lose his temper. She was supposed to get him to get angry and arrogant, to call him the Minister of Debt, Unemployment, and Taxes, and had to avoid stepping into any technical field.[16]

It didn't work. They underestimated Macron.

The debate was quite similar to the first one between Donald Trump and Joe Biden in September 2020. Marine Le Pen has been barking around Macron as an ill-tempered pug trying to destabilize a bigger dog, but Macron stayed solid and calm in front of all attacks, even when they were outrageous. She made good points when she stuck to topics in political field. But when she drifted toward discussing technical matters, such as the methods for France to abandon the euro, she looked incompetent. In addition, her aggressive attitude, her strange permanent smile, and her refusal to debate made a serious Macron appear as the adult in the room. She was the immature child. And toward the end of the debate, she was tired, unable to concentrate, and overwhelmed while Macron stayed in control until the last minute.

Marine Le Pen explained in December 2018 on the French TV network C8 that "It happened that we were at the end of the campaign, that we did not perhaps have the experience of a second round, in any case not that of a debate." She added that her "agenda was overloaded in the days preceding."[17] Emmanuel Macron was well-prepared and took some time off from his campaign before the debate.

But her primary mistake was underestimating her opponent. Emmanuel Macron won the debate because he exemplified the presidential posture and vision. It was a test for him, and he had to avoid falling into the trap of confrontation and the controversy that Marine Le Pen was throwing at him. He demonstrated an unusual mastery during what has been mainly an attack. He quietly showed strength and harmony, embracing his opponent's roller coaster without losing his focus.

On the 7th of May, 2017, Macron won the election with more than 66 percent of the votes. The election showed that the new French president had all the qualities required by Emperor Napoleon for his generals: he has all the necessary skills; he is strong; he carefully prepares his battles; and he is lucky.

But Macron's campaign also showed that those who said that the populists had lost the election were wrong: the populists had won after the first round of the election.

Marine Le Pen, the French leader of the far-right, is clearly a populist. Steve Bannon, the former executive chairman of Breitbart News and former White House chief strategist in the administration of President Donald Trump, who tried to unite the European populists in 2018, even called her the leader of the European populists.

On the other hand, Emmanuel Macron presented himself as the defender of liberalism against the dangers of populism. For example, during his confrontational TV debate with Marine Le Pen, he presented himself as a supporter of the European Union. He described the democratic processes of the European Union as protection against populism. As stated in an article published in *The Conversation* by two European political researchers, Charles Barthold and Martin Fougère, "It's clear that Macron strongly opposes the ideologies that are typically associated with populism today. The word "populism," however, has become a useful tool for liberals. It can be deployed to disqualify any ideologies that challenge the fundamentals of liberalism automatically.

Macron can argue that he couldn't possibly be a "populist" himself since his opposition to it defines him."[18]

But populism may also be considered as "an approach that separates people into 'us' and 'them.' 'Us' refers to the people inside the populist movement, while 'them' typically refers to established elites." For example, Donald Trump has appealed directly to the American people during his 2016 campaign by promising to "drain the swamp" in Washington (meaning get rid of established elites), which is undoubtedly populist. He apparently tweeted "Drain the swamp" seventy-nine times and said it countless times more.

Macron did the same during his campaign. According to Barthold and Fougère, "He has opened a radically new political frontier by calling for a "revolution" against the established elites. His campaign book, itself titled *Révolution*, stated: "The real cleavage today is between backward-looking conservatives... and reformist progressives...." There were Macron's partisans, and 'them,' the backward-looking established extremes on the right and on the left. It allowed him to aggregate "the unsatisfied demands of many groups into one movement. He offers something for everyone."[19] To support this approach, he has left his program quite vague in several areas, and he has strongly advocated for ideas that could please all these groups from the right, the center, and the left of the political scene.

At a meeting with the French mayors in November 2018, in one of his typical shapeshifting moves, Emmanuel Macron himself declared that his movement was populist: "We are not united. So we are offering an easy way, not to populists, I don't like that term [...] but to demagogues, those who would like to simplify things..." and he added, "We are the real populists, we are with the people, every day."[20] Macron sees himself as a populist, in the same way as Abraham Lincoln referred to the people in his Gettysburg address, stating that democracy is "that government of the people, by the people, for the people."

In Macron's attitude, there was a carefully planned scheme. A defining motto for the Rassemblement National, the Marine Le Pen movement, has been "Neither Right nor Left, French!" from a book written in 1996 by Samuel Maréchal, a prominent member of her party. Macron used a similar approach with the same objective of defying the parties from the left and the right. It was very apparent on a TV show during his campaign when he had to answer the question "What is the difference between right and left in politics."[21] He replied that the right is a French political family for which the most important tenet is freedom and that the left is a French political family for which the most important tenet is equality. For the right, people have to be free, but not necessarily equal, and for the left, they must be equal, but not necessarily free. He added, "for me, I think that we need a part of equality, a part of freedom," before adding that he intended to take the best ideas from the right, and the best ideas from the left. Instead of positioning himself as a politician against the right and the left, as Le Pen did, he embraced both in a deadly kiss.

And when Macron declared in a meeting, "we are the real populists," it was not spur of the moment, but rather a carefully considered rocket launched in the direction of the far-right "Front National." Thus, he denied his opponent any monopoly on directly addressing the French people, and put back the Front National to its image of a demagogic far-right party. He also recognizes the specificity of the French president, elected directly by the people.

Macron's success in his first elected position, for president no less, could be attributed to an original cocktail: incredible beginner's luck, surprising political know-how for a beginner, a touch of geek-style originality, and a hint of populism. But it would not have been sufficient if Macron's team had not been able to bring the modern Nordic dream to French people tired of their traditional political system.

Chapter 5
A Nordic Pragmatist

"What we have in mind and what my policies most closely resemble are what we see in the UK, in Norway, in Finland, in Sweden."

— Congresswoman Alexandria Ocasio-Cortez, 2019[1]

"I was tremendously interested in what they had done in Scandinavia along those lines. In Sweden, for example, you have a royal family and a socialist government and a capitalist system, all working happily side by side."

— President Franklin Delano Roosevelt, 1936

On July 31, 2017, shortly after he acceded to the presidency of the Republic of France, the young president received the Swedish Prime Minister, Stefan Lövfen, at the Elysée Palace. It was a sunny day, a smiling Macron, adapting to his newfound status as the French President, welcomed the Swedish Premier under the impressive palace's columns, surrounded by French Republican Guards in their parade uniforms. It was a special day for him — he would meet the prime minister of a country he had quoted all along throughout his presidential campaign.

After their meeting, he insisted at a joint press conference that Sweden was a source of inspiration: "I have always considered that there was in what some may have called the Swedish model a real source of inspiration in several respects... Sweden has been able to evolve its social model without ever betraying it, by reconciling a model of competitiveness whose figures today alone testify to its success and a genuine requirement for social justice. This 'at the same time' is not to my displeasure, and I have always considered that what some people have called the Swedish model was a real source of inspiration in many respects."

It had been his campaign leitmotif. On February 1, 2017, on the national radio channel France-Inter, he reaffirmed his attachment to the "Scandinavian model, which combines flexibility in the labor market and protection of career paths." Later, during the presentation of his party's program, Emmanuel Macron and his advisor, economist Jean Pisani-Ferry, declared that it was "inspired by the Scandinavian model."[2]

On August 30, 2017, En Marche, the president's political party, published on its website under the title "The Swedish Model: What Exactly Is It?" a video presentation of the Nordic model by Émilie Bourdu. She is an economist who wrote in 2013 a book entitled *Les Transformations du Modèle Économique Suédois* (Translated: *The Transformation of the Swedish Economic Model*). In her book, she explains: "Sweden's current economic and social performance is reviving the interest of foreign observers in the Swedish model. Already, in the mid-twentieth century, Sweden was the archetype of a democratic and consensual society, combining economic efficiency, redistribution, and protection of individuals. More recently, from the mid-1990s to the present, it has attracted interest because of its economic vitality, resilient industrial base, and healthy public accounts. One might almost forget that the country experienced a serious economic crisis in the early 1990s, which led to a thorough review of the organization of its social model. When France is wondering how to return to growth and recover its industry, there is much to learn from the ingredients of Swedish success."[3]

The references to Sweden and the Nordic countries have substantially impacted Macron's image as it was a disruptive position in French politics.

Indeed, there should be no shame in imitating Nordic countries, which are among the leaders in practically all international rankings. Who are the world leaders for the digital skills of the population? According to the Global Competitiveness Report published in 2020 by the World Economic Forum, it is Finland and Sweden (France and the U.S. are far behind). According to the UNESCO office for statistics, Denmark, Sweden, and Finland lead (along with South Korea) in the rankings for the number of researchers per million inhabitants. The World Happiness reports tell us that people in Finland, Iceland, and Denmark are the happiest people in the world, with Sweden ranking fifth, the U.S. fourteenth, and France twentieth. According to Transparency International, the Nordic countries are also the least corrupt countries (Denmark ranks first, Finland second, and Sweden third, while France is twenty-third, and the U.S. twenty-fifth). According to the World Intellectual Property Organization, Sweden, Finland, and Denmark are among the top ten countries for the number of patents per million inhabitants. We could go on and on; Sweden and other Nordic countries are among the leaders in fields as diverse as equality, growth, employment, research, environmental protection, and the fight against climate change.

That is why it became trendy among the progressives in the world to refer to the Nordic countries or the Nordic model. In the U.S., for example, during the first debate between Hillary Clinton and Bernie Sanders in the Democratic primary elections in 2015, Bernie Sanders, an admirer of the Nordic countries, said, "I think we should look to countries like Denmark, like Sweden and Norway, and learn from what they've accomplished for their workers." Hillary Clinton could only respond, "I love Denmark. But we are not Denmark. We are the United States of America." More recently, in January 2019, Rep. Alexandria Ocasio-Cortez (D-NY) has popularized the philosophy of democratic socialism, and she believes that it corresponds to the Nordic policies. She declared in an interview with Anderson Cooper on CBS that "What we have in mind and what my policies most closely resemble are what we see in the UK, in Norway, in Finland, in Sweden."[4] One could argue that the policies are quite different among these countries, but the reference to the Nordics is clear.

That is not new for the U.S. In the 1930s, their leaders took a serious interest in the Swedish model. The credit for this goes to the American journalist Marquis-William Childs, who after a trip to Sweden wrote "Sweden: The Middle Way," published in 1936, which became a bestseller in the United States, and then in the world, and a common reference when talking about the Swedish model. Childs explains in his book that Sweden found an effective compromise between the two political extremes of the time, the United States and Soviet Union. According to him, Sweden seemed to have been able to solve its social problems and at the same time maintain economic viability, a very "Macronian" idea.[5]

President Franklin Delano Roosevelt, then campaigning for re-election, often cited Sweden, notably at the Democratic convention in Philadelphia in June 1936. He explained, "A very interesting book came out a few months ago — *The Middle Way*. I was very interested in what they had done in Scandinavia. [...] In Sweden, for example, you have a royal family, a socialist government, and a capitalist system all working side by side. Of course, it's a smaller country than ours; but they've had some very interesting and, so far, very successful experiments." The same interest was also shown at the same time by the British Labour Party.

The French attitude was at that time quite different, even if there was interest on the left in Roosevelt's New Deal or the activities of the British Labour Party. The French showed little interest in Sweden, despite the success of the Social-Democrats, who returned to power in 1932. On the other hand, only a few right-wing original personalities were fascinated by what was happening there, such as Emile Schreiber, a liberal journalist and founder, with his brother, of the daily newspaper *Les Echos* — which is still the leading economic newspaper in France. Schreiber declared his admiration for the Swedish model in his book *Heureux Scandinaves* (Translated: *Happy Scandinavians*). For him, Sweden was home to "perhaps the happiest of the peoples of Europe, the one that has reached a high degree of social perfection, while jealously safeguarding the principle of liberty." Some other personalities shared this analysis, notably the contributors to the *Nouveaux Cahiers*, an economic and political journal that brought together bankers, industrialists, senior civil servants, and trade unionists, to put an end to the communist and socialist class struggle.

But the majority were against these ideas: they were criticized by the French left, communists, and socialists, because it came from the right, and by all the French right, who were traditionally opposed to any socialist idea, even one brought on to fight communism. And this opposition to anything social-democrat has been a constant attitude of the majority of French political parties and politicians since then — which explains why Emmanuel Macron surprised everybody when he began to refer to Sweden and Denmark as successes and models.

This situation, where social-democracy is rejected by the political right and by the left, is particular to France. In Germany or in the United Kingdom, the attitude of the main political parties on the left is very different. The Germans even have the Social-Democrats as a political party. But the French left has a different history.

Interestingly, social-democracy is a French invention. In 1848, there was no communism or Marxism in Europe, but something called republican-socialism. Known variously as social-democracy, democratic-socialism, or simply radicalism, republican-socialism was the main popular movement for social reforms following the French Revolution of 1848, resulting from an alliance between the democratic-republicans and the socialists against the right (the bourgeois). Karl Marx ironically commented after the event: "the party of the workers and the party of the petty-bourgeoisie form the social-democratic party." He did not like it because "The revolutionary point was broken off and a democratic turn given to the social-demands of the proletariat."[6]

The 1st International (1864-1876), the first political organization of the workers' movement, was primarily social-democratic. It claimed to be the first to conquer political power and defined itself by a close alliance with trade unionism, as it is still more or less the case in Nordic countries. But in the following years, the different social-democratic currents argued about the methods used against the bourgeois state, about the choice between reform and revolution. There was, therefore, a split following World War I, and then the October Revolution in Russia. Some of the militants created parties that used the name of communist and joined the Communist International after its creation in 1919. In most countries, alongside the revolutionary communist parties (who have dominated the Soviet Union), there were socialists (in France, for example), who were not denying the revolutionary approach in the long term, and social-democrats (in the Nordic countries and Germany) who were on the reformist side.

The consequence is that the development of reformist social-democracy in Germany and the Nordic countries has always been a problem for the French left, who considered the movement a traitor to the socialist cause. Even today, a part of the French left still agrees with Lenin's contemptuous reflection: "If the revolution breaks out in Stockholm, the insurgent leaders will invite to dinner the members of the bourgeois government, which they will have overthrown, to congratulate them on the efforts they made when they were in government,"[7] a sentence that was used for a long time in the French Socialist Party to mock those who were social-democrats.

In Sweden, social-democracy came to power, stayed there, and quickly became non-revolutionary: from 1920 to 1976, social-democrats ruled the country almost continuously. They closely collaborated with the trade unions. Far from carrying out a revolution, they created a welfare state system based on principles of equality and redistribution. While the German Social-Democrats waited until the Godesberg Congress in 1959 to reject any reference to Marxism and recognize free competition and entrepreneurial initiative as essential elements of economic policy, their Swedish counterparts were more flexible. They quickly embraced social-capitalism by maintaining a well-functioning market economy and private ownership while ensuring redistribution of wealth.

That was not acceptable for the French socialists, who officially remained left-wing reformists, that is, socialists who sought by legal and democratic means the progressive substitution of capitalist property by social property. Those who, like the Nordics, accepted the capitalist system and just wanted to control and reform it for the benefit of the workers were a minority and avoided calling themselves "social-democrats" as they would have been ostracized in their party. It lasted for the main part of the twentieth century. According to the historian Irène Théroux, the theme of social-democracy "seems to have appeared in the 1970s, when the Socialist Party, undergoing rapid and profound restructuring, decided to conclude a common government program with the enemy Communists, which aroused a very strong anti-totalitarian hostility" from a minority in the party.[8] This group was called the second left and was social-democrat without daring to say it loud.

Why is that? There are different explanations. One is historical: the French Socialist Party has not developed from the workers' unions. It has been dominated by intellectuals who were working based on the theory of socialism. In the Nordics and Germany, the social-democratic parties have had leaders and members mainly belonging to the working class and were aware of the industrial realities and production constraints. It has facilitated the negotiations with the employers and developed a successful economic model based on compromises of mutual interest.

Another reason may be French conservatism. The history of the "French" pension system is an interesting illustration of the difficulty for France to take on new ideas. Seen from abroad, the French pension system, more generous than the Nordic ones, seems to come from the French political left, who is leading frequent demonstrations to defend it. This is not the case: in reality, the base of this system comes from Germany, more particularly from German conservatives. In 1889, German Chancellor Otto Von Bismarck adopted a social insurance program for old age, based on an idea presented in 1881 to the German Parliament. The objective was the promotion of the welfare of workers to maintain the efficiency of the German economy. But above all, it was created to avoid a Bolshevik revolution by cutting off those who called for more radical socialist alternatives. The Nordic countries quickly followed, as it is an idea that social-democrats loved, as this kind of compromise between the interests of the workers and those of the employers is the base of social-democracy. The French did not want it.

But then, during World War II, France was occupied and Germany obliged France to adopt its social insurance system. After the war, everybody wanted to change the pension system imposed by the Germans: the mutual insurance companies and a large part of the left, which before the war managed funded pension schemes for their members, pushed for pension funds similar to those in the U.S.. Others wanted a minimal tax-based universal pension system, with the possibility of encouraging the development of voluntary individual or collective supplementary pensions, an approach adopted by the United Kingdom under the impetus of the economist William Beveridge. In the end, the supporters of the pension scheme created during the war under the Germans won because it was popular among the people.

Today, almost seventy years after this event, every time the government envisages changing it, the French take to the street. Considering this high level of conservatism, it is not surprising that it took more than half a century for the leaders of the French left to abandon the revolutionary dogma.[9] Even then, the idea of social-democracy is considered by some as heresy. That is why Macron's declaration in favor of the Swedish or Danish solutions appeared to be political suicide.

Others have tried in the past to inject a dose of social-democracy into the French political system. Jean-Jacques Servan-Schreiber, a graduate of the prestigious French Ecole Polytechnique, a journalist, a specialist on the United States, the founder of the magazine *l'Express*, and a close friend to presidents Valéry Giscard d'Estaing and John F. Kennedy, was the Golden Boy of the 1950s, just as Emmanuel Macron is today. His book, *The American Challenge*, first published in 1967, remains today's biggest international bestseller for a political essay. It has been translated into fifteen languages and sold millions of copies worldwide. As Nobel Prize-winning economist Paul Krugman noted in 2014, *The American Challenge* was a seminal work that heralded in the 1960s American dominance, the importance of the knowledge economy, decentralization, European integration, the euro, and the move to the internet.

Servan-Schreiber was in frequent contact with the Nordic and especially the Swedish social-democrats. *The American Challenge* ended with a "Note on the Swedish Experience," praising that country's success. Servan-Schreiber explained that Europe could only be strong by uniting and adopting a model similar to the Swedish one. But even if he had national and international stature, he was never very successful in politics. During his ten years as the President of the Radical Party, a centrist party opposed to the left and to President de Gaulle's conservatives, he never reached his dream to lead France. He was living proof that it was suicidal for politicians, even the most brilliant ones, to take the prosperous Nordic countries as a model.

So why has Emmanuel Macron chosen to refer to the Nordic social-democracies as his inspiration? The success of the Nordic policies and the Nordic model in the last twenty years has undoubtedly played a role. The model, which includes flexibility on the labor market, a high level of education, and excellent social protection, has been highly efficient economically. In addition, the Nordic countries do very well in the majority of international rankings, and that may have convinced Macron to choose them as his model. But it was risky: his opponents have tried to adopt the same attitude as Hilary Clinton in front of Bernie Sanders: we love Denmark and Sweden. But France is not Denmark. France is not Sweden. It is the usual attitude in France when somebody makes the mistake of referring to Sweden.

But still, it did not prevent Macron from praising the Nordic countries. He did not have the choice if he wanted to depart from what the two governing parties have been proposing for several decades: his program could be neither right-wing nor socialist. But there were not many alternatives, except for the extremes. It was also necessary for Macron to be cautious and avoid following in the footsteps of Jean-

Marie Le Pen, the previous leader of the extreme-right who declared in 2002, "Socially I am of the left, economically I am of the right."

Therefore, referring to the Nordics must have seemed a good compromise for someone who wanted to satisfy both the right and the left. It was also a clever move: the media compared Macron with foreign politicians popular in France, such as Justin Trudeau in Canada or Bernie Sanders in the United States, who themselves have often referred to Sweden, and sent their teams to the Nordics to pick up ideas. It gave Macron access to the center-left voters, who have up until that point voted for the Socialist Party in the absence of a social-democratic alternative.

Emmanuel Macron's choice was also due to the influence of the economists with whom he surrounded himself during his campaign. He had studied philosophy at Paris University, later completing a master's degree in public affairs, and he had a strong personal interest in literature and history. Even if he worked as an investment banker at Rothschild & Cie Banque and learned about mergers and acquisitions, he was not very knowledgeable about economics. He was sufficiently wise to understand that he had to progress in this field and propose an economically credible program.

When Macron decides to do something, he invests himself fully. Philippe Aghion, Professor at the College de France and the London School of Economics, and a fellow of the Econometric Society and the American Academy of Arts and Sciences, readily recount that at the beginning of the campaign, Emmanuel Macron immediately showed a genuine desire to understand economics and regularly dropped by his house to study these issues in the evening.[10] In addition, Macron quickly surrounded himself with a prestigious group of economists: in the media, he became the economists' candidate. In April 2017, before the second round of the election, forty French economists signed an article to support him in the Le Monde newspaper.[11] It was unprecedented.

But he was not the candidate of all economists. He was the candidate of those who admired the Nordic models. First of all, Philippe Aghion said when preparing Macron's pension reform: "My compass is the Swedish model."[12] Jean Pisani-Ferry, a renowned French economist, was responsible for preparing his presidential program, and explained to the press on March 3rd, 2017: "With pensions and unemployment, we are proposing a new approach to work. It is the Scandinavian model."[13]

Marc Ferracci, his friend and the best man at his wedding, and a professor of economics at Paris' Panthéon-Assas University, also has a strong interest in the Scandinavian social models and inspired the candidate's proposals for major social reforms such as unemployment insurance or vocational training. One of the French media's favorite economists, Elie Cohen, a specialist on markets and economic crisis, also participated in his campaign and declared in December 2017, "It is the flexicurity system of the Danish model that we are trying to import in France."[14] Philippe Martin, professor at the Institut d'Etudes Politiques de Paris and chair of the French Council of Economic Advisers, brought in Macron's team his views on using the Nordic mix of liberalism for international trade social support to help the people adapt to a changing world.

But Macron still knew that there were risks in presenting himself as the candidate of the Swedish model. In addition to a dogmatic attitude toward social-democracy, leftist politicians traditionally deny Swedish successes. They point out that the price of the Swedish success is the failure of the social system, with rising inequality and a failure to integrate immigrants. Critics among right-side politicians focus more on the fact that taxes are very high and discourage private initiative, that the public sector is bloated, and unions have too much power. As a consequence, the admirers of the Swedish model try to avoid these attacks by staying very discreet: for example, the sociologist and historian Wojtek Kalinowski, co-director of the Veblen Institute, published a very positive book on the Swedish model in October 2017 but preferred to adopt a questioning tone for the title of his book: *Swedish Model: What If Social-Democracy Is Not Dead?*[15]

Macron understood that he should not appear naïve and idealize Sweden or Denmark: he has never announced that he wanted to transpose the entire Nordic model. For example, he avoided making proposals inspired by Sweden for education or healthcare because he was well aware of Swedish shortcomings in these areas. His team was also cautious in their choice of words. They were inspired by the Swedish model. They would adapt it to the French culture, but they would not copy it.

That is different from the attitude of the American Democrats' left, led by Bernie Sanders and Elizabeth Warren, and more recently by Alexandria Ocasio-Cortez, who appears to support "modeling the United States after Nordic countries such as Finland, Sweden, and Norway."[16] In the idea of modeling after Nordic countries, there is an almost extremist intention of globally copying the model, which may lead to a failure because of the cultural, social, and economic differences between the U.S. and the Nordics. Macron, in contrast, learned to be moderate in his youthful enthusiasm, and to be cautious.

Macron's Nordic strategy worked. It had been carefully presented, it had the support of mainstream economists, but one other factor helped: the French people were well-prepared, as the idea of Nordic superiority has gained traction among the French general public. The mainstream media has presented the global rankings with the Nordics as the world or European leaders in many areas. In addition, social media has been a sounding board for the dissemination of information. Many French people travel more to Nordic countries. Visits to the Nordic capitals are easy: direct flights from Paris are inexpensive, thanks to the intense competition among the low-cost and traditional airlines. Those who have made the trip generally have a favorable opinion of the Nordic way of life: it is difficult to hide that the real wealth per capita after adjusting price levels is 20 percent higher in Denmark and Sweden than in France. After all, growth in Sweden has been double that seen in France over the last ten years. It makes it easier to convince the French to adopt Swedish-inspired reforms.

There is also a continuous migration movement from France to the Nordics. Several sites aimed at the French community in Sweden, such as *Les Français en Suède* (Translation: The French in Sweden), successfully support the newcomers. According to the Swedish statistical office, the number of people of French origin has doubled since the beginning of the twenty-first century to reach more than 10,000 people. Young French students go to the Nordics to study and are attracted by the lifestyle, the salaries, the responsibilities entrusted to beginners in Swedish companies where hierarchy is minimal, and with modern management that changes them from France. All these emigrants stay in touch with their friends and families in France and tell them about Sweden. In addition, young people, who played a crucial role in Macron's campaign, also travel more than older generations.

In the end, nobody knows if Emmanuel Macron won the election because he promised to adopt the best of the Nordic countries or if he won despite it: the determinants of a vote are challenging to analyze. But this episode shows that Macron does not hesitate to challenge the existing order and take risks that few politicians would accept — if it is for the right cause. Young French voters appreciated it in the 2017 election.

The interesting question is whether he has kept his promises to implement what works in Sweden or Denmark and if it worked. The answer is not a clear "yes" or "no," as is often the case in politics. Some of the reforms were implemented as planned, such as the flexibility of the labor market. Others were not implemented because they were not ready when the coronavirus pandemic began.

The iconic reform for Emmanuel Macron was that of the pension system. But it did not go as planned for a surprising reason: even if France is not far from Sweden, Macron's teams, including his economists, did not know the actual status of the pension system in Sweden at the time the reform was announced during his campaign. Macron thought that he'd played it safe: the main French trade union, a majority of his opponents on the right and some on the left, plus the European Commission pushed France to adopt a system similar to the Swedish pension system, which, according to the experts, promoted equity and long term sustainability.

But when Macron declared that he would push for the Swedish system in March 2017, the Swedish Pensions Agency published a comparative study showing that the system was not as fair as previously announced. After the Swedish reform, 92 percent of women and 72 percent of men had lost a portion of their pension under the new system compared to the old system, losing sometimes more than 30 percent. This new information changed the mind of large groups of supporters of the reform. One piece of advice for anybody wanting to implement Nordic policies: follow Franklin D. Roosevelt's method and send a specialized team to Sweden for several weeks before proposing anything. Macron was obliged to postpone his reform.

In other domains, Macron's government has been able to implement his reforms inspired by the Nordic countries: between 2017 and 2019, his government loosened labor-market rules to encourage hiring, redesigned professional training, expanded apprenticeships, and reworked benefit incentives to encourage the unemployed to return to work, all reforms which were a direct copy and paste of the Nordic labor market model. It may explain why France's rate of growth was higher than Germany's in 2019.

What does this Nordic tropism say about Macron? The main lesson seems to be that he has been the first French politician independent of either leftist or conservative ideologies. It makes him difficult to read because he is a pragmatist, like the Nordic leaders.

The notion of pragmatism is not Nordic. It is American. It was born in the 1870s in Cambridge, Massachusetts. The term appeared in a Metaphysical Club founded by the philosopher Charles Sanders Peirce. William James, a member of this club, popularized the notion in the early years of the twentieth century, denying the existence of pure and absolute truth: "Ideas are not true or false," he argued. They are either useful or not. "They are mental tools created by our brains for the purpose of solving problems and must be judged by their practical effectiveness."[17]

Even if it comes from the U.S., pragmatism is, with transparency and tough-mindedness, one of the keywords for the success of the Nordic country. It could be attributed to the fact that, until the first part of the twentieth century, life in the Nordics was tough due to the cold and the lack of natural resources except wood. Millions of people left the Nordic countries for the new world because of food shortages. In such a situation, pragmatism was privileged over ideology. Later, the social-democratic ideology dominated the country's life and put a strain on the way people and politicians should think, until the big Nordic economic crisis in the 1990s. The social-democrats and the conservatives were obliged to find realistic solutions which were not necessarily in line with their doctrines, and pragmatism replaced ideology.

One of the best descriptions of the importance of pragmatism in the Nordic success can be found in a 2013 article in *The Economist*: "On discovering that the old social-democratic consensus was no longer working, they let it go with remarkably little fuss and introduced new ideas from across the political spectrum. They also proved utterly determined in pushing through reforms. It is a grave error to mistake

Nordic niceness for soft-headedness. Pragmatism explains why the new consensus has quickly replaced the old one. Few Swedish Social-Democratic politicians, for instance, want to dismantle the conservative reforms put in place in recent years. It also explains why Nordic countries can often seem to be amalgams of left- and right-wing policies. Pragmatism also explains why the Nordics are continuing to upgrade their model. [...] And they are doing all this without sacrificing what makes the Nordic model so valuable: the ability to invest in human capital and protect people from the disruptions that are part of the capitalist system."[18]

A typical example of a Nordic pragmatist is Fredrik Reinfeldt, to whom Macron has been compared, undoubtedly because he became the Swedish Prime Minister when he was forty-one (Macron became president at thirty-nine). He was popular among the younger generations, as Macron was when he was elected. Fredrik Reinfeldt won the 2006 Swedish election by a wide margin and became the youngest head of government in Swedish history. As the conservative Moderaterna party leader, he transformed it into a centrist liberal party, which he renamed the New Moderaterna, just as Macron created his centrist liberal party, La République en March (Translation: Republic on the Move). To win the elections against the left, Reinfeldt pledged not to question the Swedish social model, but rather improve and adapt it to the world as it is. Before him, conservatives systematically criticized the Swedish social model and lost election after election. Reinfeldt won again in 2010, becoming the longest-serving non-Social-Democratic Prime Minister in Sweden since 1900.

He was in favor of the European Union, as Macron is. He is known for his listening skills, his pragmatic attitude, his refusal of conflicts, and his will to privilege common sense over ideology, which accentuates the resemblance. Macron won in the same way: his pragmatism has been his main argument during the campaign. According to the French newspaper *La Croix*, "he repeated it throughout the campaign and until the last few days: he will be above all pragmatic. Emmanuel Macron has made this his line, the mark of his independence from the dogmatic right/left approach." He wanted to free himself "from the ideological blocs of the right and the left and to have the liberty to take from each the measures and ideas that can work. Success is at the heart of his program."[19]

Macron's speeches have certainly had some impact, but one of the most important shows of the 2017 French presidential campaign has been *Présidentielle: Candidats au Tableau!* (Translation: Presidential Election: Candidates to the Blackboard!). During the show, the candidates for the 2017 presidential election had to answer the questions of a class of children from eight to twelve years old. The children had prepared for Emmanuel Macron a list of measures from the left and from the right on which they wanted him to indicate if he would adopt them or not. He took them one by one, saying "I think this could work," or "I don't think it could work," and explaining why. In the end, he had supported as many measures from the right as from the left, and he added: "I will decide on a measure because it works, not because it is from the left or from the right."[20]

Being a pragmatist has an advantage, but it is not without risks. Saying "I will take this measure because it works" entails being sure that it will indeed work, being certain that people agree with the objective of the measure, and that the means to reach this objective are acceptable for people.

When Emperor Napoleon decided to re-establish slavery after the French Revolution abolished it, it was mainly to reconstitute a French colonial empire in America as an economic asset. He knew that 10 percent of French people made their livings through colonial trade before the French Revolution, supported by slave labor in the plantations: a million slaves arrived in the West Indies in the eighteenth century. Napoleon was a pragmatist, and his objective (to improve his nation's wealth) was acceptable. But the method was flawed and a majority did not accept the means. In politics, the objectives chosen by politicians who reach positions of power are generally shared by the people who elected them. The devil lies in the choice of the methods: will they work? Will there be unwanted side effects? Are they in line with the people's values?

This has been a challenge for Emmanuel Macron. And a difference from the Nordic countries. When the Swedish Government prepares an important reform, it generally begins by creating a special investigative committee which listens to interested parties over several months, makes a report, and proposes new legislation and regulations. Specialists and interested parties are involved and analyze the method and the means carefully. It avoids surprises in the implementation and failure in the end.

Emmanuel Macron has proceeded differently because as President, he has inherited some of traditional powers of the ancient monarchs. Reforms are announced and a rapid consultation mechanism with the stakeholders is implemented. Some of the critics of different stakeholders are included in the project, and then the President's comfortable majority in the Parliament approves the reform. It is faster in the short-term but may not necessarily be as efficient as the Nordic countries' methods.

***

Since Emmanuel Macron and his team do not refer to the Nordics anymore, it would be easy to forget about his links with these countries. However, he has implemented some fashion of almost all those "Nordic" reforms in France, in particular the changes to the labor market, and he has been able to force flexibility within the French economy, when, until now, rigidity was the rule. He has also developed relations with Nordic leaders, visiting their countries several times to discuss European and international affairs, and gaining useful allies with whom he shares common values and attitudes.

It also says a lot about Macron, that he appreciates the pragmatic attitude of the Nordics, which makes them adapt rapidly to the world's changes. Interestingly, there seems to be convergence between a renovated social democracy, found in the Nordic countries, and in other parts of the world such as New Zealand, which has been obliged to change its way of protecting people in order to make them adapt to the needs of a modern economy. And Macron's type of pragmatic liberalism could inspire future young international leaders.

Chapter 6

Machiavellian or Inexperienced: The First Steps of the Apprentice

"If you're looking for an embodiment of what we commonly understand the word "Machiavellian" to mean, it's hard to go past the House of Cards character Francis Underwood. Using, where appropriate, a combination of double-crossing, blackmail, acute political nous, ruthlessness — murder doesn't faze him in the least — he rises to the top political position."[1]

— Loretta Barnard,

Emmanuel Macron has frequently been accused of Machiavellianism. His enemies believe he used clever but dishonest methods that deceived people into voting for an outsider. In France, it provides excellent material to journalists wanting to write about Macron, and it sells among both his opponents and his supporters who tend to think that he is particularly clever.

There is often discussion that he was able to win only by setting a trap for President Hollande, who chose him as a Minister of Economy when he was a political unknown. The story told is that he betrayed Hollande by announcing he was running without waiting to see if Hollande would declare. One of his colleagues, Christian Eckert, who had been Minister of Budget with Macron in Hollande's government, explained in 2018 that Macron had secretly and methodically prepared, since the beginning of his appointment as Minister of Economy, to be a candidate for the Elysée. Eckert considered it a "Machiavellian approach" and even accused Macron of being a traitor. It was harsh, as one could also assume that Macron's decision to run could be explained by other reasons, such as Hollande's tricks to sideline Macron as soon as he became too popular.

Whatever Macron does, there is always a suspicion that he has a secret plan, a hidden intention behind the apparent transparency about his objectives. Véronique Descacq, a leader of the French trade union CFDT, declared in May, 2018 that "Macron is Machiavellian." Annie Genevard, Secretary-General of the Republicans, the main party on the right, said in 2018 on the French television that Emmanuel Macron "is a slightly Machiavellian tactician." And there is even an essay called "Machiavel et Macron: Correspondance Improbable," (Translation: Machiavelli and Macron: An Improbable Correspondence) which is a well-documented fiction with an exchange of imagined letters between Machiavelli and Macron.

Calling Macron Machiavellian did not stop at French borders. In July 2020, Turkey sent its Oruc Reis research ship supported by Turkish warships to carry out a drilling survey in Greek waters close to the Greek island of Kastellorizo, a short distance from the coast of southwest Turkey. Then Greece sent a fleet soon supported by French warships to prevent further exploration. The Turkish Ministry of Foreign Affairs wrote on the 10th of September, 2020, that "Macron is attacking Turkey because of the internal sense of discontent he feels because we have disrupted his Machiavellian foreign policy plans."[2] *Al-Araby Al-Jadid*, a news website funded by Qatar and headed by former Israeli-Arab member of Parliament Azmi Bishara, an advisor to the new emir, wrote that, "the influence of Machiavelli on Macron's political practices is evident. And perhaps the greatest moment of Machiavellianism was his visit to Beirut in the aftermath of the explosion in the city's port on the 4th of August."[3]

Being accused of Machiavellianism is not necessarily a handicap for a world leader. There is even a modest presentation on *Prezi* ("Contemporary World Leaders & Their Relation to Machiavelli") in which the authors have compared John F. Kennedy's characteristics with Machiavelli's recommendations for a leader in his most famous book *The Prince*. Machiavelli states that a prince should be war-wise and handle war not only for the gain of territory, but also for self-defense and lawful stability. According to the presentation authors, Kennedy fought in Vietnam "not for the gain of territory, but for self-defense against the spread of Communism." According to Machiavelli, a prince should be noble and kind-hearted in order to be both feared and loved, and Kennedy "was one of the most well-loved presidents in U.S. history." The list goes on, and the authors conclude that "based on what a Machiavellian leader would be, John F. Kennedy could almost be considered one."[4]

That shows that being Machiavellian is not necessarily a bad thing if you look at the genuine concept put forward by Machiavelli. According to Australian writer Loretta Barnard, Machiavelli's *The Prince* describes the various states or principalities that were part of Italy in which he lived and being desirous of stability of governance and ultimately a united Italy, its author proposed some characteristics he felt were important for a prince — read: political leader — to be an effective head of state. Among those characteristics were a strong connection with the military and powerbrokers, the assembly of a trusted team of advisors, and a willingness to act expediently if necessary, so if it was crucial to tell the occasional lie (or worse) to achieve a goal then the prince should go ahead and do that." Barnard concludes that it is part of daily politics: "there's nothing new there — governments have always lied by obfuscation or omission, twisting the facts or keeping information from the public when it suits their interests."[5]

In France, linking the President to Machiavelli is even quite normal for successful French presidents, at least those re-elected. In 1986, Professor Roger Baillet, a research specialist of Italian Renaissance, analyzed the convergence between the life and the philosophy of de Gaulle and Machiavelli, concluding that "their respective trajectories reveal almost identical experiences and events insofar as they both advocated — unsuccessfully, it is true — military reforms and coordination of political and military action. From this point of view, Machiavelli and de Gaulle appear above all men of action and reflection."[6]

Former President Mitterrand, who was highly skillful with a strong dose of finesse and, sometimes, cruelty, has been called "*Le Machiavel de Latché*" (Translation: The Machiavel from Latché). Latché was his holiday house in the southwest of France, used for meetings and planning with his close friends and allies. He was nicknamed the "Florentine" in reference to the art of dodging, illustrated during the Renaissance by natives of Florence, like Lorenzo the Magnificent and Machiavelli.

It appears as a privilege and a mark of respect for his intelligence and political skills for Macron to be associated with these two successful presidents. It is better than being called "small-minded Machiavellis," as ex-President Sarkozy and Hollande were in 2016 in an article in *L'Obs*, one of the leading French political magazines.[7]

But one fascinating fact is that Macron is probably the head of state with the best knowledge of Machiavelli in the world, which gives some validity to the hypothesis that Machiavelli influences him. When he was a student at the Paris Nanterre University, Macron wrote his master's thesis on "The Political Fact and the Representation of History in Machiavelli." However, as nobody can find it today because old archives in French universities are not digitalized, it is impossible to understand Macron's thoughts about Machiavelli and his recommendations for politicians. However, of great legislators who founded great peoples or great cities, Machiavelli writes in his book, *The Prince*, "It cannot be seen that they received from fortune anything other than the occasion which gave them a subject on which to introduce the form which seemed good to them."[8] It is difficult not to see a link with Macron, who understood the French political crisis before anyone else, and has seized that opportunity.

Even if Macron focused his studies on Machiavelli, and if he declared "with a smile" in 2014 to Liz Alderman from *The New York Times* that it was a "good background for navigating power politics in Paris," it had not prepared him to be accused of inexperience and naïvety. During the first months of his campaign, nobody would have said that he was Machiavellian; in fact, quite the opposite. Because of his young age, his inexperience in politics, and his boyish looks, he had the image of a naïve young politician who would not be able to manage a complex and old country. That was an image supported by his opponents, and in the media. On the most popular political show on French TV, "Les Guignols de l'info," a satirical puppet show, Macron was caricatured from 2014 to 2017 first as a crying baby, having fun insulting the poor, and doing his business on François Hollande's political program. Later he was presented as an insolent teenager before becoming a screaming young adult. And the show ran every evening, in front of millions of French voters.

Yet his lack of experience may have been an asset. Many French people were tired of politicians, and he appeared to belong to a different category. However, it has also likely cost him a lot when he had to face his first severe crisis, some weeks after being elected. It was, as in most crises, a story with many twists and turns, featuring unreliable allies, and ultimately an unconvincing result that severed Macron's relation with people who wanted a change in French politics.

After the French Parliament adopted the laws on transparency in public life in 2013 to fight against conflicts of interest and democratic openness, all parliamentarians must fill a public declaration of interest. Several journalists of the French media followed in 2017 the example of the *Canard Enchaîné*, the newspaper that broke the story of former Prime Minister François Fillon, the right-wing candidate and the frontrunner for the 2017 presidential election, who had been accused of having organized a system of fictitious jobs for his wife and his children. They investigated the situation of the 900 members of Parliament (National Assembly and Senate). The French people discovered that 10 to 15 percent of them employed at least a spouse or a child paid for by public money in the Parliament. There were no other indictments: these spouses and siblings were employed for shorter periods than Ms. Fillon, and, sadly for democracy, it was considered not worth spending public money on investigations to determine if they were working, which would have been legal, or if, like Ms. Fillon, they could be suspected of being paid for doing nothing. It was a missed opportunity for Emmanuel Macron to show that he was different from the usual politicians.

It created turmoil in France, and showed how much France has changed. Twenty years ago, there would have been no transparency law allowing investigative journalists to access the records and archives of the Parliament. Even if such behavior had been discovered, it would not have triggered reactions, as it was generally accepted that politicians got special privileges. But French people have changed, and they became very suspicious of politicians. According to the European Social Survey, more than 65 percent of French people do not trust politicians, with 13 percent not trusting them at all. In addition, even if they were first reluctant, French people have learned to use social networks, which have played an essential role in amplifying the Fillon case and obliging justice to act on it.

During the last presidential campaign, all the candidates had been pushed to present corrective measures to improve the transparency of institutions in France, with, according to the NGO Transparency International, an advantage to Emmanuel Macron compared to his opponents. When Macron was elected, there were strong expectations, especially with a new and modern president.

All the French media, TV, radio, and newspapers sent journalists worldwide to analyze what was done elsewhere to fight corruption and improve transparency in public affairs. After many weeks, they systematically took Sweden as a reference, with headlines such as "Fillon Affair: Why Is Sweden Considered a Model of Transparency in Politics?" or "Moralization of Public Life: In Sweden, Transparency in Politics Is a Deep Value." France was waiting for the first Swedish reform of the President.

The Swedish solution looked simple to implement and would have solved the problem: the principle of transparency (*offentlightet-sprincipen*) has been enshrined in a constitutional text since 1766. It is based on the idea that public money does not belong to the state but to the taxpayers. And it means, among other things, a universal right of access to all administrative and financial documents paid with public money. There is an obligation for any public official whom a citizen or journalist approaches to give without delay and directly any information in his possession, except in cases where this would threaten the country's security. As a result, transparency is total and immediate: anyone can obtain, for example, the expense accounts or official bank card purchases of any political figure, at the national, regional, or local level. The main media have specialized journalists who scrutinize these expenses, thus forcing politicians to be very honest.

In Sweden, everyone remembers the Toblerone scandal: at the end of 1995, Mona Sahlin, the second-in-command in the Social-Democratic government, was forced to resign for some groceries, including a chocolate bar, paid with her official credit card. Such control of the media is sufficient to ensure that any ethically questionable behavior has a good chance of being discovered and stigmatized.

After hesitating on this solution, which would have gone a long way to reconciling the French with their political staff, Emmanuel Macron backed down for two reasons. The first one was the opposition of almost all elected officials. They felt citizens should not have access to all their activities paid by public money, including with whom they had lunch and for what reason. And second, there was the Bayrou scandal.

François Bayrou was a well-respected politician, President of a French Center Party, the Democratic Movement (MoDem), and the European Democratic Party (EDP). He was a candidate in the presidential election in 2002, 2007, and 2012 and got a sufficient number of votes to influence the final result by systematically supporting the candidate from the right. During the 2017 campaign, he surprised everyone by backing Emmanuel Macron and became his most important ally. He was appointed Minister of Justice in the government after Macron's election, and some members of his party were a part of the government announced on the 17th of May, 2017.

Then Macron had to face his first bump: a preliminary investigation into the Bayrou's party, Macron's ally, was opened by the Paris public prosecutor's office in early June 2017 for "breach of trust and concealment." The party was suspected of having financed salaries of its headquarters employees in France through the budget allocated by the European Union to its Parliament's members. It was illegal. After some days of denying any wrongdoing, François Bayrou, who, as Minister of Justice, oversaw the preparation of a law in the field of transparency and ethics for public officials, announced that he was leaving the government.

That was hard on Macron. The law prepared by Bayrou was supposed to be his first act to show that politics in France would change with him at the helm. Also, Bayrou's support and advice have been one of the main reasons for his successful campaign. Bayrou was highly determined to propose a strong law for the moralization of politics to Parliament. Losing him in this manner was a defeat for Macron. He finally settled for having Parliament vote on two laws consisting of a juxtaposition of heterogeneous measures to avoid new problems and specify the prohibition of certain practices.

The consequences were evident. Macron looked weak and unable to take the necessary measures to optimize France's democracy. It influenced his relationship with Parliament and with the people. French statistical institute IFOP, which regularly measures the president's popularity, found that, in June 2017, 64 percent of French people were satisfied with the new president. In September, it went down to 45 percent. Hard beginning for somebody who looked more like an adolescent in politics than the new Machiavelli... But he was beginning to learn. You could say that it was harsh on-the-job training.

After that, the presidency went on without too many hiccups, but the next major event arrived during the following summer and profoundly changed Macron.

When a new president is elected, one of their first acts is to choose a core team of key advisers. When you have a long career in politics, it is easy, as you know many people who meet your standards and have the required experience. If you look at the people in charge in President Biden's White House Office, none of them were beginners when they were chosen: Ron Klain, Assistant to the President and White House Chief of Staff, was previously chief of staff to two vice presidents, Al Gore and Biden; senior adviser Mike Donilon served as Counselor to

Vice President Biden in the Obama administration; Cedric Richmond, who serves as Senior Advisor to the President and Director of the Office of Public Liaison, has been a congressman and chairman of the Congressional Black Caucus; Senior Adviser Anita Dunn has been a successful political strategist, who has worked on two winning presidential campaigns (Obama and Biden), has worked for several members of Congress, and served as acting White House Communications Director under President Obama; Steve Ricchetti served as Chief of Staff to Vice President Biden during the Obama administration and Deputy Chief of Staff for Operations under President Bill Clinton. This list could go on, but one element is common to all these advisers: they were not beginners and had already served in similar positions.

Macron had limited experience in the political world. He had only been minister of economy for a short time. He chose a chief of staff, Alexis Kohler, who had been his chief of staff at the Ministry of Economy, and who, according to different observers, could be his clone. He then surrounded himself with relatively young people who have worked with him during the campaign, a friendly attitude aiming to reward their loyalty more than recognizing their competencies at the highest level of power.

On the 8th of April, 2019, less than two years after Macron's election, there was a farewell party in the Elysée Palace for seventeen of Macron's advisers who were leaving the team. Among them, Sylvain Fort, who ran Macron's media campaign as a presidential candidate and served previously as his speechwriter and communications director. He had not been successful in managing his relationship with journalists or at managing Macron's communications during difficult times such as the Yellow Jackets movement. Ismaël Emelien, the co-founder of Macron's party and President Macron's special advisor for strategy, communication, and speeches, left after being embroiled in the Benalla scandal.

Stéphane Séjourné, another of Macron's close advisers during the campaign and then at Macron's presidential office, also had to leave. Macron finally understood that his close guard composed of his main campaign advisers, an influential but discreet group nicknamed "the Mormons," needed to be replaced by professionals. It was the end of the first part of Macron's presidency, at a time when his polling was at its worst (29 percent of positive opinions in March and April of 2019, according to the IFOP polling institute). Apprenticeship ended.

Interestingly, this was seen as a victory for Brigitte Macron, who, according to the French media, was not liked by the "Mormons." They considered her influence on the President too important and too disruptive, probably because she advised her husband daily. Above all, she never hesitated to give him negative feedback. In particular, the departure of Ismael Emelien, with whom Brigitte Macron's relations were not easy and incidents were frequent, was a relief for the First Lady. According to the magazine *Gala*, a close friend said, "They dream that she dies. (...) They dream of making her disappear."[9] But there is no question of letting it happen, and after their departure, she was still there, and her relations with the President's team were not an issue any longer.

Why was Macron so unpopular? There was certainly the impact of the Yellow Vests movement, which has disturbed French social peace and the economy. It likely could have been prevented, and certainly could have been better handled by Macron's team. But it should not have been sufficient to undermine his presidency. It was the Benalla scandal that could have destroyed the presidency and led to more severe consequences than a team change.

Alexandre Benalla was the embodiment of the President's ideal, showing that you can come from immigration and succeed in France. His parents were educated immigrants coming from Morocco. After his parents' divorce, he spent his childhood with his mother in a so-called "sensitive" suburban neighborhood of Évreux, in Normandy, or, in other words, a French ghetto for poor people. In addition, Benalla was under the threat of being kidnapped by his father, who went back to Morocco.

What makes Benalla special is not his success in the educational system, but his determination. When he was fourteen and in the ninth grade, he wrote to Nicolas Sarkozy, the Minister of Interior, to request an internship with the Service de protection des hautes personnalités, an equivalent to the branch of the U.S. Secret Service in charge of protecting the president and other personalities. He got the internship, which confirmed his calling: he would one day be the president's bodyguard. It was something he'd dreamt of since he was ten and saw *In the Line of Fire* for the first time, a political thriller where Clint Eastwood's character is a bodyguard for John F. Kennedy.

All went according to his plans. In June 2007, then fifteen years old, he provided security services at the Cabourg Film Festival. Becoming a member of the Socialist Party, he soon worked for the party's security service. At age twenty, he was a member of the security team of François Hollande's campaign but was not recruited when Hollande became President. Then, when Emmanuel Macron left the Ministry of Economy in August 2016 but before announcing his candidacy for the presidential election in November, he did not have any official protection. He met Alexandre Benalla, liked him, and accepted Benalla onto his security detail.

On the 5th of December, 2016, Alexandre Benalla was hired as head of security for En Marche and became very close to the future President. After Emmanuel Macron's victory, he joined the Élysée Palace as a project manager in the presidential cabinet. He became one of the two deputies of the chief of staff, playing a coordinating role between the various departments responsible for the president's security. A close relationship developed between Macron and Benalla, who was among the few able to access the French president. Benalla shared holidays and free time with the presidential couple, skiing at La Mongie, a ski resort in Pyrenees mountains, or taking a vacation at Le Touquet, where Brigitte Macron has a holiday house. Benalla was even said to be in charge of a project to create a new security service under the direct command of the president instead of the Ministry of Interior.[10] Surprisingly, he was promoted to Lieutenant Colonel in the French police force (gendarmerie), which fed rumors that he could become the head of this equivalent of the U.S. Secret Service. This was later denied by Macron and his teams.

Then all hell broke loose — a story with violence, lies, generals, Russian billionaires, indictments, and a dancer.

On the 1st of May, 2018, during clashes between demonstrators and the police, a man equipped with a police helmet with a visor was filmed molesting a man and a woman. According to the newspaper *Le Monde*, he was wearing "a helmet and a light-colored sweatshirt, and pulled a young girl with brown hair by the neck, then returned to attack a young man violently, already on the ground, surrounded by police. In one of the videos, the young man beaten is heard begging him to calm down, shouting: "I'll explain." In vain. The helmeted man, visibly in a state of rage, drags the victim on the ground, seizes him violently in the neck by behind, then strikes him several times.[11] The video was visible on social networks.

A month and a half later, on the 18th of July, his identity is announced by journalist Ariane Chemin in *Le Monde*: his name was Alexandre Benalla. According to Patrick Strzoda, the president's head of advisors and number three in the hierarchy after Macron and the chief of staff, Benalla had informed him that he wished to participate in an intervention at the Police Headquarters to see how the police managed a large demonstration. He got a green light, but it was made clear that he was going only as an observer. Usually, in a democracy, if an adviser to the president had violently beaten two citizens, he would have been immediately fired and be obliged to face justice.

But the investigation by *Le Monde* revealed a different story. Patrick Strzoda explained that the day after the demonstration, on the 2nd of May, he was informed that Mr. Benalla had been recognized participating in law enforcement operations. He looked at the video, told Macron, who was traveling in Australia, and asked for sanctions. Benalla immediately got a letter referring to "manifestly inappropriate behavior" having "undermined the exemplarity that is expected, in all circumstances, of agents of the Presidency of the Republic."[12] The letter also announced the penalty: a simple temporary suspension for two weeks. And no one communicated this information to the public or informed a prosecutor.

It caused an uproar in the press, the political world, and the population. The Paris Public Prosecutor's office immediately launched an investigation, but, panicking, Macron and his government continued to avoid discussing Benalla, with the message "there is a sanction, case closed." The National Assembly, dominated by Macron's party, and the Senate, in the hands of Macron's opponents opened, on July 21 and 24 respectively, inquiries to shed light on the actions of Alexandre Benalla. And things became worse for Macron as the press followed all possible leads.

The first line of inquiry for journalists was to investigate the real role of Alexandre Benalla in the Elysée Palace. They discovered that the presidency had minimized it to limit the consequences of the outrage for Macron. They rapidly found out that he was not a simple bodyguard. He had access to important meetings and had developed a solid network of relationships at a high level. They even found a picture of Benalla with the General Bio-Farina, head of the Elysée security forces and military adviser to the president, at a party of former SWAT team members in a cabaret in Paris with a half-naked dancer.

It became amateur hour. One day after the scoop from *Le Monde*, Bruno Roger-Petit, Macron's spokesman, made an official statement, explaining that Alexandre Benalla had obtained an authorization to "observe the police operations planned for the 1st of May" and he said that this authorization had been "largely exceeded" before confirming the "disciplinary action."[13] One hour after this press conference, the Minister of Justice Nicole Belloubet contradicted it, stating in the National Assembly that Benalla "was at this demonstration without authorization." Questioned by investigative journalists from the website *Mediapart*, the Ministry of the Interior indicated that he had not dealt with the request to let Benalla participate in the police operations. He added that Paris police headquarters had given the authorization, which contradicted Macron's spokesman's declarations.

At the prosecutor's request, Benalla had been put in police custody for a preliminary investigation, and the police were authorized to search his apartment on the 20th of July. He agreed to it, but curiously he declared that he did not have the keys. Only his wife, who, he said, was abroad, would have them, and he refused to give her phone number. In the evening, the police employed a locksmith but he was unable to open the sophisticated door. Light seals were placed, but the police did not guard the apartment. When they opened the door the following day, there was nothing to find in the apartment, and in particular not the strongbox where Benalla's three pistols and the pump-action shotgun were supposed to be kept. Benalla declared that "It had to have been taken to someplace by a person, but it is not me who took care of that."[14]

In police custody, as well as before the senate commission of inquiry, Benalla stayed vague. "On the 19th of July, my wife called me to tell me that there were many journalists in front of the house and in the corridor leading to my home," he said when he was first questioned. Then he said that he "asked a friend to go and get [his] wife and recover everything that could be stolen, valuables, and in particular weapons."[15]

Neither he nor his wife, who was not abroad, but near Paris, gave the name of this friend, and, curiously again, the prosecutor did not investigate who he or she was or what was in Benalla's safe.

It was only in February 2019 that a team of investigative journalists from another French newspaper, *Libération*, declared that they found the name of this friend: it was a thirty-four-year-old sergeant in the French army, Chokri Wakrim, who was is in a relationship with Marie-Elodie Poitout, a commissioner in charge of security at the prime minister's office. The Paris prosecutor was obliged to launch an investigation. In his testimony, Wakrim denied having moved the safe but declared that he had seen two members of Macron's team in the presence of one of these safes in a Parisian apartment belonging to a businesswoman who helped Alexandre Benalla's family when he was arrested. These people involved from the Elysée were a member of the Presidential Security Group (GSPR), who was also adviser to Emmanuel Macron's chief of staff, and a former director of the president's party of En Marche.

Chokri Wakrim was also linked to another investigation concerning Benalla, who had played a significant role in the conclusion of two security contracts to protect two Russian oligarchs. A first contract concluded in June 2018 — while Alexandre Benalla was still officially employed by the Elysée Palace — provided for the protection of Iskander Makhmudov, an oligarch reputedly close to Vladimir Putin and the Moscow mafia. It was signed by a friend of Alexandre Benalla working at the Elysée Palace, Vincent Crase, who was also head of security for Macron's party. Several elements show that Mr. Benalla was personally involved in the negotiation while still working at the Elysée. The financial prosecutor services (Parquet National Financier) launched an investigation for corruption in January 2019.

Benalla was also under investigation for using illegal diplomatic passports after being fired on the 20th of July, 2018. He had two diplomatic passports and was asked in May by his supervisor to give them back after the events on the 1st of May. But Benalla did not return them. Instead, he allegedly used them until December for business trips to Africa and Israel as part of his new consulting business, having meetings with top officials, including Chadian President Idriss Deby. Benalla says he has been working legitimately as a business consultant, but it seems that he tried to profit from his former insider status. Justice will decide.

The parliamentary inquiries in the "Benalla scandal" or "Macrongate" have had different consequences. In the National Assembly, dominated by Macron's party, there was no agreement between the majority and the opposition on the process, and the inquiry ended rapidly. In the Senate, despite clumsy attempts from Macron and his Minister of Justice to stop it or modify it, the report published in January 2019 was devastating for Macron and his team. The senators indicated "major dysfunction" among the top ranks. They noted that Alexandre Benalla and Vincent Crase, but also, to a lesser extent, Alexis Kohler, chief of staff of the Elysée, and Patrick Strzoda, Macron's head of the president's office, "withheld a significant part of the truth during their hearing." It could be an offense punishable by five years in prison and a fine of 75,000 euros. The president of the senate committee in charge of the inquiry concluded that "We have gathered enough elements to estimate that the security of the President of the Republic was affected." He stressed that "there would have been no Benalla affair if an appropriate sanction had been taken on the 2nd of May, 2018."[16]

Macron reacted strangely. He did not address these issues on TV, as he usually does when there is a problem. Instead, he used a political meeting organized by his party some days after the story was leaked and, in front of his supporters, he said: "If they want someone responsible, he is in front of you, let them come and get me! " It appeared as a challenge to his opponents rather than the excuses the country was waiting for. This attitude made him fragile politically, and key ministers, such as Nicolas Hulot, Minister of Environment, and Gérard Collomb, Minister of Interior, left the government in the following months, officially for personal and political reasons, but perhaps as a consequence of Macron's attitude about the Benalla scandal.

Then something happened in October 2018 that finally triggered a reaction from the President. Journalist Frédéric Helbert posted a story on Twitter: "Bad times for Macron. According to a source, some time ago at the Elysée Palace, the President suffered a real scolding, a "beating" from his wife, Brigitte Macron, who reviewed everything (Benalla, etc.). There was such loud yelling behind the door that we heard everything," a member of the President's protection team said." Brigitte Macron was heard saying: "It is time to stop your bullshit."[17]

She rarely speaks about her husbands' actions and policies, except for supporting his communication. But in June 2019, after Macron had reacted by totally reorganizing his team of advisers, particularly in the field of communication, she gave an interesting interview on RTL, a French radio station, giving her views on the mistakes made by her husband during the Benalla scandal. She declared: "We have certainly downplayed it. That, I confess, [...] I didn't see it coming... Emmanuel has an affection for all the people who work for him. Yes, he does — a huge respect and affection. Sometimes, perhaps, affection disturbs reason. [...] Perhaps it would have been better to say right away, "there is a problem." But [...] it's not that easy! The people who work with us, you can't tell them overnight, "[...] You don't work with us anymore."[18]

What happened with Benalla was perfectly analyzed in the report from the Senate. However, one could also prefer the analysis made by Benalla's friend, Vincent Crase, who was also indicted, and wrote a book on the scandal in 2019. In an interview with the newspaper *Le Parisien*, he explains the reactions of Macron's team in front of the storm,

"I have the impression that everyone knew and that they passed the buck. If there had been a direct, firm, definitive sanction, there would not have been a Benalla affair. They waded through the mess." The special relationship between Macron and Benalla may have been the reason, according to Crase. He explains that Benalla "was an essential transmission belt at the Château [the Elysée Palace]. I saw him enter the office of the "PR" [the President of the Republic] and say to him: "Perhaps you should go and cut your hair! Things that no one would dare say to a president. He did it. Emmanuel Macron knew that he could rely on Alexandre [Benalla]."[19]

The Benalla scandal showed that far from being the mastermind who has read Machiavelli and was a genius of politics, Macron began his five-year term with a dose of naivety and has suffered from his dramatic lack of experience. When elected, he claimed that everything would be different with him. Yet he behaved just like an old-fashioned French politician by trying to hide the scandal and minimizing the consequences for his friend. He reacted only when the scandal was exposed by denying its importance. Instead of courageously recognizing the mistake, he tried to find who leaked the story to the press. He reacted to the attacks by saying that they were purely low-level politics and that he had more important things to do than focus on such a secondary matter. He made a show about the report of the inquiry of the Senate, pretending that the senate had exceeded its authority in this investigation. It is a very classic response in the political context, but it fooled no one: Macron's popularity took a nosedive in the opinion polls, and many people thought that the President was on his way out.

He was not, he was wobbling, but he was still standing. Macron is not a Machiavellian president, but he is highly resilient, and he learns fast. Even before the publication of the Senate report, he had entirely reorganized the administration of the Elysée Palace under the responsibility of a new general director. New recruitments were now scrutinized, as it appeared that Benalla had had problems when he was the driver of a former Minister of Economy, and there was no background check when he was recruited. Old friends left Macron's advisers group, and a new, professional team arrived.

For those looking today for weaknesses in the French President, it is sufficient to say that he is the only President since de Gaulle who has had to weather so many storms, with a political scandal with Benalla, a national revolt with the Yellow Jackets, and a pandemic with COVID-19. But, he survived, and his popularity has since gone up again. He was naïve. He has become harder. As his wife said, they understood that "Now, unfortunately, we are alone. It is the Elysée that wants this: we can no longer trust anyone. [...] I trust Emmanuel, and Emmanuel trusts me. That's it."[20] He was not a politician, but he learned fast in the brutal French political world. His predecessors Sarkozy and Hollande finished their presidency worn out and unpopular. Macron is not.

Chapter 7
A Story of Resilience

"Remontada (Spanish language) means a comeback. The word is often used when a team is behind on goals and needs to turn things around in order to win. They need a big comeback or remontada. Emmanuel Macron continues his incredible "remontada." It is rare in the history of polls that a politician who has fallen in popularity manages to regain points while still in power. It is however what happens with the current Head of State."[1]

— Benoît Lasserre, journalist

Why are safety vests generally yellow in France as in the other countries?

It is probably for the same reason that school buses are yellow in the U.S.. The *Smithsonian Magazine* explains that Frank Cyr, an American educator and a specialist in rural education, organized the United States' first national standards conference for school transportation in 1939.[2] The meeting decided on the standardization of the color for school buses and their markings. Strips of different colors were hung from the wall, and the participants talked until they narrowed the color down to three slightly different shades of yellow.

It was a good choice. According to the same article in the *Smithsonian Magazine*, Ivan Schwab, professor of ophthalmology at the University of

California Davis School of Medicine, explained that, "The best way to describe [the color] would be in wavelength." The wavelength of the popular school-bus color is "right smack in the middle" of the peak wavelengths that stimulate the photoreceptor cells our eyes use to perceive red and green. The red and green photoreceptor cells, or "cones" as they are commonly known, are the two most predominant ones in our eyes. Schwab says, "If you get a pure wavelength of one color and you hit just one cone with it, you're going to have x amount of transmission of a signal to the brain. But if that [wavelength] were to stimulate two cones, you'll get double the amount of transmission to the brain." Swab added that remarkably "That color that we are calling school bus yellow hits both peaks equally."[3] It makes it easy for other drivers to see and recognize a school bus.

In France, school buses are not yellow, which is a pity, but safety vests have been since 2008. According to specialists, visibility is only thirty meters without these yellow vests, whereas, with a high visibility vest, it is 150 meters, five times higher. As everybody owning a car is obliged to have one, they are highly available and not expensive (under four euros for some of them). Everybody has one, and it was a genius move for people to use these yellow jackets as a kind of uniform to launch the demonstrations against the price increase on gasoline enacted by Macron's government for environmental reasons in 2018.

There had been another colorful revolt before, in 2014. President Hollande, a socialist, wanted to create a heavy-duty trucks tax, called the ecotax. Its objective was to reduce road transport, deemed to be polluting and energy-consuming, and to finance the development of transport by barges and rail. Long story short, the opponents to this tax decided to use red beanies to identify themselves. The Red Beanies Movement destabilized the government by demonstrating and destroying the expensive equipment necessary to implement the reform. The ecotax was withdrawn, and one billion euros in equipment was lost. In addition, the government was obliged to finance a plan for the economic development of Brittany, which was the French region where the movement was most active. It was one of the main failures of President Hollande, stressing his weakness and his lack of ability to implement reforms.

Macron had to face the same type of challenge with the Yellow Jackets.

Everything began in September 2018 with the announcement by the French government of the 2019 budget. The increased taxes on gasoline were meant to promote more sustainable ways of transportation. There were immediate protests on social media, with tens of thousands of followers. On the 18th of October, Jacline Mouraud, a hypnotherapist, metapsychist, parapsychologist, and accordion player, posted a video on social media criticizing the government. Her four-minute testimony was viewed more than five million times in a few days. In the video, she declared that she was "outraged by the increase in fuel prices [...], the tightening of roadworthiness tests, the attacks against diesel vehicles, and the introduction of tolls at the entrance to major cities." She added, "I have few words to say to Mr. Macron and his government. When will the hunt for drivers that you have put in place since you came to power end? We've had too much of it, is that clear? [...] What are you doing with the money? Apart from changing the dishes at the Elysée Palace or building swimming pools.[4] [...] We can't take it anymore."

Small movements and demonstrations developed here and there in France, but for the first time in the country social media played an essential role in gathering citizens in a national protest. It was a surprise because it did not begin with a trade union, a professional association, or a political party. People adopted the yellow jacket, not by a national decision of some leaders, but because they were initially demonstrating on the streets, roads, and motorways and did not want to be killed by accident. They invaded the roundabouts, stopping cars, giving leaflets to drivers and passengers, and explaining the reasons for their revolt.

The movement rapidly became popular. In the middle of November, 2018, 73 percent of French people supported or were sympathetic toward the Yellow Jackets. On the 17th of November, 2018, protesters used social media to organize demonstrations in a significant number of towns. They called it "Act I" of the process. Almost 300,000 people participated, which was a lot less than demonstrations organized by the trade unions or political organizations. However, it still had a strong impact. France had never known such a movement, which incorporated a collaboration between national demonstrations with thousands of people invading the Champs-Elysées, and small actions developed at the local level.

According to the French historian Gérard Noiriel, Director of Studies at the "École des Hautes études en Sciences Sociales" in Paris, social networks have played an important and unprecedented role in the success of the initial movement.[5] He theorized that social media had the same impact that, at the end of the nineteenth century, when the written word became widely accessible to the working classes, and has allowed the development of communities with the same interests and the creation of trade unions. The algorithms created by Facebook allow fast access to content from your first circle of friends and other content that seems to be like-minded according to the artificial intelligence managing the social network. Facebook helped the Yellow Jackets create a virtual community of interest in a matter of hours.

For Gérard Noiriel, this would not have been sufficient to provoke a serious social movement. There are millions of ideas exchanged on social networks daily. To have a real impact on opinion, they have to get support from the leading media that dominate political coverage. In France, the twenty-four-hour news networks have developed extremely fast. After a summer devoted to disseminating and repeating news concerning the Benalla scandal, they needed a new topic to boost their audience. The Yellow Jackets got almost 100 percent coverage of their demonstrations, with a cascade of interviews of Yellow Jackets leaders and followers, and hourly analysis of their doctrine and the situation on the roundabouts. No rally organized by political movements or by trade unions had ever had such massive coverage.

Who were the yellow jackets, and what did they want? The answer to these two questions is not an easy one. If you study their leaders, they were initially pretty different from the usual leaders of French protests. In addition to Jacline Mouraud, the hypnotherapist whose video went viral, there was Eric Brunet, a French journalist politically on the right side, who called in the French television to participate in the first major demonstration of the movement, on the 17th of November, 2018. He justified his engagement by saying that "France is the most taxed country in the world."[6] He stopped supporting the movement in December when it became violent.

Eric Drouet, another leader, was (and still is) a truck driver who, at the end of October 2018, launched a call for a rally of motorists on the Paris ring road. This call is considered one of the main events announcing the Yellow Jacket movement. Drouet was presented in the media as one of the main founders of the movement. It gave him a singular media stature within the movement. He represented the radical aisle of the Yellow Jackets but was obliged to leave the movement at a later stage: he has been suspected of violence during the demonstrations and has been condemned for beating his stepson, who was just thirteen years old. He left the Yellow Jackets in 2019 and announced in 2020 that he would be a candidate for the 2022 presidential election.

Maxime Nicolle, another Yellow Jackets leader, was also working episodically as a truck driver. He used the name Flyrider on social networks, chosen because of his passions for aeronautics and motorcycle riding. He had been discharged from the army because of alleged psychiatric problems and was sentenced to eight months in prison in 2012 for death threats, kidnapping, and violence. He played an essential role in launching the protest because of his Facebook group, which had more than 174,000 subscribers at the beginning of December 2018.[7] He had been coordinating regularly with other movement figures.

Priscillia Ludosky, probably the most recognized leader of the Yellow Jackets, launched, in October 2018, a petition condemning the hike in fuel prices and the government's lack of transparency about how taxes are spent. It also criticized the lack of public transport. After being employed for eleven years in a bank, Ludosky was at the time of the revolt running a small business selling organic cosmetics and aromatherapy from home and had a small shop selling perfumes. She was chosen as Woman of the Year for 2018 in a poll among French people, at the same level as German Chancellor Angela Merkel.

The sociological profiles of those leaders and of the initial Yellow Jackets were a surprise for the French and foreign observers and a shock for Macron's government. These people were not involved in politics; they were not in a trade union. They had not previously been in demonstrations, and they were generally working, either as self-employed with low incomes or in poorly paid jobs. They were not poor, but were in the lowest part of the middle class. They could generally not afford to live in towns and lived at a distance from their work, which obliged them to use a car daily. They were the invisible people for whom a slight increase in the gasoline prices meant restrictions on food, clothes, or holidays.

Suddenly, these invisible people appeared with their high-visibility Yellow Jackets on the roundabouts, organizing demonstrations, and on all the TVs and radios with very moving testimonies. For example, Maxi, from eastern France, declared, "I am fed up with being treated like a dog. I am a temporary welder. It's a job that is in demand. There is work to be done. Despite that, the wages do not follow. [...] But beyond that, I'm demonstrating for my parents, my brothers, and sisters who are struggling, who can't find a job, or who have one but are very poorly paid."[8] Another Yellow Jacket in the same demonstration declared: "I have just enough to live with dignity. But I'm not here for myself. I'm here for my grandparents who have worked all their lives and are left with 1000 euros between them. It's a good thing they have their house; otherwise, they wouldn't even be able to afford a place to live. And the government continues to tax them. It's a shame." It would have been difficult for the majority of French people not to sympathize.

What were the motivations of the Yellow Jackets? In the beginning, they were fighting against the gasoline tax, but it changed with time and with the government's decision to withdraw the tax hike on the 5th of December, 2018. Then the demonstrators' motives changed, too. As stated by Priscillia Ludosky, the respected Yellow Jackets leader, "What unites the Yellow Vests is that we condemn the widening gap between rich and poor and the rise in living costs. The fact is that four main factors unify the Yellow Vest movement. Democracy is one, and we have created a structure that enables people to participate more easily in decision-making. The environment is another issue that we agree needs urgent action, so we have come up with solutions we think are socially fair. We are also demanding more public services and fairer taxation."[9]

The movement became less and less popular with time, especially after the riots on the 1st of December, 2018. During previous demonstrations, there had been acts of violence because the Yellow Jackets were not organized with a security squad, and groups called "the Black Blocs" joined the demonstrators to commit acts of violence. What happened on that day was the worst riot in France in fifty years: in Paris alone, the fire brigade had to intervene against 250 fires set by the demonstrators, about a hundred vehicles went up in smoke (including two police cars), and six buildings were set on fire.[10] Groups of rioters destroyed street furniture, construction equipment, and fences; they demolished fire hydrants, vandalized a French landmark, the Arc de Triomphe de l'Étoile, and damaged or looted more than two hundred shops, offices, and bank branches, (142 of which were severely damaged). Clashes between police and demonstrators left 133 people injured (twenty-three of whom were police officers).

The police arrested 412 people, of which 378 were taken into custody. The titles of the British tabloid, *The Sun*, said it all: "START OF A REVOLUTION: Paris riots 'worst in 50 years' as thousands of masked thugs carrying weapons smash city leaving 133 hurt." The police were not prepared for such an event; there was no real demonstration, just attacks from everywhere. The police teams were insufficient, and their management had weaknesses, leading police officers to be put at high risk of being hurt or killed. Police officers on the streets were obliged to use extreme means to defend themselves. Even the presidential palace was under threat, and one policeman posted in front of the Elysée Palace explained later, "we had 3,000 yellow vests who marched in front of us, and we were only three."[11] An evacuation of the president by helicopter was prepared, but it was not necessary in the end. Calls for declaring a state of emergency were made by some political parties, and the intervention of the army was considered.

During this same time, there was a wave of unprecedented anger and even of hate against Macron. His predecessors had been extremely low in the polls — they had been mocked and despised, but it was mainly political, not personal. But none were hated as Macron was.

As once written by philosopher Cornelius Castoriadis, "one of the main sources of hatred in the human psyche comes from the tendency to reject and hate that which is not itself."[12] French people could identify with President Chirac, who loved women and food and had difficulties with one of his daughters. Hollande also had a good touch with a fork and loved women. Sarkozy spoke like people in the streets and loved chocolate.

But Macron looked like a superman, who had it all: brilliant academically, he had a high-level position in the presidential palace, a well-paid job in a famous business bank, and a rapid ascent to a ministerial post, and then to the presidency. He was accused of being the president of the rich, mainly because of his work as an investment banker at Rothschild & Cie.[13] All presidents before him have had difficult times, and, except de Gaulle, they have spent years in local politics having to deal with real problems of people. Macron did not. He did not have any real drama in his life. He has no children, seems to have money, is young, is good-looking, and is thriving. Many French people and the Yellow Jackets in particular considered Macron as an outsider who could not understand their problems, and they hated him for that.

One member of Parliament from the extreme-left party La France Insoumise, François Ruffin, explained in a book why he hates Emmanuel Macron. He explains that he considers Macron as "the product of social segregation, outside the people, far from the people, and now against the people." He adds, "I despise your look [...] this physical, visceral rejection; we are millions to feel it. It is now a political fact. Why is it so? Where does it come from? You exude class. You carry within you a smugness that arouses in the common people, in me, in us, both respect and revolt. Respect and revolt, a strange mixture."[14]

In January 2019, Macron had still not recovered from the Benalla scandal. This unprecedented revolt allowed his opponents to follow the Yellow Jackets who were chanting *"Macron démission!"* (Translation: Macron resign!), but the riots were so impressive that only one of them, on the extreme-left, said: "What do the French people I meet say? That Mr. Emmanuel Macron must leave now. That he must leave by car, by motorcycle, on horseback, on a scooter, in a helicopter, as he wishes, but that he must leave."

But Macron brilliantly turned the table. At the beginning of January 2019, he was at a 23 percent approval among the French people, according to the polling company IPSOS, his lowest ever. Everyone in France thought he was politically dead. The moderate attitude of his opponents was motivated by the fact that, in France, you do not kick a man when he is down. During the summer of 2019, he passed the 30 percent mark, then the 40 percent mark during the summer of 2020 — a much better result than his predecessors.

Why this "remontada?"

First, he stayed calm. On the 8th of December, his Minister of the Interior changed the strategy in the face of these new types of urban riots. He increased the number of police officers to manage the demonstrations and organized them into mobile teams to face the diversity of actions. Demonstrators arriving in town were checked for weapons or Black Bloc uniforms. Also, the police purchased riot control guns and were authorized to use them in case of a direct threat. It made the police more efficient against the most dangerous rioters, even though bystanders or journalists have been occasionally seriously injured as well. This demonstration of strength by the government was appreciated mainly by people on the political right. However, there were many people hurt in the process, feeding the anger among the demonstrators.

At the same time, Macron, like the rest of France, discovered these people living on the brink of poverty, too poor to have a decent life, but not sufficiently poor to access social benefits — those who resented the idea that immigrants may access social benefits without having paid taxes and who may listen to the extreme right. In addition to canceling the increase in the price of gasoline, he announced in December a significant increase of the minimum salary, a new benefit for the lowest-paid workers, and the elimination of taxes and social contributions on overtime work. At the beginning of 2020, he also eliminated a tax on pensions and decided to increase small pensions. There has also been an acceleration of income tax cuts. All these measures were in direct response to the Yellow Jackets crisis and have resulted in 17 billion euros being injected into the economy. The result was an increase in purchasing power that has not been seen in France for over ten years.

Macron understood that showing strength and distributing public money would not be sufficient to appease people's anger. He launched for a Great National Debate, which was an extraordinary idea that French people criticized but also appreciated. It was a two-month-long nation-wide debate designed as a participatory democratic exercise open to all citizens willing to engage on one or more of the four themes selected by the French government: "Democracy and Citizenship," "Fiscality and Public Spending," "Ecological Transition," and "Organization of the State and Public Services." The Great National Debate started on the 15th of January, 2019. And during those two months, Emmanuel Macron stopped his usual activities to participate in and follow this national debate.

People could participate in the debate in different ways. First, they could go to their town hall to write their insights in a register. They could also contribute online by presenting their opinions and proposing their solutions. Anybody could also organize a local initiative meeting to discuss in public any of the topics or all of them, using tools provided online. There were also regional meetings with citizens selected at random and elected officials to debate the same topics. After the last sessions, national summaries were drafted (with the support of artificial intelligence) and published.

For France, this type of direct democracy was very new compared to other countries. The world champion in this domain is probably Switzerland, where the people participate extensively in political

decisions. The population votes four times a year on an average of
fifteen issues. In addition to the right to vote, citizens have the
opportunity to make their demands through three instruments that
form the core of direct democracy: the popular initiative, which allows
citizens to propose an amendment or an extension of the constitution;
the optional referendum, that allows 50,000 citizens to request that a law
passed by the Federal Assembly be submitted to a popular vote; the
mandatory referendum for any constitutional amendment decided by
Parliament; and Switzerland's membership of international
organizations is also subject to a mandatory referendum.

In the U.S., there is also a tradition of direct democracy. According
to the *Encyclopedia Britannica*, "The most important historical reference
of direct democracy is assembly democracy in ancient Greek city-states,
particularly Athens, where decisions were taken by an Assembly
(Ecclesia) of some 1,000 male citizens. Later, people's assemblies were
used in many Swiss cantons and towns, and town meetings in some
American colonies and states. Early U.S. states also started using
procedures in which constitutions or constitutional amendments were
ratified by referenda, which later became common in the country."[15]

Today, in twenty-six U.S. states and in Washington, D.C., citizens can
use three types of citizen initiatives: they can draw up a proposed law
and put it on the ballot, and if it is approved, it becomes law; they can
put a veto referendum on the ballot to repeal a law that the legislature
passed; and they can propose, and vote on, a change to the state
constitution. In 2020, some states only allowed some of these initiatives,
and some don't allow citizen initiatives at all. Some citizen's initiatives
have had a significant impact, such as the decriminalization of drugs, or
changes to a state's tax system. Like, for example, the Taxpayer Bill of
Rights (TABOR) in Colorado. In 1992, citizens proposed and passed a
ballot initiative that changed the state's constitution to oblige state and
local governments to get direct voter approval to raise taxes, and to

return any tax surplus to citizens, unless otherwise approved by a ballot referendum (it happened). But the system has its limits: American journalist Kelsey Piper, who lives in California, complains about the necessity to vote frequently, on "unclearly written ballot propositions on a dozen niche issues," and she states that a system "that funnels lots of issues, both big and small, directly to the voters leads to bad policy judgments because under-informed voters don't have time to research and form opinions on all the issues."[16]

But France is far behind in implementing direct democracy.

The French Revolution is one of the ancestors of modern democracy, together with the American Revolution, that gave birth to democratic elections in the late eighteenth century. But little progress has been made toward direct democracy, which is a problem when confidence in the political parties is at its lowest.[17] There is a possibility of consulting French citizens on legislation at the initiative of the president, or of 20 percent of the members of Parliament supported by 10 percent of the voters, and only if the Parliament does not deal with the topic in the meantime. Local authorities can also decide to consult their citizens, but citizens have no power to force a consultation.

Macron's Great National Debate had an element of direct democracy in its organization, allowing a direct expression of the people at the national level. However, it did not go the entire way, as Macron did not promise to put forward any piece of legislation based on its conclusions. However, the desire of the people to express themselves and be heard was so strong that it was a success. Even if the total cost of the Great National Debate is estimated at only 12 million euros, more than 1.5 million people participated in 10,000 local meetings or conferences, posted a comment on the web, or went to the town hall to write their opinion.

There was considerable work done using artificial intelligence to produce an analysis of all the contributions in a few weeks. The main priority for the people who replied was taxes. People indicated that taxes are too high and that higher taxation of the wealthiest people is necessary. People also asked for better transparency on the use of taxes. Another strong concern was to step up the fight against fraud and tax evasion by banning tax havens and increasing the taxation of capital. The second problem for people was that "We use too much energy, especially from fossil sources," and they are intensely aware of the urgency of doing something — 62 percent of the contributors to the platform said that their daily lives are already affected by climate change (such as heatwaves or other climatic events); 86 percent indicated that they could help protect the environment, proposing several solutions such as a tax on kerosene, the banning of pesticides, the improvement and promotion of circular economy, the development of public transport, carpooling, or even creating more bicycle paths and cycling.[18]

As usual in France, consensus is difficult, even about the method. Macron's political rivals criticized the Great Debate, but many of them still participated. Experts showed that the participants in the Great Debate, whose objective was to solve the problems raised by the Yellow Jackets, were sociologically not comparable to the Yellow Jackets and did not face the same issues. The Yellow Jackets themselves decided that the debate was fake and decided to have their own Great Debate called The True Debate, during which one million voters curiously arrived at almost at the same conclusions about the tax system and the environment as the participants in the Great Debate. They added a need to have more direct democracy in France with the possibility of citizens' initiatives on legislation. They stated that public services such as transportation, health care, energy, insurance, and waste collection should not be managed by private companies.

These national debates have proven that French people could reach a consensus on a large number of topics. The main obstacle may be that the political parties do not have the same positions as the people they are supposed to represent...

Emmanuel Macron was remarkable during this period. At the beginning of the Great Debate, he decided to cancel all his international activities and focus on proving to his fellow countrymen that he was taking the debate very seriously. According to his team, Macron participated in sixteen debates during the two months, most of which took place in the regions. He spent eighty-four hours and fifty-one minutes listening and speaking during local meetings. He met with 2,310 elected officials, primarily mayors, 1,000 young people, 400 citizens and NGOs involved in preserving the environment, 60 intellectuals, and 150 specialists in urban policy. The longest meeting lasted eight hours, the shortest one hour and fifty-five minutes. Macron listened when people expressed their ideas and critiques. Then, he replied in detail on each topic, one by one, sometimes going on for three hours. The method has been criticized, but not the fact that he spent so much time actively listening to people. The president could not be accused of staying in his office or failing to listen to citizens any longer. His commitment was confirmed.

For Macron, who had never been elected in a local election, this contact with people was energizing. His advisors described a man who could say after five hours of debate, "Come on, I'll take new questions," when it was already late in the evening and people had begun to leave. The president had taken off his jacket and clearly had no desire to stop. Emmanuel Macron was beyond fatigue in these moments, as if exhilarated by the exercise, intoxicated by his performance as described by journalists following him.[19]

It was the turning point of his presidency. He put the Benalla scandal and the Yellow Jackets movement behind him. It was the beginning of his comeback. Certainly, when he presented the actions to be taken following the debate, there was a general feeling of deception. They were less ambitious than what people desired during the debate. But politicians were relieved. For direct democracy, Macron proposed a change in the rules for electing the Parliament's members and the possibility for 1 million citizens to oblige the Parliament to discuss a topic. It was far from the request to organize a referendum directly to adopt legislation based on citizens' initiatives, as is the case in California. Macron accepted the request to develop public services in the rural parts of the territory, which had been abandoned for decades, but the details were not disclosed. He proposed decreasing taxes for the middle class but refused to increase taxes for the richest, which in France are already among the highest in the world and the most redistributive.

Macron scored a big win with the Great Debate, and he got back the respect he lost with the Benalla scandal. But the reactions to the proposed measures, which were far from being enthusiastic, are a sign of the discrepancies between the president, the politicians, and French society, which today lacks homogeneity. The people on the left and the so-called populists want more public services, a reduction of financial inequalities, particularly an increase in taxes for the rich, and more direct democracy. Others, particularly young people, would like to see immediate and robust action in favor of the environment. Many people just want the more traditional requests of lower taxes and security. And then, there is a growing minority of people who want to develop businesses.

Macron was elected in such a divided country by trying to convince the people that he can satisfy everyone, taking the best from the right and the best from the left. But that was a deception, and the Yellow Jackets have been the proof of that deception. Macron is a liberal in the European meaning: he does not think that you create jobs by a government decision, but by giving more freedom to private companies and motivating their shareholders by allowing them to make money. He does not think that you can reduce inequalities with more taxes on the rich, but by developing the education system to guarantee equality of chances among children. He tried to compensate for his weaknesses on the environment by hiring Nicolas Hulot, a renowned environmentalist in the government, but Hulot left during the Benalla scandal. And Macron was personally interested in direct democracy, but nothing could be done without the members of Parliament, who were not in favor.

It would not be honest to say that the Yellow Jackets revolution has been a damp squib because it did produce some results and inspired important conversation. More money (17 billion euros) went to people who were near poverty. There were changes to the tax system to decrease taxes for the middle-class. People got substantial subsidies to exchange their diesel cars for a new hybrid or electric vehicle. Also, direct democracy has progressed. Macron created the Citizens' Climate Convention in 2019, an assembly of 150 citizens drawn at random from the French population, to "define the structuring measures to achieve, in a spirit of social justice, the reduction of greenhouse gas emissions by at least 40 percent by 2030 compared to 1990." It has been a successful initiative with 149 measures proposed and generally agreed with by French people, even if lobbyists have reduced their impact by pushing to limit them in Parliament.

During the Yellow Jackets movement, Emmanuel Macron showed a surprising capacity to recover from a compromised situation, which had been impossible for his predecessors. Part of this could be due to his youthful energy, which had been highly visible during the campaign. But there is also his capacity to be disruptive and abandon the old way of thinking and the outdated ideologies of the older generations of politicians.

Chapter 8
Reformer

"We only manage to make reforms by pretending to make a revolution."

— Jacques Chaban-Delmas, Former French Prime Minister

If you want to be the President of France, you need to propose reforms; people love it. These reforms should preferably deal with the main problems of the society, and politicians are supposed to propose strong measures showing a capacity to manage the country and change it. They should be positive and preferably avoid any reference to a possible negative impact on specific groups. You can propose to "improve the public administration's efficiency" but not announce that you will fire 100,000 public servants. You will "reduce the administrative constraints for companies," but never say that you will lower the environmental standards. It is not specifically French, but the difference compared to other countries is that, in France, even those who have voted to elect a president react strongly when the announced reforms are implemented. The French are armchair revolutionaries because they back off when they have to face the changes, and then they take it to the street.

Likewise, demonstrations in France are very different from those in other countries. The U.S. has long been home to vigorous protests, with spectacular events: the demonstrations such as the Women Marches of

2017 and 2018, or Black Lives Matter in 2020 have been about societal dysfunctions. It was not, as is generally the case in France, against a president implementing his program after his election.

Now, imagine that you are French.

It is Sunday morning, and you wake up with a pleasant feeling of expectation. It is a sunny day. Soon all the family is getting their breakfast around the table, and you enjoy your coffee and your butter toast with homemade jam. There is a good atmosphere, and your children seem to appreciate that it will not be a regular Sunday. The morning goes as usual, your wife and children go to mass, and during this time you prepare sandwiches with salami and pâté, not forgetting to add some boiled eggs, tomatoes, fruits, and cheese. That should do.

When the rest of the family comes back, they all change their formal clothes for more relaxed outfits and take backpacks with food and water, their caps or hats, and some windbreakers in case it becomes cold. Together, you walk to the bus rented by a trade union for the event, and you meet up with your colleagues from your work and their families. Everyone greets you, and you are happy to meet them again, even if you see them daily at work. The children sit together at the back of the bus, and the adults discuss the day to come. The noise level is high.

You arrive Quai de Valmy, in Paris, because it was decided to have a picnic on Square Frederic Lemaître, on the canal Saint-Martin, one of the most pleasant places in Paris, and where there are not too many people. Everything goes well, all appreciate the food and the company, and even the wine brought by a colleague from Burgundy. At 2:30 p.m., all leave, happy and full, and walk to the Place de la République, which is packed to bursting point. Your group remains together because it is nice, and it allows you to continue the discussions.

At 3:00 p.m., the procession starts, and for two hours you advance slowly, singing songs that everyone knows and shouting in unison slogans against the government. In the past, it was *"Sarko, facho, le peuple aura ta peau,"*[1] (Translation: Sarkozy! Fascist! People will get you!) now it is often *"Macron! Demission!"*[2] (Translation: Macron! Resign!). Next to you, there are colleagues from Marseille, who came by train and are accompanied by several elected officials, magnificent with their tricolored scarves in the colors of France. A sign makes you laugh; it says, *"C'est quand que tu vas me mettre des paillettes dans nos retraites Manu ?*[3] (Translation: When are you going to put glitter in our pensions, Manu?) as the President, who is said to regret not having been an actor, is famous for liking all that glitters, including the glittering robe of his wife when she went to a G7 meeting some days prior. Others are more serious, like the one that announces, *"Elu pour nous servir, pas nous asservir!"*[4] (Translation: Elected to serve us, not enslave us).

When you arrive at the Place de la Nation, it is the end of the demonstration. You leave quickly to avoid the thugs, the infamous Black Blocs, who came only to fight against the police and begin breaking into stores as a provocation. Before the end of the demonstration, they will be prevented from doing further damage by the trade unions' security forces, who are very efficient. You find the bus in a nearby street. Everybody is happy but exhausted, especially the youngest ones, because of the excitement and the long walk. It will be a day that you will all remember, as a family, this day of demonstration against Macron's pension reform.

This description may appear stereotypical. But it shows one side of the reality: demonstrations develop a feeling of camaraderie and togetherness and are a means of catharsis for the French who doubt or oppose the President's policies. It is socially accepted and good for the morale of the country. But this ritual is also and mainly a necessary part of French democracy, which lacks other mechanisms for solving conflicts.

In the Nordic countries, Germany, and other social-democratic countries, there is a strong tradition of collective negotiation between responsible trade unions representing the people (more than 50 percent of people working are unionized), and well-organized associations of employers used to collective bargaining. When the government plans a reform, these social partners are generally involved in its preparation. Trade unions are on the boards of private and public companies and are well aware of economic issues. They adopt a reasonable attitude while safeguarding the interests of people. In most cases, people do not need to take the streets to demonstrate.

In France, people are not more unionized than in the United States: less than 8 percent of the working force is unionized, which is low compared to other European countries. The government does not consult the trade unions in preparing labor market and economic reforms like they do in Germany and the Nordic countries. Demonstrations are therefore the only way for the trade unions to show that they have the support of French people when the governments present their reforms. Curiously, there is a standard: 1 million people or more in the streets means that people do not support the proposal, and the government comes back to the trade unions to negotiate new measures.

The same results are sometimes obtained through strikes, but this occurs only for the reforms linked to the labor market. Strikes exist in France — depending on the year, France has previously ranked third and tenth in the world on labor conflicts and number of days per 1000 workers that were not worked due to strike or lockouts. But the most impressive demonstrations in France are different. They are seldom connected to labor conflicts and have been more related to political reforms and social and societal issues in recent years. They are the way to remind the country's leaders what their citizens think.

But why would the French government or a president fear demonstrations, which, after all, are peaceful events without anything but a symbolic impact?

First, the nature of the demonstrations has changed and they are no longer always peaceful. There have been increasingly violent events at protests, increasing the population's worries, particularly when the media are mostly focus on the acts of violence and not the actual demonstration. They are perpetrated by violent groups who originate from Germany. In France, they are called the Black Blocs. They were initially small groups of German *Autonomen* (autonomous activists) occupying West Berlin squats in the 1980s. Reacting to eviction operations by police forces, they started organizing street protests, wearing black and hiding their faces — hence the name *Schwarze Block* (Black Blocks in German).

The Black Bloc technique was progressively developed through fanzines, specialized websites, and punk counterculture. They have spread worldwide, and they are present at major international events such as meetings of the World Trade Organization, summits of the European Union, the International Monetary Fund, or even NATO. This transnational dissemination is also reflected in the presence of foreign individuals — mainly Germans and Italians — at demonstrations taking place outside their own country. They have been a serious problem for Macron's police. They have obliged them to develop a reinforced strategy and use stronger weapons during and after the demonstration, with the risk of hurting peaceful demonstrators, which has harmed Macron's popularity.

Governments also fear demonstrations because they can be the beginning of something else, something more serious. Just look throughout history. In the U.S., the War of Independence came after several decisions taken by the British King, which the people in the U.S. did not appreciate. The first may have been the royal proclamation setting the eastern limits of the thirteen colonies, which forbade Americans to settle on the lands located west of the Appalachian Mountains, considered as the property of American Indians. Later, it was primarily decisions concerning taxes, and the fact that those changes were decided without Americans having any say in the matter since they had no representation in Parliament, that provoked the revolution: the 1764 Sugar Act extended taxes on molasses to other products; the 1765 Stamp Act created a mandatory tax stamp on all documents, including newspapers, books, and playing cards; the 1765 Quartering Act forced the colonies to finance the English troops in charge of keeping peace in America; the Townshend Acts established a tax on raw materials imported into the American colonies; and finally, the famous Tea Act, passed in May 1773, that allowed the English East India Company to sell its tea to the North American colonies without paying taxes. There were demonstrations immediately, and some demonstrators boarded the ships of the East India Company and threw the chests of tea into the Boston Harbor. The British King did not see it coming.

In France, the country celebrates the 14th of July, 1789, as the symbol of the revolution and our national day. It is called the day of the storming of the Bastille, a fortress used as a prison in Paris. There were undoubtedly structural causes for the uprising, such as the increase in the price of bread. There were also some troubles due to a fear of a decrease in salaries and the firing by the King of the popular Minister of Finances, Jacques Necker. On the 27th and 28th of April, 1789, thousands of workers, artisans, small company owners, dockers, and unemployed people rioted near the Bastille, and the army killed hundreds of rebels. The King more or less ignored it, which was a cardinal mistake. Some weeks later, when the demonstrators stormed the Bastille, killing its guards and freeing the prisoners, the French revolution began. The King was hunting and ignored it until the night when one of the nobles around him woke him up. He exclaimed, "But is it a revolt?" "No, Sir, it is a revolution!" the noble replied.

This episode is present in the minds of the French during demonstrations taking place on the 24th of January, 2020. The demonstrators chanted: "Louis XVI was decapitated, Macron, we can do it again." Some were wearing masks bearing the effigy of the President of the Republic hanging on top of a pole, a reference to the execution of France's king during the French Revolution, on the 21st of January, 1793.

All this is history, but more recently, French politicians also have been caught by events that they did not consider serious initially and which had damaging consequences for them.

The May 1968 events, for instance, began with political fights between student organizations from the extreme-right and the left, with physical aggression, punishments, provocations, and even a fire started in the Paris Sorbonne University by a student group. Without any intervention from the politicians, it became "a vast spontaneous anti-authoritarian revolt, cultural, social and political in nature, directed against traditional society, capitalism, imperialism and, more immediately, against the Gaullist government in place."[5] With almost ten million strikers just before the negotiation of the Grenelle Agreements, which raised the minimum wage by 35 percent, it remains the most important social movement in the history of France in the twentieth century. And a nightmare for any president. De Gaulle, the emblematic French President, was not able to face the French rebellion and even left France for Germany during the uprising. He remained

President, but one year later, he organized a referendum, lost it, and resigned.

Another president, Jacques Chirac, had to face the same type of revolt as de Gaulle when his Prime Minister, Dominique de Villepin, pushed his party, who had a large majority, to adopt a law creating a *contrat première embauche* or CPE (Translation: first employment contract). It was a new form of employment contract, available solely to employees under twenty-six, making it easier for the employer to fire employees by removing the need to provide reasons for dismissal for an initial "trial period" of two years, in exchange for some financial guarantees for employees. It was so controversial that millions of French people demonstrated, and the government led by De Villepin withdrew the law voted on only weeks before. De Villepin then ended his political career, and Chirac's second term did not finish well.

Any French president who wants to reform France faces the risk of demonstrations. Events may turn for the worse, a revolt becoming uncontrollable, as happened in May 1968, or the loss of credibility for the President and his Prime Minister. Francois Hollande, Macron's predecessor, had to face demonstrations from the left against a law improving the flexibility of the labor market, inspired by the Minister of Economy, Emmanuel Macron himself. There were also large-scale demonstrations from the conservatives against the so-called "Marriage for all" bill, which extended marriage and adoption to same-sex couples in France. Hollande did not recover politically from these difficulties and did not even try to run for a second term.

What is frightening for politicians is that it is difficult to predict if a protest will expand or not. Political researcher Frank L. Wilson wrote in 1994 about France that "the dynamics that change isolated and specific protests into regime-threatening mass collective action remain mysterious. At times, multiple, widespread, and well-grounded dissent portends threats to the existence of the regime and then nothing happens. Other times, seemingly small disputes escalate very rapidly into outright revolts that threaten or bring regime change. Only days before the Events of May [1968] exploded, a columnist in *Le Monde* reported that the French seemed bored with politics. [...] Politics in France seem to have a dynamic of their own; in many cases, no one — not the participants, their leaders, or the government — can control the flow of events. This uncertainty means that knowledgeable observers of France must pay especially close attention to the otherwise common protest phenomenon."[6]

That is undoubtedly one of the reasons why everybody is convinced that France has more protests than anywhere else in the world, even if in the last years' protests in other countries like Hong Kong or the U.S. have outmatched those in France. Another reason is that French protesters are very good at communication and, in particular, at symbols. In May 2021, after the implementation of Brexit, around fifty French fishermen's ships threatened to block the British island of Jersey's harbor, and, even though they did not do it, the British government sent two warships as a deterrent. The French Navy did the same, provoking a media frenzy in Europe and in the world. Solutions were found, the demonstrators got the attention they wanted.

For all these reasons, when Macron became President, everybody in France was waiting for the first clashes when the newcomer would try to pass his reforms.

After all, he was not a seasoned veteran; he was essentially a greenhorn in politics. Also, he had in his program almost four hundred proposals, with several of them likely to be unpopular. In particular, he promised to limit public spending: his program planned €60 billion in budgetary savings by 2022 with €25 billion on the state budget, notably through measures to "modernize" the civil service and the elimination of 120,000 public sector jobs over five years (50,000 in the state civil service and 70,000 in the local authorities). It was a challenge because trade unions are powerful in the French public services. Macron had also proposed to reduce the unemployment insurance budget by €10 billion, which meant a reduction in the unemployment benefits, a provocation for the trade unions. He wanted to cut €15 billion on the operation of health insurance when the trade unions were publicly fighting for the public hospitals. Local government spending would be substantially reduced, which would be very unpopular among the 560,000 elected municipal officials, including 36,700 mayors and approximately 100,000 deputy mayors.

In addition, everybody expected the worst due to his program of reforms that were mainly pro-business and liberal, beginning with two topics that have always been the trigger of massive demonstrations.

The reform of the labor market was the first obstacle. There is a mechanism in the French Constitution allowing the government to ask Parliament for authorization to take, by ordinance, measures usually regulated by law. The Parliament, dominated by Macron's party, which had more than 50 percent of the members of the National Assembly, authorized Macron to change the labor law by ordinances. The compulsory negotiations with the social partners, trade unions, and employers took place in summer, which is traditionally not convenient for demonstrators. In addition, Macron convinced several moderate trade unions to support his measures.

The first demonstration was organized on the 12th of September, with limited success: 230,000 demonstrators were in 180 towns. It was a success for Macron, and on the 22nd of September, he signed five ordinances, which contained 117 measures. The implementing measures were gradually adopted, and the legislative work ended on the 31st of December, 2017. It was probably the first time a major reform has been adopted in such a short time.

It was huge, and the changes were important. It became easier and less expensive for employers to hire people on short-term contracts and to lay off employees. People dismissed got lower unemployment benefits, and employers making mistakes when dismissing somebody were not punished when they made an honest mistake in administrative formalities. Negotiations have become easier in private companies and could lead to greater flexibility than what was previously defined by law. Teleworking was now included in the labor law.

That was a big success for Macron, but it did not last. While previous presidents, like Chirac, had been very cautious after their first reform — it is even said that reforms you do not implement in the first 100 days of the presidency are doomed because resistance increases — Macron accelerated.

His method has been relatively consistent before the COVID crisis. First, he rattles the cage: he starts each reform with a wake-up call, explaining bluntly why the present situation is unacceptable, and then suggests some extreme solutions. Then, he discusses compromises to limit opposition, but he never abandons his primary objective.

With the French railway workers, Macron began "rattling the cage" on the 1st of July, 2017, when he inaugurated the Paris-Rennes TGV line, a new high-speed train line. He met with railroad workers and discussed the problems at French national railway company (SNCF): the increasing and unsustainable debt, the good pensions of the railway workers compared to those of other French people, and their highly protected status. And he seemed to hint that, if they wanted the French State to provide the necessary financial support to the company, everything should be discussed, including workers' benefits. There were negative reactions. In addition, as the people working for the

French railways are highly unionized and known for their strikes that are able to paralyze the transport system, there were fears that there would be demonstrations and strikes in the coming months if Macron launched his reform.

After this agitation, there was a period of calm. Macron promised that there would be a serious negotiation, and he ordered two reports, one on the railways' infrastructures and one on the future of the railways. They were published in February 2018 and provoked fierce reactions from the trade unions and the French political left: they included measures such as an end to the advantages for newly recruited railway workers, a substantial staff reduction, and the elimination of unprofitable small railway lines. There was a public outcry, to which Prime Minister Edouard Philippe answered by explaining that "The situation is alarming. [...] The French, whether they take the train or not, are paying more and more for a public service that works less well."

Then came the time of confrontation, which is a period that Macron seems to enjoy, probably because it corresponds to the final negotiation. He likes negotiating and winning. But everybody knew that the strength of the reactions would define what he would be obliged to accept. However, he did not hesitate, even when facing an unavoidable conflict: he got the Parliament to vote a law to allow him to use ordinances for his reform, which avoided a long discussion. It gave his opponents less time to organize the social movement against the reform. However, it was a breach of tradition that ordinances are used only to implement reforms that are part of the program presented during the election.

But Macron made what appeared to be a mistake: at the same time, he launched a reform of the French public service. In February 2021, he created a committee called CAP22 whose mission was "to offer a better service to citizens while making savings."[7] Macron asked for measures to eliminate 120,000 civil servant positions with the objective of a 4% reduction in the share of public spending in GDP by 2022! Prime Minister Édouard Philippe indicated that CAP22 should identify structural reforms and significant and sustainable savings across the entire field of public administration to the tune of €4.5 billion by 2022.

There was nothing new here. Such reforms had been implemented under the previous presidents, under different mottos: "modernize the public service," "general review of public policies." They all were projects aiming at cutting jobs in the public service, with little results because decentralized authorities have been wildly recruiting at the same time. But there was now a difference: the CAP22 committee was mainly composed of personalities from private finance, large industrial groups, and liberal economists without any knowledge of the public service. A first draft was even considered too timid by the government. Macron wanted to have some ability to let go of some decisions proposed by the committee to allow the reform to finally be accepted.

In France, 20 percent of people work in the public service because most hospitals, schools, and universities are a part of the public service. Post-offices are public. Railways are a public monopoly. When you ask French people if they want to reduce their public administration and make public service more efficient, there is a general agreement. When you want to implement such measures and reduce the number of teachers, policemen, firemen, and nurses, people disagree and refuse the "dismantling of our public service." In the last twenty years, people have seen schools, post offices, police-station and hospitals closing around them. In 2018, they could no longer believe that the reform would bring better public service and understood very fast that Macron meant that he would continue to cut it. They did not like it.

It could have been dangerous for Macron, as there could have been a convergence of the conflicts leading to a major crisis. In addition, students were agitated because the government had defined criteria for admission to the university for the first time. But Macron was able to avoid trouble with students by being transparent about these criteria.

As if all this was not sufficient, something very French happened. In 2008, Nantes, in the west of France, needed a new airport, and the decision was taken to build a new one in Notre-Dame-des-Landes, a small municipality nearby. It was a 580 million euro project, and the construction was expected to start in 2012, with an opening date in 2015. But there were local opponents, mainly some farmers who refused to leave, and environmentalists who considered that the airport was a nuisance. People began to live on the site, building cabins and demonstrating against any attempt to begin construction. It lasted ten years, and gained some sympathy from the French population.

In April 2018, police officers clashed with activists trying to maintain a camp, using grenades, and hurting both inhabitants and journalists. Police officers were also wounded and one ended up in the hospital. The police prevented journalists from filming the incident. Later, more than 2,500 riot police were deployed to remove the occupants from the fields, putting an end to an anarchist utopia and provoking demonstrations against police violence across the country.

In the Spring of 2018, fifty years after the revolutionary events of 1968, there was a risk of seeing all these discontents coordinate against the government. It would have been a worrying convergence of the strikes and demonstrations. Macron's political opponents on the left as well as on the right hoped that it would be the end of young Macron. Some of those on the extreme left organized anti-Macron parties and events, but there were not many participants. On the 22nd of March, a little more than 320,000 people were demonstrating in all France, and less than 5 percent of workers were on strike. From then, it went down. The opponents' dream faded away.

France saw that Macron still had the magic touch. The young president found that trade unions were not interested in organizing old-fashion movements. Instead, the CFDT (French Democratic Confederation of Labor), who had just become the most important of the trade unions, was moderate and favored negotiating the reforms instead of striking and demonstrating.

After ten years of hesitation from President Sarkozy and President Hollande, Macron decided to abandon the Nantes airport, and after the coronavirus epidemic, it shows that he was lucky. He understood that he could not reduce the number of civil servants by 120,000 and change their contracts to allow more flexible management: he abandoned the cuts, but he was able to negotiate and make Parliament adopt a critical Public Service Transformation Act. And on the 13th of June, the French Parliament validated a law on the railways: the company became a private company owned by the State, the people newly recruited now receiving a classic private sector contract. Competition was opened to private operators in 2019 for regional trains and in December 2020 for TGV. Liberalism won.

It was not the end of the reforms launched during the first years of Macron's presidency. In January 2019, he asked the social partners to negotiate a plan for improving the professional training for the workforce at a moment when digitalization was transforming the economy, destroying and creating jobs at a fast pace. Trade unions and employers were not happy to negotiate on this topic because they managed billions in training funds until Macron's presidency and thus financed their own activities with public money. Still, they prepared an agreement, but Macron was not happy with it. He announced in March a major reform, which provided each employee with an account financed by the employer and the State. People can freely use this account to follow the training of their choice. The social partners lost control of the funds, but people got more freedom.

In addition, Macron's reform promoted apprenticeship, which allows people to work, thus learning a trade, and at the same time to follow relevant training courses, a system popular with artisans, industry sectors, and construction. The success of German industry inspired it. The reform was negotiated in the Spring of 2018 and voted on in September 2018.

There were other laws voted and decisions taken during this period. The law for the State to serve as a trust society aimed at simplifying procedures and changing the relations between the public services and their customers was presented in November 2017 and voted on in August 2018. There was also an increase in the subsidies for people with a disability and people with small pensions.

Then the Benalla scandal arrived, and Macron seemed to have lost his magic touch. The pension reform, one of his major objectives, more or less failed. And then COVID-19 hit.

When COVID-19 arrived in France, Emmanuel Macron was not only this young President who, as the British newspaper *The Guardian* described it, was able to "speak impressively on everything from class sizes to rural railways" if he was put in front of a crowd of hundreds. Or the expert president who would "present a brilliant joined-view of his policies on Brexit, E.U. reform, hi-tech protectionism, Russian and European Defense" for the benefit of two foreign journalists.[8]

He has known success: he had been able to push through more economic reforms than any president since de Gaulle. At the end of 2019, France's economy was in good shape, with a growth rate twice that of Germany; unemployment was at its lowest rate since 2008, more than 260,000 new job opportunities were created in 2019, mainly in the private sector, and there were 825 000 new businesses created during the year. The future looked bright.

But, after almost two years of rollercoasters, he seemed bored or tired. He did not show his usual capacity to bounce back when his pension reform was at risk. Was he more interested in international issues and the future of Europe? He let his rigid Prime Minister, Edouard Philippe, deal with the rejection of the pension reform by the trade unions. And the reform lacked Macron's usual touch.

Then he had to deal with an epidemic. On the 16th of March, 2020, Macron announced the containment measures following the COVID-19 pandemic — he declared the suspension of all reforms starting with the pension reform. In the summer of 2021, when the COVID-19 epidemic began to be less of a problem in France, he announced that he would push for new reforms during the months before the presidential election: he did not want to be known only as the president of a pandemic era, but as the only one able to implement the necessary reforms in the country. A fourth wave in France in 2021 limited his ambitions.

Chapter 9
Crisis Manager

"So it is interesting that a political leader like Emmanuel Macron is interested in listening, and by meeting with different religious leaders he is sending an important signal that secular society can coexist with religion."

— Sherin Khankan, Imam of the Mariam Mosque in Copenhagen

On the 14th of October, 1962, a U-2 spy plane photographed SS-4 missile installation sites on the island of Cuba, two hundred miles from the U.S. Florida coast. Soviet launch pads, missiles, bombers, rockets, and advisers were spotted in Cuba. Also identified were twenty-six Soviet ships carrying nuclear warheads (operational in ten days) en route to the island. It was a major threat to the U.S. — a missile strike from Cuba could not be detected in time for retaliation.

The challenge was clear: nuclear missiles had to be driven out of Cuba, and John F. Kennedy was, according to his brother, determined to have the missiles removed peacefully.[1] According to Guillaume Gonin, a French biographer of Robert Kennedy, the lack of an American response to this deployment would have proved that the Soviets "could act with impunity in the very heart of the American vital interest zone. Soviet missiles in Cuba might not have upset the strategic balance, but they would have certainly upset the political balance and had a profoundly destabilizing effect on the world's balance of power — not to mention the impact on domestic politics, a consideration that a president never really puts out of his mind."[2]

President Kennedy was an admirer of British military analyst Basil Liddell Hart. In a review of Liddell Hart's book *Deterrent or Defense*, he wrote that "we should bear in mind a few impressive lines of advice from Hart's book: Keep strong, if possible. In any case, keep cool. Have unlimited patience. Never corner an opponent, and always assist him to save face. Put yourself in his shoes — so as to see things through his eyes. Avoid self-righteousness like the devil — nothing is so self-blinding."[3]

Kennedy implemented these recommendations, even though he was surrounded by a majority of hawks who preferred a bellicose stance instead of diplomacy. He opposed an airstrike recommended by the Executive Committee of the National Security Council because he worried about losing control of the situation. He kept very tight control of the armed forces because he feared an incident that would lead to war.

First, he asked his close team of advisers to put themselves in Russian President Nikita Khrushchev's shoes. They concluded that there was probably no interest for the President of the Soviet Union to launch a nuclear war that he could not win. At the same time, Kennedy thought about the necessity of giving his opponent the option to save face if he was obliged to withdraw the nuclear warheads from Cuba. He saw early on that the exchange of American rockets in Turkey for Soviet missiles in Cuba was a possible way out. He secretly asked Robert Kennedy to meet with Ambassador Anatole Dobrynin to arrange this exchange. It was a solution that most of his advisors opposed.

He was then well-prepared to discuss the issue with Khrushchev, who had the same problems with the hawks among his closest advisors. They exchanged ideas and letters, and, after thirteen days, the crisis ended with an agreement that included the withdrawal of Soviet missiles and bombers from Cuba, the commitment of non-invasion of the island by the Americans, and the dismantling of all (ageing) Jupiter missiles from Turkey, Greece, and Italy. This agreement put an end to the crisis. Nuclear war was avoided.

As described in his brothers' book, John F. Kennedy showed during this crisis all the qualities expected from a leader: a well-educated and remarkably calm president, a thoughtful leader, not giving in to rapid decisions suggested by his advisers, keeping his cool, aware of the weight of his choices, incisive in his questions, firm in his judgments, commanding at all times, leading his advisers with perseverance to the position he wanted to take them to. And these should be the qualities expected from modern leaders, including President Macron.

But Macron is not Kennedy. There are significant differences between the two men. Kennedy's father was a diplomat, giving him an international culture, whereas Macron is purely the product of the provincial bourgeoisie. Kennedy was into sports, Macron literature. Kennedy traveled and worked as a trainee around Europe during his studies, and Macron traveled mainly between Amiens, Paris, and the Pyrenees. Kennedy focused on political philosophy and international affairs, Macron on philosophy and public affairs. Kennedy enrolled in the Marine Corps and fought during the war. Macron avoided military service (as did the majority of young French people at the time).

Despite what could be considered a lack of preparation for a country's leadership, Macron's destiny shows that his personality has nevertheless played a role in his capacity to manage crisis.

Initially, in ancient Greek, the word "crisis" meant a decision, and Hippocrates used it to mean "a turning point in a disease, that change which indicates recovery or death."[4] Translated into a political context, it would imply a situation with a dangerous disturbance in the ordinary course of events, with a high risk for the country, but that with the right response could be avoided and could even offer opportunities to improve the initial situation. But today, "crisis" is one of these words used for any event that disturbs the ordinary course of life. If the annual budget of the U.S. or the E.U. is not passed in a timely manner, it is a political crisis. If the French constitutional court rejects a part of a law passed by Parliament, it is another one. Suppose the polls are at their lowest for the president in power — another crisis.

But the most important ones are those events that define a presidency, when decisions taken have a tangible impact on citizens. Those reveal the capacity to lead a country.

During the last few French presidencies, these key moments have been scarce. After the revolutionary movement of 1968 that almost pushed President de Gaulle to resign, successive presidents primarily had to face terrorist attacks or economic downturns, with Presidents Sarkozy and Hollande provoking wars in Libya and Syria, but to no avail. Emmanuel Macron has had to face fierce terrorist attacks, the coronavirus crisis, and its consequences, the most significant economic crisis since the Great Depression of 1929, and additional minor challenges such as the Yellow Jackets demonstrations. These main difficulties have been an opportunity to judge his capacity to handle crises.

Sadly, France is familiar with being the target of terrorist attacks. In the thirties, the Secret Organization for National Revolutionary Action, better known by the nickname "La Cagoule" (Translation: The Hood), was extremely right-wing, anti-communist, anti-Semitic, anti-republican, and close to fascism. They committed assassinations, bombings, sabotage, and disseminated false rumors about a communist insurrection to destabilize the country. In the fifties and the beginning of the sixties, terrorist attacks were common and mainly linked to the war for independence in Algeria and organized by pro-independence and anti-independence groups.[5] The latter even organized an attack against French President Charles de Gaulle with twelve men, equipped with automatic weapons, explosives, and four vehicles, who fired fourteen bullets into de Gaulle's car. They missed him, his wife, his driver, and his stepson who were in the car.

In the sixties, seventies, and eighties, the number of groups fighting for their causes by using terrorist attacks in France increased. In 1982, a terrorist attack perpetrated by a Palestinian extremist group in a Jewish restaurant in the old district of Marais in Paris was followed by several others in the eighties and nineties.[6] Terrorist organizations in French provinces such as the Basque country, Corsica, and French Brittany have organized bombings to push for independence, and some of them continue today. Extreme-left and extreme-right groups have also expressed themselves with terrorist attacks and bombings. Islamic terrorism began developing in the eighties, linked initially with events happening in Algeria, a former French colony.

The wave of Islamist terrorist attacks that touched the world had tragic consequences in 2015, two years before Macron became President, when a group attacked a satirical weekly newspaper, *Charlie Hebdo*, in Paris, killing twelve people. This event was followed by other coordinated attacks in the following days, including an attack on a kosher supermarket where four French Jewish people were murdered. It has triggered in France a strong reaction, with more than 4 million people marching to express their support to the victim's families, including a large number of heads of state from the world, and the feeling that something should be done.

For these reasons, every French president has had to prove that he was efficiently dealing with terrorism. In the case of a terrorist attack, the program is always the same. First, the prime minister and the minister of the interior visit the scene of the episode, accompanied by the media. They meet the relatives of the victims and the injured in the hospital. Then the president makes a solemn speech on television, during which he presents his condolences to the victims' families and announces vigorous measures against terrorism. He receives the families at the Elysée Palace to show his support. Finally, he proposes a bill to reinforce the efforts against terrorism. The result is extravagant: since 2000, the French Parliament has voted on twenty-six laws against terrorism, more than one each year. In five years, President Hollande proposed ten pieces of legislation that the Parliament adopted.[7]

As France has a lot in common with the U.S., French presidents have been active in sending soldiers abroad to fight Islamic groups in Iraq, Syria, and Libya. Since 2014, the French army is present in Africa's Sahel region with the support of several African countries and some European partners. It is considered part of the global fight against terrorism, but the impact of these initiatives on terrorism is frequently discussed without a solid conclusion.

During Nicolas Sarkozy's presidency, there was another element that provoked negative reactions in the Islamic world: in 2010, after long debates, a law was passed that prohibited the concealment of the face in public places when that makes it impossible to identify the person. This prohibition applied to all individuals, regardless of age, sex, religion, nationality. It included tourists. In particular, wearing hoods, full veils (such as burqa or niqab), or any other accessory or garment which, taken alone or in combination with others, has the effect of concealing the face, is prohibited. As for the "traditional veil," which allows the face to be seen, a special exception exists — it is authorized in public places and universities, but is forbidden in public schools, colleges, or high schools. Public service employees are also prohibited from wearing the veil, based on the principle of secularism.

This decision has provoked negative reactions in Muslim countries, such as Pakistan.[8] In July 2010, al-Qaeda's second in command, Ayman al-Zawahiri, called on Muslim women in France to resist the ban, "even if it costs you your money, your education, and your jobs. You are *mujahedat* (holy warriors) on the most important battlefield."[9] France is a target because of the importance of secularism (called *laïcité* in France). This French constitutional principle discourages religious involvement in public affairs and is the constitutional base of the law forbidding any accessory that has the effect of concealing the face. For the Islamic movement, Islam is not only a religion but also a holistic socio-political system, and Sharia (Islamic) law must become the law of the state. For Islamists, France, with six million Muslims, is a target.

The worst fear of the Islamist movement is the development in France of a model where Muslims are endorsing a secularist model and keep their religion in private life, as is the case for other religions. It would be a nightmare for them, as this kind of compromise would prevent the development of Islamism and the implementation of the Sharia. That explains why France has been the main target in Europe between 1979 and 2019, suffering nearly 44 percent of Islamist attacks, with 42 percent of the victims.[10]

After the 2015 terrorist attack against the newspaper *Charlie Hebdo*, Islamist attacks in France have mainly become domestic and committed by lone individuals. The first attack during Macron's presidency took place on the 6th of June, 2017 at Notre Dame de Paris when a man attacked a police officer before being subdued by police. The assailant was armed with a hammer and two kitchen knives. He was an Algerian-born journalist named Farid Ikken, who won an award for work on human rights in Sweden. He returned to Algeria to manage an online news site before moving to France. He was pursuing a doctorate in communications at the time of the attack. He told investigators that he had radicalized himself over a period of ten months. They found at his home outside Paris a manual for "lone wolves" issued by the fundamentalists of the Islamic State (ISIS). There were also images of the London attack that took place three days before and a recorded message of support for ISIS that Mr. Ikken had tried but failed to upload to social media on the eve of his attack.[11] Since then, more than fifteen of these lone-wolf attacks have been committed by people who have been radicalized through the internet or by direct contact with other Islamists in France.

What is Macron's policy to fight terrorism? It has been a perfect example of how he deals with crises. His proposals during the presidential election did not differ from his opponents' ideas. He also did not specifically address the question of terrorism in his program but picked ideas here and there. He confirmed that he would strictly apply the principle of secularism. He wanted to develop the knowledge of different religions in school by providing specific lessons on religion. He did not propose to extend the ban on the veil to universities, as requested by the extreme-right, but would dismantle the associations which, under the auspice of religion, attack the Republic, and would definitively close down any places of worship in which they preach the apology of terrorism. It was not very original, except for the promise to organize university training in secularism, the values of the Republic, and the French language for priests of all religions.

He added measures from the left: he planned to make the fight against discrimination a national priority, and he would encourage hiring people living in priority neighborhoods by financing jobs and providing tax reliefs. Macron also promised to increase controls to prevent discrimination for access to employment or housing. These measures aimed at addressing the daily problems of immigrants and their children, with the understanding that it would facilitate their integration and increase their sense of belonging in French society in the long term.

This program was "classic Macron" — borrowing the ideas on the right and on the left and refusing to let ideology lead him. Then reality struck — an attack almost every two months. It had a strong political impact by developing a feeling of danger in the French population. He understood that he had to modify his approach, and he decided to focus his activities on the religious question, mainly on Islam, as Muslim fundamentalists performed nearly all the deadly attacks.

One can guess that he has probably proceeded, as is typical for him, by reading books about Islam and immigration, and meeting many specialists and religious leaders to make up his mind on the topic. He met the main French religious leaders on the 21st of December, 2017, to discuss the situation. After that, he organized regular meetings with them, discussing ethical questions and asking them to disseminate the idea that he will never ask "any French citizen to be moderate in his religion or to believe moderately in his God, it would make little sense" But he added that he would ask "everyone to absolutely respect all the rules of the Republic."[12]

In the same meeting, he remarked that "France has become accustomed in its dialogue to a religion that is structured in a much more vertical way, because it is the history of France with the Catholic Church," and announced his intentions to the representatives of Islam in France: "We must work to give a structure to Islam in France, which is the very condition for you not to fall into the trap of the divisions of your own religion and of the crisis that it is experiencing internationally." He declared that he intended to reorganize Islam in France or, as it became clear, to create a French Islam. It was not a new idea, Presidents Chirac, Sarkozy, and Hollande had tried to do something about it, but they could not implement it, mainly because of the divisions among the representatives of the Muslim religion.

It seemed like a strange idea that the president of a country where secularism obliges to separate religion and the state would intervene in how Islam is organized in the country. However, there were important reasons to push for changes. Young Muslim children of immigrants tend to turn to Islam, looking for their roots and some form of protection, because they are often living in difficult neighborhoods and experience feelings of exclusion.[13] They go to the local mosque and their imams to get a religious education, which means that the imams are vital for defining young people's attitude toward their country and its republican values. As Islam is not structured in France, imams are chosen by the mosque's congregation and are seldom paid for it or even trained. There are dangerous exceptions: three hundred foreign imams are paid by their governments (Turkey, Morocco, and Algeria) to teach Islam in France. Being a full-time imam has a significant influence on how Islam (and its relationship with the French Republic) is taught. The result is worrying: in a poll published in 2020, 57 percent of young Muslims consider the Islamic law (Sharia) to be more important than the law of the French Republic (+10 percent since 2016), and this proportion is much higher among Muslims as a whole (38 percent) than among Catholics (15 percent) for example.[14]

As with other reforms, Emmanuel Macron waited until the 2nd of October, 2020, to present his ideas to avoid further degradation of the situation.[15] To prevent the phenomenon of illegal schools, often run by religious extremists, he announced that from the start of the school year in 2021, school education would be made compulsory for all children from the age of three. Homeschooling, which is frequently used for teaching Islamic law and affects nearly 50,000 children, will henceforth be limited to children with health requirements. He also announced an increase of oversight of private religious schools "because the school must first teach the values of the Republic, not those of a religion, to educate citizens, not followers." The most spectacular measures were included — within four years, the system of foreign imams would be abandoned and mosque financing (used in particular by Saudi Arabia and Turkey to develop their religious control of French Islam) would be changed.

These were harsh measures. Macron has had to use threats and all his powers of seduction to influence the French Council of the Muslim Faith (CFCM), whose vocation is to represent the Muslim faith before the state authorities for questions relating to religious practice, such as relations with the French political powers, the construction of mosques, the halal food market, the training of certain imams, the development of Muslim representation in prisons and the French army. Macron's strategy worked: the CFCM adopted a charter taking a clear position against political Islam and recalling the compatibility between Islam and the values of the Republic. But four of the nine associations members of the CFCM refused to sign it, particularly the ones managing the four hundred Turkish mosques and other worship places.

In 2020, President Macron presented a draft law for "reinforcing the respect of the principles of the Republic," including, in particular, the neutrality of the public service, a reinforced control of associations, better transparency of all religions and their financing, restraining homeschooling, and combatting the virginity certificates system and polygamy. Finally, the measures adopted in Parliament were even stricter than those proposed initially by the government. An important one is the fight against hate on social networks: an "offense for endangering the life of others by disseminating information relating to the private life, family, or professional life of a person that allows him or her to be identified or located"[16] was created. It is punishable by three years imprisonment and a fine of 45,000 euros. The code of criminal procedure has been amended to allow for immediate appearances to judge hate speech on social networks.

What can be concluded about Macron's actions against the permanent crisis that terrorism is for France? His program for the presidential election was not original and did not show a deep understanding of the complexity of the topic. But in the end, he had to face reality and felt pressure due to the accumulation of terrorist attacks in France. He announced his will to act. He has been a thoughtful leader, not giving in to rapid decisions suggested by his advisers, keeping his cool, being aware of the weight of his choices, staying firm in his judgments, listening, and commanding at all times.

It was easy to determine if John F. Kennedy was successful: there was no nuclear war, and the Soviet Union withdrew its nuclear weapons from Cuba, which was the objective. But for Macron, it is difficult to know today if his decisions have been correct. Especially since the measures he has promoted are not focused directly on preventing terrorism: most terrorists did not come from France, were not recruited in a local mosque, and one-third of them had previous psychiatric problems. There was nothing about mental health in Macron's action plan. That does not mean that he was wrong when he was fighting to better integrate Islam in the French society, even if his left-wing opponents accused him of limiting the freedom of association, and his right-side opponents blamed him for not adopting tougher measures.

It is unlikely that terrorist attacks will stop any time soon in France. For one, many of these measures will not have a significant impact for the next fifteen to twenty years. However, Macron's measures may lead to an Islamist's nightmare: France may become a country where a moderate version of Islam compatible with western democratic values develop, a showcase for countries who want to limit foreign influence from extremists. In fact, it may lead to even more attacks, as France appears as the primary enemy of Islamists.

***

Recently, President Macron has had another opportunity to show what kind of leader he is: he had to face the COVID-19 crisis, an excellent test of the quality of his leadership. And his way of managing the crisis has followed the same pattern.

COVID-19, a contagious disease caused by coronavirus 2 (SARS-CoV-2) was identified in Wuhan, China, in December 2019. The virus first reached France on the 24th of January, 2020, when the first COVID-

19 case in Europe and France was identified in Bordeaux, a town in southern France. The first five confirmed cases were all individuals who had recently arrived from China.[17]

Almost all French people benefit from the public health insurance system, except those who are not employed and do not want the insurance. It is paid for by taxes and contributions from households (52.7 percent), employers (38.9 percent), and public administration (8.4 percent). This public health insurance pays 70 percent of the cost for medical procedures, 60 percent for paramedical procedures, between 15 percent and 100 percent for pharmaceuticals, and 80 percent for hospitalization (100 percent after 30 days). Health insurance provides 100 percent coverage for most severe or chronic diseases. This is the case for cancer, diabetes, HIV, Alzheimer's, Parkinson's, and kidney failure. In addition, 96 percent of French people have additional private insurance that allows them to get treatments from health practitioners, pharmaceuticals, and hospitals for free. If their resources are low, this private insurance is financed partly or totally by the public health insurance system. Treatments are delivered by public and private hospitals and private health professionals, and people can freely choose their providers. In France, current health care spending represents 11.2 percent of GDP, far behind the United States (17 percent), at a level comparable to that of Germany (11.7 percent), Sweden (10.9 percent), or Japan (11.1 percent). The results are considered good: in France, life expectancy reached 82.8 years in 2018 (it was then 78.7 years in the United States[18]). The French are very proud of their health care system, and problems occur any time politicians try to change it.

However, health crises have been frequent in the country and should have better prepared France for the coronavirus pandemic. Since 1945, France has experienced the Distilbene scandal, a treatment that caused genital malformations in children; the growth hormone scandal, that caused Creutzfeldt-Jakob disease and the death of 111 people; the chlordecone scandal, an insecticide that promotes prostate cancer; the contaminated blood scandal, following the distribution of batches of blood infected by the AIDS virus; the asbestos scandal, due to its use even when it was known to be dangerous; the Isomeride scandal, an appetite suppressant causing severe health problems; the Mediator scandal, a drug that caused hundreds of deaths; and the Depakine scandal, a treatment that caused severe handicaps in children. These events have had political consequences. Ministers' careers were ended, complaints were filed against ministers, doctors, and senior public servants. It would have been a good reason to be very careful about possible health threats.

Despite these warnings, Macron's program for the presidential election was quite vague, as Macron himself had never shown any interest in health matters.[19] There were some promises about prevention, a promise to maintain the treatments paid for by the public health insurance, some improvements in the payments for eyeglasses and dental care, and support for health professionals ready to settle in regions where they are lacking. He also promised to look into the efficiency of the health system, which meant the continuation of the budget restrictions for public hospitals. It has been a serious handicap for France: hospitals were not able to easily handle the increase of activity provoked by COVID-19, obliging Macron to order costly shutdowns. Macron was not alone: nobody among the candidates for the French presidential election had anything about health threats in their program.

Then COVID-19 arrived, and it did not go well for France. Macron, who was not prepared for such an event, suffered politically. France's failures are explained in a report by an independent commission to evaluate the management of the COVID-19 crisis and the anticipation of pandemic risks, set up in June 2020 at the request of the president. Published in March 2021, the report included an evaluation of the health, economic, and social impact of the crisis experienced by France since the beginning of the year 2020 (with international comparisons), an assessment of the relevance, speed, and proportionality of the response to the crisis compared with other countries, and recommendations for improvement.

Macron's failure to protect France against the consequences of the COVID-19 epidemic was emphasized: in June, 2021, France, with three shutdowns, had almost 1,700 death for every 1 million inhabitants, which is nearly as high as the U.K. or the U.S. (about 1,900 deaths), but more than Sweden (a little more than 1,400 deaths) where there were almost no restrictions, Germany (less than 1,100), Finland (174) and Norway (145),[20] which means that the reactions to the crisis were inadequate, and employed too late compared to other countries. In addition, the report of the independent commission indicated that, as hospitals' resources were insufficient due to years of austerity, "the crisis has led to delays in diagnosis and treatment, which are likely to have a strong health impact for the people concerned. This is particularly the case for certain cancers, for which delays in diagnosis are likely to result in excess mortality." And the independent mission added: "All the restrictions decided in 2020 have led to a loss of economic activity unprecedented in recent history. France is particularly hard hit, with an estimated recession of 8.2 percent in 2020 (eurozone: 7.5 percent; Germany: 5 percent; United Kingdom 11.2 percent) and despite a significant rebound after the first wave."[21]

Macron's reactions were slower than usual. The President relied on his Minister of Health, Agnès Buzyn, a Professor in hematology who had no experience in communicable diseases. She even declared on the 24th of January, 2020, that "In terms of risk for France, [...] the risk of importing cases from Wuhan is moderate, and is now practically zero because the city is isolated. The risk of secondary cases around an imported case is very low, and the risk of spreading the coronavirus is very low."[22] The Ministry of Health did not make any preparations, expecting that there would be no cases in France: between 2002 and 2004, there was an outbreak of SARS caused by another coronavirus and that provoked the same type of symptoms. It was first identified in Foshan, Guangdong, China, but it did not spread to Europe. When the World Health Organization declared a Public Health Emergency of International Concern regarding COVID-19 on the 30th of January, 2020, the French government did not take immediate action. In particular, nobody checked if France had the masks and protective equipment necessary for healthcare professionals and the public.

On the 17th of February, 2020, twelve cases were confirmed in the country. On the 29th of February, 2020, one hundred people were infected with the virus, and two had died. On the 5th of March, all French metropolitan regions and French Guiana, a French territory in South America, were affected. On the 6th of March, Emmanuel Macron went with his wife to the theater to encourage the French to continue to go out despite the pandemic: "Life goes on. There is no reason, except for fragile people, to modify our habits of going out."[23] On the 8th of March, a milestone was passed with one thousand cases. And then, Macron realized how serious the situation was. On the 12th of March, he announced the first set of measures, and on the 16th, in a solemn address to French people, a total shutdown of the country, with fines for violations.

It was too late, and, as a consequence, France was in a difficult situation — hospitals were obliged to limit their other activities to be able to face the flow of COVID patients, there was not a sufficient stock of masks to equip the healthcare professionals dealing with COVID patients, and the shutdown harmed the French economy more than necessary by comparison with its neighbor, Germany.

Other heads of state made mistakes, and Macron cannot be blamed entirely for it. Asiatic countries that had to deal with the 2002-2004 SARS outbreak have done better because they had the experience. Some countries could isolate themselves because of specific geographic characteristics, such as New Zealand and Australia. Some relatively isolated countries, such as Finland and Norway, have also managed the pandemic efficiently. But it could have been better in France if Macron had been more careful about public health.

France is also a very centralized country, particularly in the field of public health, and that delayed the response to the COVID epidemic. Some Regional Agencies are in charge of health, but they are purely bureaucracies and only report to the Minister of Health, without local connections. The French regions, which are relatively independent of the government, have no competence in health and could not act when everything was on stand-by in France, waiting for the bureaucracy of the Ministry to decide. Multiple regions, however, ordered and got masks and protective equipment for health professionals, but they were not legally able to do more.

In addition, the organization of the French response to the crisis has been erratic, as the country lacks high-level, solid, and established tools immediately available in case of a health emergency. In the U.S., President Trump had a medical adviser, Anthony Fauci, a professional with extensive experience in public health. Fauci has participated in the management of several health crises and has been involved in the fight against viral diseases like HIV/AIDS, SARS, the Swine flu, MERS, Ebola, and now COVID-19. Donald Trump created a White House Coronavirus Task Force to combat coronavirus, and Dr. Fauci was a key member. With President Biden, Dr. Fauci remains a prominent member of the White House COVID-19 Response Team, which includes public health specialists and the country's political leaders.

It has happened that French presidents have had health advisers with public health or medical backgrounds. Instead, Emmanuel Macron had chosen Marie Fontanel, a lawyer who had worked in administrative positions in the healthcare system. Ms. Fontanel resigned on the 31st of January, 2020, one day after the World Health Organization (WHO) declared "a public health emergency of international concern" for COVID-19.[24] She was replaced by another health adviser with a purely administrative profile. In addition, the Minister of Health, Professor Agnès Buzyn, a French hematologist, who had been previously the head of the National Health Authority in charge of giving independent advice on health matters, left the government on the 16th of February, 2020, just as the outbreak was developing in France.[25] Olivier Véran, who has had a short career as a neurologist in a University hospital before becoming a member of the Parliament, replaced her as Minister of Health. Near Macron, there was no Dr. Fauci who could have advised him on epidemiology.

But don't imagine that there was no possibility to use existing people and organizations. The President could rely on Pr. Jerome Salomon, the Director-General of Health (the head of the public health department of the Ministry of Health and Social Affairs) and a specialist in communicable diseases. He also had the option to use all the agencies and committees created in France in the field of public health, including epidemiology: the National Public Health Agency, Santé Publique France, which is the French equivalent of the Centers for Disease Control and Prevention; the High Health Authority, which, among other missions, is in charge of giving public health recommendations, and issuing opinions as part of its mission to help public authorities make decisions; and the High Council for Public Health (HCSP) which has to provide the public authorities, in collaboration with the health agencies, with the expertise necessary for the management of health risks and the design and evaluation of prevention and health security policies and strategies. It also provides the public authorities with forward-looking thinking and advice on public health issues, and has a specialized committee on "Infectious and Emerging Diseases" and a permanent working group on "Influenza, coronavirus, emerging respiratory infections."[26]

It did not work because there was no stable organization with clear mandates for these structures, especially in case of an epidemic. Also, this organization is very complicated, as French administration generally is. All of France, even during health crises, is managed by its administration. Four of the eight French presidents of the Republic since 1958, Macron included, are alumni from the famous ENA, National School of Administration, a special place where people who have a university degree train to become senior civil servants. They are very good at managing public service, but they seem to like complexity.

Instead of simplifying the already complex French public health system, Macron did the opposite: he decided to create another committee, the COVID-19 Scientific Council established on the 11th of March, 2020, "to inform public decision-making in the management of the health situation related to the coronavirus."[27] And Macron's decisions have been taken in a task force called Health Defense Council with the main Ministers and the Heads of the Public Health Agencies.

Such a system makes it complicated to have a unified scientific position, and there have been divergences among the different organizations and committees involved. The COVID-19 Scientific Council and its president gave thirty-two recommendations, but some have not been very clear, letting some leeway for the only one who decided, the President.[28] Parliament protested that it should be involved, and it has sometimes been consulted. Once the president made any decision, it had to be passed on to people who had to implement them. It created misunderstandings and delays — like the vaccination situation. France got started later than in neighboring countries.

When he decided on the first shutdown, Emmanuel Macron declared, "One principle guides us in defining our actions, (...) and it must continue to do so: it is trust in science. It is to listen to those who know."[29] It did not last long. He understood that he needed to know the pandemic better to make better decisions. He began to consult all the studies as soon as they were published and read about public health and epidemiology. The Minister of Education even said that "The president has acquired real expertise on health issues. This is not a difficult subject for a mind like his, taking into account the significant time he has spent on it for several months."[30] The president of the National Assembly, Richard Ferrand, also declared, "He looks for anything new every day to make sure he doesn't miss anything. One day, he will be able to compete for the aggregation of immunology."[31]

The result has sometimes been positive. In June 2020, he decided to reopen France after the shutdown faster than the COVID-19 Scientific Council recommended, and it worked. In December 2020, experts anticipated a new peak of contaminations in France in February. Macron refused to act on it, and the February peak did not happen. But when scientists asked at the end of January to take measures to avoid a new rise, he refused and postponed them until April, when it was too late. Le Monde, a leading French newspaper, has calculated that this decision provoked more than 14,000 additional deaths, nearly 112,000 additional hospitalizations, including 28,000 in intensive care, and about 160,000 other cases of COVID-19.

Macron's methods do not always work. Behind an appearance of modesty and attention to others, there is a form of arrogance. The French President tends to think that his superior intelligence makes his judgment more reliable than that of specialists. This is not the case, as shown by his handling of the coronavirus crisis. It could cost him the reelection if he is not able to recognize it and show some humility.

Even if Macron has handled the coronavirus better than Donald Trump and Boris Johnson, he has not shown the leadership ability expected of him during the COVID-19 crisis, particularly if you compare him to Angela Merkel and other European leaders. And months after the report's publication on the management of the crisis, he has not yet acted to correct the structural deficits of the French public health system.

Compared to John F. Kennedy, he has yet to prove his leadership abilities.

***

The Benalla scandal, Yellow Jackets, terrorism, rebellion against his disruptive reforms, the COVID-19 crisis... The young French President has had to face more problems than any of his predecessors since de Gaulle, and he will undoubtedly be judged by historians based on his capacity to face them. When the French reelected Macron as their president in 2022, they seemed to have forgotten about Macron's uncertain attitude during the Benalla scandal, the media did not focus either on the police violence during the Yellow Jackets movement. But the management of the COVID-19 crisis and the increase of the French debt due to Macron's management of the COVID crisis were the main focus of his competitors, and of the media. It shows the capacity of the French to change their mind rather quickly: one year before the election, spending without limits seemed to be the motto of the opposition, as Macron was accused of not following President Biden who explained that he intended to use the health crisis to "re-found the nation by launching a real "Marshall Plan" of 1,900 billion dollars (nearly 1,600 billion euros) and by promising a more ecological and fairer world."[32] At the time, the opposition accused Macron, their forty-year-old president, of not having the guts to try to make the same bold move as his seventy-nine-year-old counterpart on the other side of the Atlantic...

Chapter 10
Foreign Policy

"In the event that misfortune should befall and the freedom of the world should be at stake, who would automatically be the best allies of nature if not France and the United States, as they have often been in such cases?"

— President de Gaulle[1]

"We are in 50 B.C.; all of Gaul is occupied by the Romans... All of it? No! because a village populated by die-hard Gauls is still resisting the invader. And life is not easy for the garrisons of Roman legionaries of the entrenched camps of Babaorum, Aquarium, Laudanum, and Petibonum..."[2] This Gallic village in Armorica, the residence of the comic book hero Asterix, resists the invader thanks to the magic potion prepared by the druid Getafix, which momentarily gives superhuman strength to anyone who drinks it. As a result, these resistance fighters live free and happy and regularly have banquets where they eat and drink together.

Even if it seems strange, most French people still see themselves as these besieged Gauls, and it has an impact on their relations with the rest of the world and an influence on their President.[3]

According to historians, until the French Revolution in 1789, the Gauls had a rather negative image, as they were described by the Romans who invaded their territories and colonized them.[4] The Romans considered them their enemies, a violent people, illiterate and devoid of artistic sense. Gauls were said by their invaders to practice human sacrifices. They appeared to be inferior beings on the intellectual, social, and political levels and needed to become civilized. But then, in 1828, French historian Amédée Thierry brought the Gauls back into fashion in the first book devoted to a history of the Gauls in French, in which he spoke about "our ancestors the Gauls."[5] From 1828 to the end of the twentieth century, millions of French children have learned that: "In the past, our country was called Gaul, and the inhabitants were called Gauls. [...] One day, Gaul was attacked by a people who lived in Italy. These people were called the Romans. They were commanded by a great general, Julius Caesar. The Gauls chose as their general a young man from the Auvergne, Vercingetorix. [...] He talks to the Gauls. He speaks very well. He tells them: 'The Romans want to take our country from us; we must defend ourselves. Let's march and drive them out of Gaul, our homeland.'"[6] And children were happy to identify with this legendary image of the Gauls: tall, robust, and fierce warriors, blondes with a long hair, living in the forests, adoring nature, brawlers, refusing any authority except their priests, fearing nothing except that the sky falls on their head....

The French have lived with this total fabrication for almost two centuries. It was a fiction: Gaul does not correspond to France: it was a region of Western Europe populated mainly by Celts, Belgians, Aquitanians, Ligurians, and Iberians, which would today cover France, Luxembourg, Belgium, most of Switzerland, northern Italy, as well as parts of the Netherlands, and the part of Germany located on the west bank of the Rhine. The Gauls did not live in forests but in cities or in the countryside (mainly in large farms housing aristocrats).[7] They were not primarily fierce warriors, they were renowned craftsmen and tradesmen, and they had commercial links with Rome and Greece ever since some of the Gauls joined Alexander the Great during his conquests. Two thousand years before the success of the French prestige brands Christofle and Louis Vuitton, they were famous for tableware (in ceramic and bronze, and even gold and silver objects linked to a prestige brand), and jewels (rings, bracelets, fibulae, and pendants). They were not organized as a unified country with a king but had a clan system similar to the Scots.

Also, for centuries, so many people have moved to France or from France that it would be challenging to find one actual descendant of the Gauls without external blood. After the Celts, the Romans arrived, and they facilitated the arrival of the so-called barbarians from Germany: the Franks, who gave their name to France, the Burgundians, who settled in the present-day territories of French-speaking Switzerland, Franche-Comté, Burgundy, and the Alpine and Rhone regions, the Alamanni, and the Visigoths coming from a group of tribes from around the Baltic Sea before migrating to the Black Sea, who obtained the right to settle in southwest of France. These movements of populations went on, with the Vikings who settled in Normandy and the Arabs who took some parts of the south of France. In the twentieth century, the movements continued: millions of Spanish, Portuguese, Polish, and Italians arrived in France before World War II; after the war, it was mainly people from Northern Africa. In 2019, immigrants represented 11.5 percent of the French population according to the French National Statistical Institute.[8] This is not that different from the U.S., whose immigrant population (44.9 million in 2019) represented 13.7 percent of the U.S. population.[9]

However, the French still see themselves as the heirs of these proud and irreducible Gauls, even if the school system changed history books in 2015 to reflect the historical reality. During the campaign for the right-wing primary in 2016, former President Nicolas Sarkozy, himself the child of an immigrant, declared: "as soon as you become French, your ancestors are Gauls."[10] This sentence was criticized, as it hinted that immigration should aim for assimilation instead of integration. Later, on a trip to Copenhagen during the campaign, Mr. Macron said his admiration for flexicurity, regretting that it could not be implemented in France because of cultural differences: "These (Danish) Lutheran people, who have lived through the transformations of recent years, are not exactly the Gaulish people who are resistant to change."[11] Again, there were protests in France because he criticized the Gauls.

This image of the French being these independent, strong, and proud warriors may explain why France has kept a strong army, which can intervene alone, or with the U.S. and other partners in Africa and the Middle East without serious opposition from the French population. Moreover, France is the only E.U. country that has made an effort to spend 2 percent of its GNP on its Defense programs, an objective proposed by President Trump. The result is that the French army is second only to the U.S. in NATO, according to the Global Firepower Website[12], and in July 2021 it was engaged in external operations in Syria, Iraq, and more than fifteen African countries.[13]

Emmanuel Macron inherited this situation, and he has not shown any strong will to change it. It is undoubtedly because most of these actions, either directly managed by France or under the U.N., NATO, or E.U. umbrellas, are meant to protect France and the E.U. against the development of terrorism. His two predecessors hoped to boost their popularity by launching or being involved in a war (it did not work), but Macron seems to prefer to find negotiated solutions. Thus, for example, his announcement in May 2021 that ended the Barkhane military operation in the Sahel, where French troops had been engaged since 2013 in the fight against jihadist groups. They will give way to an "international force" whose composition is yet to be determined. It was a way to relieve the French troops and pressure the countries in the region to ensure their security independently.

***

A main reference for the French foreign policy is Charles de Gaulle, the founder and the first President of the Fifth Republic in 1958, and a source for Macron's inspiration. He is also the most admired French war hero. He refused defeat in 1940, organized the resistance, regained control of the French empire, and recreated a powerful French army that participated efficiently in the allies' campaigns in Italy, France, and Germany to end World War II.

De Gaulle embodies the French spirit. In the mind of the French, he was able to restore France's grandeur and then to behave independently from the great powers, dealing with Russian and American leaders on an equal footing, which satisfied the ego of the Gauls hiding in French souls. To understand Macron's foreign policy, de Gaulle is the key — the standard to which all the French presidents who succeeded him are compared. De Gaulle's Minister of Culture, André Malraux, a famous novelist, had said one day that everyone has been, is, or will be a Gaullist. That is true for French Presidents, and particularly for Macron.

Before going into more details about the consequences of this alignment with de Gaulle's foreign policy, it is essential to underline that, according to the Constitution and the practice established by De Gaulle, the French President has exclusive powers in foreign affairs and defense. He is responsible for accrediting French ambassadors abroad, negotiating and ratifying treaties, entering into direct contact with foreign heads of state, and representing France on the international scene (for example, within the G7).[14] He guarantees national independence and territorial integrity; he is the head of the armed forces and decides to use the French nuclear force. As the head of the government, the prime minister is competent in all the other domains, even if the president can always influence his prime minister because he chooses him and can dismiss him. French foreign policy, however, is solely in Macron's hands.

What was de Gaulle's doctrine, which is so essential that French politicians from the extreme-right to the left adore it and judge all other presidents by its standards? It is a mix of pragmatism, long-term vision, stubbornness, arrogance, balance in the relations with the great powers, and search for France's grandeur, sovereignty, independence, and strategic autonomy. More than fifty years have passed since de Gaulle died, and what is left is some benevolent ghost who gave back to France a significant rank in the world while setting up a robust and efficient political system.

It is also about political pragmatism: after World War II, he nationalized large companies and created Social Security, which left a positive memory for left-leaning people. But when France's economy improved, he turned to liberalism. He wanted his country to be independent, so he respected a balance between the east, dominated by Russia, and the West, led by the U.S., even though his attitude showed that France was clearly on the side of the West: de Gaulle was the first one to express his support for the U.S. during the Cuban missile crisis.

In addition to the solid cultural and scientific cooperation between France and the Soviet Union, and his frequent meetings with Soviet leaders, de Gaulle showed his independence by refusing American hegemony within NATO, particularly concerning nuclear issues and the integration of member countries' armed forces within a unified command.[15] He made France leave the integrated command of the organization in 1966, and NATO's headquarters had to move from Fontainebleau, near Paris, to Brussels in Belgium. It was made possible by the fact that France had developed an independent nuclear force and had a permanent seat at the United Nations Security Council, with the ability to veto any decision presented there. France, however, remained a member, not only of the Alliance proper, but also of NATO.

After de Gaulle, there were initiatives from his successors to bridge the gap and improve cooperation between France and the U.S. on NATO matters. After a meeting with President Gerald Ford in Martinique in December 1974, President Giscard d'Estaing pushed for the French defense doctrine to gradually shift from the sanctity of the national territory to the sanctity of Western Europe.[16] There were agreements between France and NATO to coordinate in case of tactical nuclear weapons being launched. Later, President Mitterrand, who had opposed the 1966 decision to withdraw from the integrated military organization, increased French collaboration with NATO. He strongly supported the installation of Pershing II and Tomahawk missiles in West Germany. However, after the collapse of the Soviet bloc, the relevance of NATO was questioned by the French. In particular, they suggested giving more autonomy to Europe within NATO. It was refused by the U.S.

France and Germany decided in 1992 to create the European Corps (later the Eurocorps) — in other words, to "equip the European Union with its own military capacity"[17] and, according to Vaïsse and Sebag, the U.S. pressured Germany to add: "The European Corps will contribute to the reinforcement of the Atlantic Alliance." Later, with President Clinton in the U.S. and President Chirac in France, cooperation developed. However, France maintained its non-participation in the integrated military structure as the French request for more European autonomy was denied by the U.S. It was not until 2009 that Nicolas Sarkozy organized France's reintegration into NATO. However, France did not join the Nuclear Planning Group, wishing to maintain its independence for nuclear deterrence. President Hollande, who in 2009 was an opponent to France's reintegration into NATO, completed the full integration of France into NATO in 2016.

Then Macron arrived, and France's foreign policy changed.

***

When he was elected, Emmanuel Macron was a beginner in the field of foreign policy. However, his program for international affairs began with: "I wish to implement clear and resolute diplomacy, in the de Gaulle and Mitterrand tradition, to make France an independent, humanist, and European power." The reference to de Gaulle was classic among the candidates. Even Sarkozy used to quote him. Nobody cared much what Macron said because he was a newcomer without any experience. It was a mistake, and Emmanuel Macron proved that even a young and seemingly inexperienced leader can quickly change the country's international policy. It required a competent entourage, a vision to guide the action, and courage.

He organized his campaign team using the impressive network of those he sympathized with during his years in the administration at the Elysée Palace and as Minister of Economy. The presence in his team of Jean-Yves Le Drian, a very popular Minister of Defense in the previous government and Macron's future Minister of Europe and Foreign Affairs, has undoubtedly boosted Emmanuel Macron's credibility in international matters. He also had several high-level diplomats on his campaign team. Jean-Claude Cousseran, who served in several ambassador positions in the Middle East (Damascus, Ankara, Cairo) and has been the Director of the DGSE, the French intelligence service, participated in Macron's campaign. Last but not least, Gerard Araud, a French diplomat for more than three decades, a former Director-General for Political Affairs and Security and Director for Strategic Affairs, Security, and Disarmament at the Ministry of Foreign Affairs, has been another source of knowledge in foreign affairs for Macron.[18] Araud also served as the French negotiator on the Iranian nuclear issue from 2006 to 2009 and France's Permanent Representative to the United Nations in New York. After the campaign, Macron made him France's Ambassador to the U.S. Macron may not be a specialist in foreign affairs, but Team Macron was the strongest possible.

He needed a vision, and he had one. It was not apparent in his program, which focused on some traditional topics for French politicians: i.e., we live in a world of threats and opportunities, France's declining influence despite considerable assets, France is supposed to be an independent power, humanism should be at the core of foreign policy, and France is a leading European power. That is nice to hear, but the question is: can they address these matters?

Few people knew that Emmanuel Macron had been very impressed during the clash between France and the U.S. in the United Nations.[19] It happened with a slow rise in tensions that began in the summer/autumn of 2002 with the vote on Security Council resolution 1441, which aimed to seek peaceful means, through a united international community, to organize inspections and resolve the uncertainties concerning Iraq. The negotiations between Colin Powell, the U.S. Secretary of State, and representatives of the international community allowed for real progress. But the U.S., apparently convinced that Iraq was hiding "weapons of mass destruction," refused to vote on the resolution and presented what they considered proof of the existence of these weapons. They asked for the support of the U.N. Security Council for military operations against Iraq, and for the first time in history, France, a permanent member, vetoed the proposal.

The French Prime Minister, Dominique de Villepin, made a moving, intellectual, and very French speech in the Security Council. The audience applauded it, which is a rare event.[20] All France loved it, and time proved De Villepin right: there were no weapons of mass destruction, and the fall of Iraq may have facilitated the emergence of Islamism. But the relationship between France and the U.S. was strained for several years.

Before De Villepin, who is a right-wing conservative, declared his support to Macron, he also stated in March 2017 that he was close to him: "Emmanuel Macron is someone I know well, he's someone I have a friendship for, who has a bold, original path, he's a Republican."[21] Macron had positioned himself as an admirer of De Villepin: "I happen to have read his book, [...] I had several discussions with him and he is someone whose vision I share, I must say, on international issues."[22] De Villepin has sometimes criticized Macron, but seldom on his foreign policies, except for his attempts to befriend President Trump.

When the young president took the lead of French foreign policy, a French-style neoconservatism dominated the Ministry of Foreign Affairs, quite similar to American hawks: these diplomats saw the world in black and white, divided into friends and enemies of the western world. They advocated the use of force against the latter. With President Sarkozy and President Hollande, they have pushed for the wars in Iraq, in Syria for attempts to overthrow the regime of Bashar El Assad, and for the intervention in the Sahel.

This diplomatic vision of the world changed with Emmanuel Macron. Just elected, he declared in June, 2017: "With me, it will be the end of a form of neo-conservatism imported into France over the last ten years. Democracy is not built from the outside without the support of the people. France did not participate in the war in Iraq, and it was right. And it was wrong to wage war in this way in Libya."[23] The meaning of this sentence was also that France should not be systematically aligned with the U.S.

This evolution has been called "friends, allies, not aligned" by Hubert Védrine, former Minister of Foreign Affairs, in his 2012 report on "The consequences of France's return to NATO's integrated military command, and on the future of the transatlantic relationship and the prospects for a European defense." Védrine thought that it was unrealistic "to think, as the Bush administration does, that maintaining absolute military superiority will be enough to preserve our interests." He considered that it had proven to be inefficient, and he recommended getting out of this Atlanticist vision, partly carried by the French right. Since Macron was elected, Hubert Védrine has frequently supported the positions of the president on the international scene.

NATO has been one of these cases where France's attitude has changed. On the 21st of October, 2019, Emmanuel Macron declared in an interview to *The Economist*: "What we are currently experiencing is the brain death of NATO."[24] President Trump reacted violently to this provocation before calming down after the 2019 NATO summit, and other NATO members also declared that they were shocked. But Macron had serious reasons to intervene: he was upset that he learned by a simple tweet of Trump's decision to withdraw his troops from northeastern Syria. Turkey's Erdogan, another NATO ally, did not bother to warn his NATO partners of his offensive against the Kurds, the allies of the coalition led by the U.S. in the Middle East against the Islamic State. Even if other European countries were worried about the U.S. attitude, nobody dared to support the French President. However, the questions Macron asked about the revision of the goals and functioning of NATO in a changing world where a military attack by Russia should not be the only scenario, have had an impact. One step forward was the decision by NATO Heads of State and Government on the 14th of June, 2021, to agree on a set of proposals covering a range of issues: the protection of critical infrastructure, promoting innovation, boosting partnerships, and making the fight against climate change an important task for NATO.

Macron showed spectacularly that France would have an independent foreign policy: the first official Head of State invited to France for an official visit was Vladimir Putin. It was an opportunity for the two leaders to revive their countries' diplomatic relations after years of incidents. The last one had been President Hollande's unexpected cancellation of the Russian President's visit to Paris in October 2016, when the Syrian regime forces and Russian aircrafts had bombed the town of Aleppo. The meeting with Macron, which took place in the grandiose Versailles Palace, was impressive. The relationship between France and Russia was normalized, and the following discussions between the two presidents became almost friendly.

Macron has also changed the French policy concerning Syria. In the Spring of 2011, during the Arab Spring revolt, President Sarkozy supported the cause of the popular and peaceful protest movement in Syria. When the Syrian regime chose repression, President Hollande recognized the Syrian National Coalition and suspended its diplomatic relations with Bashar al-Assad, calling for the Syrian president's removal. After al-Assad used Sarin gas against his opponents, Hollande was ready to send airstrikes against the regime, as agreed upon with President Obama, but the American president reconsidered. France had a very bellicose stance.

It would have been easy for Macron to continue this policy. For most French, al-Assad was a cruel dictator who had hundreds of thousands of Syrians massacred to stay in power. Politically, he would have been safe: the notion of the "right to intervene," which refers to the possibility for external countries to intervene in a sovereign state, even without its consent, in the event of a massive violation of human rights, was dominant in France. Bernard Kouchner, the founder of Doctors Without Borders and President Sarkozy's Minister of Foreign Affairs, had made it popular for Biafra during the Nigerian Civil War and the famine in the region between 1967 and 1970.

Macron understood that there was no question: the status quo would have increased the suffering of the Syrians. War was not a solution, and neither the U.S. nor the Russians who had military units in the region wanted it. Macron declared soon after his election that "On this subject, my deep conviction is that we need a diplomatic and political roadmap.

The issue will not be resolved by military means alone. That is the mistake we have collectively made. The real aggiornamento[25] that I made on this subject is that I did not state that the removal of Bashar al-Assad was a prerequisite to everything. Because nobody presented me with his legitimate successor!"[26] That was a bold movement and a pragmatic change that has been supported by those wanting the return to de Gaulle's style policies. The aim was to put France among those working on a negotiated solution and not among the belligerents.

The situation was different with Iran, but Macron again moved to be at the center of the negotiations. France had been active in the negotiation of the Vienna Agreement on the Iranian nuclear issue (Joint Plan of Action) signed in Vienna, Austria, on the 14th of July, 2015, by the five permanent members of the United Nations Security Council (the United States, Russia, China, France, and the United Kingdom), as well as Germany, the European Union, and Iran. This agreement aimed at controlling Iran's nuclear program and lifting the economic sanctions that affected the country. On the 8th of May, 2018, U.S. President Donald Trump announced the country's withdrawal from the Vienna agreement and reinforced economic sanctions against Iran. The European countries opposed this decision and created methods to avoid the sanctions, but nothing seemed to change President Trump's mind.

President Macron has voluntarily taken the lead to find a solution with Iranian leaders and President Trump trying to discuss and mediate a negotiated solution. On the 24th of April, 2018, he was in Washington to meet the U.S. President and convince him, but it was in vain. After that, until the end of 2019, he pushed for negotiating a new agreement covering a more extensive field. In June 2019, the two presidents met in Normandy to pay homage to the 160,000 American and Allied troops who landed there on D-Day seventy-five years before, altering the course of World War II. After a private meeting, the two presidents gave a press conference — Trump declared about Iran: "I understand that they (the Iranian government) want to talk, that's fine. We will talk, but one thing is sure: they cannot have a nuclear weapon, and I think the French president would agree with me completely."

Macron made a new attempt for a dialogue at the G7 Summit organized in France at the end of August 2019. The French newspaper *Le Monde* wrote that "The arrival in Biarritz [...] of Iranian Foreign Minister Mohammad Javad Zarif was a real coup during a G7 Summit under the French presidency dominated by the Iranian issue. Mr. Zarif was not invited to the Summit but came to meet with his French counterpart, Jean-Yves Le Drian [...] The meeting lasted about three hours with the head of French diplomacy, then half an hour with Emmanuel Macron."[27] It was symbolic, but it showed that Macron wanted to promote dialogue between the U.S. and Iran.

Encouraged by this opening and as persistent as ever, Macron used the U.N. General Assembly in September 2019 to push for a negotiated solution. According to the *New York Times*, on the evening of the 24th of September, 2019, Macron and a small team made an unexpected visit to Iranian President Rouhani's hotel.[28] They proposed that he talk with President Trump on a secured line prepared by the French team. President Trump was ready to take the call. Rouhani hesitated, leaving Macron and his advisers waiting outside his room for an answer. But Macron had underestimated the constraints of Iranian internal politics: Rouhani refused, as he had no guarantee that Mr. Trump would consider ending the sanctions on Iran, leaving the Iranian President at risk of "a political backlash at home, where hard-liners were already fuming at the mere possibility that Mr. Rouhani would consider a dialogue with Mr. Trump," according to the *New York Times*. A French source reported an interesting exchange between Macron and Rouhani behind the scenes of the General Assembly. Macron told his Iranian counterpart that "It takes two to tango."[29] The sarcastic reply was that "Clerics do not dance the tango."

Was it the end of Macron's initiatives for Iran? Certainly not. He is not a quitter. The situation has changed: with France's support, President Biden has relaunched negotiations with Iran on a new framework agreement. Macron has established a strong relationship with the new U.S. president, and the positions of the two countries are now similar. On the 25th of June, 2021, U.S. Secretary of State Anthony Blinken and French Minister of Foreign Affairs Jean-Yves le Drian announced that the United States and France warned the new Iranian authorities that time was running out to save the Iranian nuclear deal and put an end to international sanctions, calling on them to take "courageous and strong decisions."

Macron's actions on Iranian files have not been successful, but they show that he is a different type of leader in foreign affairs. He knew the importance of normalizing the relations with Iran to stabilize the Middle East, and he did not hesitate to take political risks even when he knew that there was a greater chance of failure than of success. After de Gaulle, this attitude has not been common for French presidents.

The evolution of the French attitude towards China is another example of Macron's input in France's foreign policy. His predecessors have been relatively inactive, paralyzed by the fact that China is one of the main customers of French and European businesses. A visit of a French President in China has generally been organized to publicly sign billions of euros' contracts for French companies with the Chinese government, and to make some low-key remarks about human rights' breaches in the country.

Macron has changed the approach, after analyzing that it has failed. During his presidential campaign in 2017, he pledged to strengthen and rebalance relations between the European Union (E.U.) and China in the areas of security, trade and ecology through a cross-cutting agreement. As he explained in an interview with the thinktank The Atlantic Council, "This agreement is not... a huge deal, is not a transformational deal, neither for China nor for the European Union.… It presents some very important and positive items. It will improve some issues on investment and access to markets. It failed to deal with the intellectual property issue… But for the very first time, China accepted to engage on ILO regulation and to commit precisely on labor issues, which are part of our human rights package. And for me, this is very interesting because this is a test of the reality of a good-faith discussion on that". As of 31 December 2021, this Comprehensive Agreement on Investment (CAI) supported by Macron has been accepted by the E.U. heads of state, but had not been signed, pending ratification by the European Parliament. Even if there are serious doubts about the final approval of the deal, it has shown Macron's determination to push for negotiated solutions in the relations with China. As he explained in his interview, "My willingness is to have a political approach, because I want a stable and peaceful world. But it means managing together to have a fair and open discussion, sometimes to share differences".

This attitude has been largely criticized in France by people on the left because of China's breaches of human rights against their population, such as the actions against Uyghur Muslims. Macron explained in another interview with the French magazine Brut in December 2020 "I am not going to start a war with China on this subject [...] What I would like is that we Europeans, in our dialogue with China, carry this demand and that we ask for an immediate end to these camps, to this violence", an explanation which was not appreciated in China.

He uses a method which consists in applying an increasing pressure through political and economic means (Europe represents 21 % of China trade) while never stopping the dialogue with Beijing (he has already been two times in China for official state visit, and promised to continue every year). Politically, he has been progressively tougher with China: in May 2018, he warned against the risk of Chinese "hegemony" in the Indo-Pacific area; in April 2020, he criticized Beijing's handling of the

Covid-19 pandemic; in May 2020 he refused to yield to Chinese pressure to cancel an arms deal with Taiwan; in June 2020, he called on China to respect Hong Kong's autonomy; in September 2020, he condemned for the first time the repression of the Uyghurs in Xinjiang and in December spoke out on behalf of the Europeans to ask for "the cessation of these camps" of forced labor to which many members of this Muslim minority are sent.

But the Chinese government is clearly more annoyed by Macron's activism in the EU for obliging them to accept improvements in the terms of the economic relations. He has for example succeeded in pushing the EU to develop anti-dumping tools, perform investment screenings, force reciprocity in public procurement, or develop an independent 5G strategy. The EU-27 are also preparing to adopt a tax on third countries companies that get high levels of public subsidies, and an industrial strategy to limit the EU dependence in strategic sectors. All of this is aimed at better protecting the EU from Chinese ambitions. With time, Macron has been able to get the EU countries to support his views: China is now less attractive to Europe. Even in Germany, where Angela Merkel has long prevented the EU from asserting itself more strongly in relation to Beijing, the situation has changed. As for the EU countries that joined the Chinese "New Silk Roads" project, their enthusiasm has waned. Mario Draghi's Italy, in particular, has distanced itself and now also supports Macron and defends the principle of a more autonomous Europe.

It could go well with Biden's desire not to be supplanted by China. Macron said that it is a question of "not being vassalized by China or aligned with the United States on this issue," but Europe's quest for autonomy pushed by Macron may be compatible with U.S. objectives, even if the EU is still quite weak politically in front of China.

Macron's preference for diplomatic solutions does not mean that he is not strong when necessary. He has often exposed his doctrine: "When you set red lines, if you don't enforce them, you appear to be weak. That's not my choice."[30] For the Syrian crisis, he wanted a negotiated solution with the Syrian regime and the Russians. However, he warned in the same interview: "If it is proven that chemical weapons are being used on the ground and we know where they are coming from, then France will carry out strikes to destroy the chemical weapons stocks."[31] When Syrian government forces organized a chemical attack against the population of the Syrian city of Douma, near Damascus, President Macron launched airstrikes directed against the Syrian regime's clandestine chemical arsenal. It was a part of an international operation conducted in a coalition with the U.S. and the UK. He did not hesitate to do it because the Syrian regime had crossed the red line he had defined with his allies.

Macron had another opportunity to show his strength. It began with the discovery in recent years of vast gas deposits in the eastern Mediterranean off Israel, Lebanon, Egypt, and Cyprus. Turkey sent exploration ships to search for hydrocarbons in Cypriot waters, justifying it by the fact that Turks occupy a part of Cyprus following an illegal military invasion in 1974. In July 2020, they began to conduct their research south of the small Greek island of Kastellorizo, the easternmost island of Greek territory, three kilometers from the Turkish coast and 550 kilometers from the Greek mainland. Based on the U.N. Convention on Maritime Law, signed by Greece but not by Turkey, the Greek government accused Turkey of violating its territory. However, Turkey continued this exploration using one specialized ship accompanied by warships.

Greece asked for help from the European Union, citing a clause in the E.U. treaty that stipulates that if an E.U. country is the victim of armed aggression on its territory, the other E.U. countries must aid and assist it by all the means in their power.[32] As usual, the E.U. was slow to react. One of its most important countries, Germany, has a large Turkish population and feared troubles. In addition, there was a fear that Turkey would stop retaining refugees from the Middle East in camps organized on its territory (and paid for by the E.U.) and let them cross into E.U. countries.

But, as explained by Gérard Araud, a diplomat who knows Emmanuel Macron well, "There is no effective diplomacy that is not based on a balance of power. Against the Turkish actions, it was first necessary to oppose force with force. Then comes the time for diplomacy."[33] Macron reinforced the French fleet in the Mediterranean, and two vessels supported the Greek fleet, with two Rafale jet fighters. Turkish President Erdogan hated it, but he withdrew his exploration ship, and diplomacy prevailed. On the 14th of June, 2021, after months of tension, Macron and Turkish President Recep Tayyip Erdogan met in Brussels in "an appeased climate," pledging to "work together" on Libya and Syria, according to Macron.

Besides this evolution of the French foreign policy toward more independence, the preference and the push for diplomatic solutions, and a show of strength when countries cross the red lines, humanism is one of Macron's guidelines. He declared it in his program for the presidential election, and he repeated it regularly. For example, he made the following declaration at the 27th French ambassadors' conference in August 2019: "So our responsibility in this context, and I believe in this capacity to revive the spirit of the Enlightenment, is to be essential actors to make a new demand in terms of human rights, to make a further demand so that our democracies and our values are defended everywhere."

It is an echo of President de Gaulle's times. In a speech delivered on the 6th of July, 1960, the French President declared, "At the rendezvous that France gave to the universe, 175 years ago, that of liberty, equality, and fraternity... France's vocation is human to serve the cause of man, the cause of freedom, the cause of human dignity... This is the vocation of France since 1789. It has always been true; it is true today more than ever, a France at the service of all humanity."[34]

There is a contradiction between these declarations and the reality. From 1963, Franco-Soviet relations developed with a diplomatic rapprochement, particularly with the ten-day visit de Gaulle made throughout Soviet Russia. It triggered meaningful economic, cultural, technical, and scientific exchanges between Paris and Moscow, despite the human rights breaches in the U.S.S.R. De Gaulle needed to balance France's relations with the U.S. for France to exist diplomatically, and the question of human rights could not prevent him. In addition, behind the U.S.S.R, he saw the imperial Russia, which had been close to France for centuries.

Emmanuel Macron could also be criticized on the limits of his humanism. In particular, the French political left has criticized Macron for inviting Prince Mohammed Bin Salman to Paris for an official visit in 2018. Saudi Arabia had intervened in Yemen's civil war and committed serious violations of international humanitarian law. During the visit, Macron obtained his signature on €18 billion contracts for French industry. However, since the beginning of Emmanuel Macron's five-year term, there has been no love lost between Paris and Riyadh, according to the French magazine *Challenges*. Unlike his predecessors, Macron "has not made an official trip to the kingdom, apart from a whirlwind visit to Riyadh in December 2017 to secure the release of Lebanese Prime Minister Saad Hariri," who was then held prisoner by Saudi Arabia.[35] Prince Mohammed Bin Salman did not make efforts to befriend Macron. Even worse, the program of his 2018 visit to France was shortened while he had just spent three weeks in the United States, particularly in Silicon Valley.

Like Presidents Hollande and Sarkozy, Macron has not taken a strong stance about the situation of the Palestinians. Presidents de Gaulle and Chirac have always been popular in the Arabic world by defending human rights in Palestine and pushing for the two-state solution for the conflict between Israel and Palestinians — an independent Palestine alongside Israel. This solution was proposed in a 1974 U.N. resolution and opposed then by Israel and by the U.S. Macron has been accused of supporting the Palestinians too mildly: he limits his action in this field to presenting official protests when there are human rights abuses from Israel in Gaza. He was also accused of being too friendly with Benjamin Netanyahu when he received him in Paris in 2017. He explained that they have disagreed on most topics, but he had called him "dear Bibi" and called "anti-Zionism" a new form of antisemitism.[36]

These critiques do not seem very serious, as the French president alone would not be able to change the fate of Palestinians or pressure the Saudis to stop human rights violations in Yemen. However, the limits of Macron's humanism have been tested on France's territory with the reception of refugees and asylum seekers. Some asylum seekers try to cross the Mediterranean from Africa or the Middle East by boats and are taken on board by NGOs' ships. There has been a period when these ships were refused in E.U. harbors, but France and Germany have organized a mechanism to share refugees voluntarily between like-minded E.U. countries. However, Macron's France does not decently receive asylum seekers and refugees. France is regularly condemned by the European Court of Human Rights for failing to assist asylum seekers, who are forced to live "on the streets" and "deprived of a means of subsistence."[37] That is not humanism and is a stain on France's reputation.

Interestedly, Macron himself has been an asset to France's foreign policy. He is the youngest French President; he has been elected against all odds; he has not his predecessors' reluctance to take risks; he speaks English. He regularly gives interviews in English to foreign media. Besides, he knows how to make himself heard in the world, as shown with his famous slogans, "Make the planet great again!," "France is back," and "What we are currently experiencing is the brain death of NATO." According to Gilles Andréani, a specialist of international affairs, "Seen from the outside, it was said that France could still produce something new; that in the land of sclerosis a renewal was possible. This feeling of curiosity and interest contrasted with the more or less polite condescension that had often accompanied, on the part of foreign commentators, the evocation of Emmanuel Macron's predecessors. It has been the first international fallout of his victory."[38]

The reforms launched by Macron's governments have caused a stir in France, and they have been successful in convincing foreign business leaders to invest in France. Macron's predecessors, particularly from the left, have been careful to avoid presenting themselves as pro-business, as it was not very popular in France. Well, France has changed, and Macron did not hesitate. He has already invited three times high-level business people to the Versailles Royal Castle to support France's international ambitions. Louis XVI invited Benjamin Franklin there in 1778; Emperor Napoleon III invited Queen Victoria in 1855; President Felix Faure invited Tsar Nicolas II in 1896; Macron invited Vladimir Putin in 2017. But today's important people invited to the French Republic's most prestigious palace are the leaders of large companies, American (Coca-Cola, Snap Inc, FedEx, Google, Netflix...), Asian (Hyundai Motors, Samsung Electronics, Fosun, Toyota...), African (Cooper Pharma, Orascom) and European (Rolls Royce, EY, ING Bank...). Sundar Pichai, CEO of Google Inc., Vasant Narasimhan, CEO of Novartis, Bill McDermott, CEO of SAP, have replaced kings, popes, emperors, and tsars.

Macron's policy has been successful: in 2019, France became the most attractive European country for investors, and still was in 2020.[39]

***

What is the real impact of Macron's foreign policy?

It is not easy to answer because it would suppose having clearly defined the objectives of France's foreign policy for assessing the results of the government's actions. The U.S. State Department and U.S.AID have a joint strategic plan 2018-2022 with four goals: Protect America's Security at Home and Abroad; Renew America's Competitive Advantage for Sustained Economic Growth and Job Creation; Promote American Leadership through Balanced Engagement; Ensure Effectiveness and Accountability to the American Taxpayer.

Nothing similar exists in France. Major decisions are still taken on a case-by-case basis by the President, who is not limited by any strategic document. It can make it difficult for foreign observers to predict France's reactions as they depend on the president's personality. Macron, being a mix of idealism and realism, may make his decisions based on the search for France's grandeur, or pure humanism, with a striking realism when he finds it necessary for political or economic reasons. But France would need a more stable strategic vision.[40]

Chapter 11
The European

"The only way to ensure our future is to rebuild a sovereign, united and democratic Europe."

— President Macron, 2017

"Of course, one can jump on one's chair like a goat and say Europe! Europe! Europe!... but it doesn't lead to anything and it doesn't mean anything."

— President de Gaulle, 1965

On the 10th of December, 2016, Emmanuel Macron was in front of 15,000 supporters for his first campaign meeting for the 2017 presidential election. He had no program yet, so everybody expected some type of revelation from the young candidate. He was enthusiastic, spoke with passion, and showed a high level of energy. He captivated the audience, more with his style than with the content of his speech. But there was a shock: in his speech, he declared himself an enthusiastic supporter of the European Union. Corinne Lhaïk, a journalist from the French magazine *L'Express*, expressed it best: "He finished an hour and a half of speech with his voice in a slump, his arms crossed, ecstatic, as if possessed. By the devil or by God? No, by Europe."[1] Macron declared in his speech, "We love Europe, we want Europe!" And, according to Lhaïk, the room got up, was covered with blue flags spangled with yellow. That was a surprise: he was the only Euro-enthusiast among the eleven candidates in the presidential election.

French politicians are very cautious when it comes to their attitude toward the European Union because the French's attitude toward it is complex. They are at the same time against the European Union as it is currently, but they believe in the concept. A study published by the NGO Notre Europe Institut Jacques Delors in 2020 analyzed this phenomenon.[2] At the time, France was with Italy, the United Kingdom, and Greece, one of the countries whose inhabitants were the least favorable to the E.U. Only 32 percent of French have expressed confidence in Europe, which was worse than any other country except the U.K.[3] That probably explains why France, along with Austria and Denmark, is one of the three E.U. countries where political parties strongly opposed to European integration have become major political forces. That is worrying because France is a "large" member state (demographically speaking), a founding country, participating in all E.U. policies.

During the last presidential election in 2017, five of the eleven candidates representing 29 percent of the voters favored a French exit of the E.U. for reasons ranging from the restoration of French sovereignty to the rejection of European liberalism. In addition, the candidate with the majority of votes on the left (20 percent of the voters), M. Melenchon, condemned the excess of liberalism and asked for a social reorientation of the E.U. He threatened to leave the E.U. if the other countries would not accept his demands. The Socialist candidate, M. Hamon, made the same demands as M. Melenchon but did not clearly say that he would leave the E.U. if they were not satisfied. In addition, the candidate from the right, Francois Fillon, said that he supported the ongoing European integration process but stressed that the E.U. should go back to cooperation between national governments and not continue toward moderate federalism. The 10th candidate, M.

Lassalle, who had belonged to the French Center party (UDF-Modem), refused to endorse the federalist positions of his former party and did not indicate his position for the E.U.

Emmanuel Macron was the only pro-European candidate, which may have been dangerous in a country with so few people having confidence in the E.U. But he did not take such a considerable risk: the French show a solid attachment to the E.U. (53 percent), and they feel that they are European citizens (58 percent).[4] The French do not want to leave the E.U., but they expect it to be more efficient, more present, more protective. Their lack of confidence is due to the gap between their expectations and the reality of the E.U.'s actions.

Emmanuel Macron understood it. He presented himself as the defender and the promoter of the European Union, with the motto "I am the candidate of a strong France in a Europe that protects."[5] During the campaign, he explained that, by a strong France, he meant to give back to France its historic role as the leader of the European construction. By a strong Europe, he meant that the people's sovereignty could not be ensured at the national level in a globalized world: he said during the first debate for the presidential election that "true sovereignty is achieved through European action."[6] He has understood that the French wanted the E.U. to protect them, and that France would play a pivotal role in the development of the Union.

Some background about the European Union is necessary to explain why Emmanuel Macron, with this solid pro-European attitude, was able to win the presidential election.

It is typical to judge the European Union by comparing it with the United States and other big powers such as China or Russia. In 1991, the then-Belgian Minister of Foreign Affairs Eyskens famously retorted that "Europe was an economic giant, a political dwarf, and a military worm." European and foreign politicians and experts regularly use this sentence. In 2016, Andrey Kortunov, a Russian historian and the

Director-General of the Russian International Affairs Council, developed this opinion when he explained: "The European Union is sometimes referred to as 'an economic giant and a political dwarf.' This somewhat condescending definition implies that E.U. member states have always been reluctant to invest significant resources and energy into a common foreign and security policy, especially at the expense of social and economic development priorities. It is also a reference to the fact that Europeans have traditionally relied on U.S. leadership, guidance and protection for most important political and security matters."[7]

How could the E.U. be something else? It has been created so recently, and its history is so different from that of the U.S.!

In 1776, in Philadelphia, the Second Continental Congress declared the Thirteen Colonies' independence as the "United States." Led by General George Washington, it won the Revolutionary War. The Constitution adopted in 1789 established a strong government with clear powers, protection of civil rights, and clear recognition of independent States' competencies, making the U.S. a federal state. Later, the country developed by different methods. There were peaceful ones, such as purchases, the main ones being the Louisiana Purchase, which covered all the Mississippi basin, purchased from France in 1803, Florida from Spain in 1819, and Alaska from the Russian Empire in 1867. The U.S. government pushed for colonization of Indian territories and practiced annexations, such as West Florida in 1810, the Republic of Texas in 1845. The Mexican–American War in 1846 allowed the U.S. to annex California and a large area comprising roughly half of New Mexico, most of Arizona, Nevada, Utah, and a portion of Colorado. The rest of New Mexico was later purchased. All this strengthened the federal government's power, which allowed the U.S. to become the main power of the twentieth century.

The European Union is an entirely different matter. It has gone through periods of being united three times in the last 2000 years. The Romans launched the conquest of most of the known world from the third century, B.C. From the first century, they united a large part of Europe, covering today's Italy, France, Spain, Belgium, Luxemburg, Portugal, South Germany, the United Kingdom (except Scotland), The Netherlands, and all the countries of South Europe. It determined the future of Europe: the Romans brought their advanced technology of an irrigated agriculture, which has helped the future development of the civilization in Europe. They also disseminated their conception of a state, an army, an administration, a currency, provinces, and borders defined and guarded to ensure the cohesion of the whole. Other new ideas arrived in Europe, such as written laws to regulate life in society and settle disputes, and Latin, which remained the language of intellectual communication in Europe until the eighteenth century, before being supplanted by French in the nineteenth century and by English in the second half of the twentieth century. Consequently, many European countries, including France, have adopted their version of Latin as a national language.

This history has had an impact on the European Union. Several European institutions use Latin in their logos: the European Parliament (Parlamentum Europaeum), the Court of Justice (Curia), the Court of Auditors (Curia Rationum). The Council of the Union uses the word "consilium" in its web address. The motto of the European Union was initially written officially in Latin ("in varietate Concordia") in the European Constitutional Treaty. And the possibility to adopt Latin as its only official language is still considered since the Romance languages are predominant after Brexit.

Europe was later partly united in the ninth century by Emperor Charlemagne, who conquered most of Western and Central Europe. He was the first recognized emperor to rule since the fall of the Western

Roman Empire around three centuries earlier. He was initially the King of the Franks, which was the title of the King of France. He launched reforms to improve the administration of his empire, using methods inspired by those of the Catholic Church. He created a currency ratio system which was a revolution for the economy and was still used in the U.K. up until the adoption of the metric system. He took measures to develop trade in Europe, with some limitations such as a ban on arms exports. But at his death, his empire disappeared.

In 1812, the French Emperor Napoleon walked in Charlemagne's footsteps and unified most of Europe once again, except the UK and Portugal. It did not last: he was beaten in 1815 and was exiled by his enemies — a coalition of British, Russians, Austrians, Prussians, and Swedish kings. Napoleon set up numerous reforms in the societal and economic fields. He was responsible for the construction of the Paris Stock Exchange and its main regulations. He instituted the Civil Code, also called the "Napoleonic Code," promulgated in 1804, which has influenced the legislation in most E.U. countries in property, family, contracts, and obligations.

These adventures could have allowed the creation of a solid European empire or a federation of countries similar to those of the most powerful countries in the world. But, except for the Roman empire, which lasted for centuries, they were not successful. Europe has instead been the origin and the main scene for conflicts, including World War I and World War II. However, the idea of a united Europe began to emerge slowly. The Congress of Vienna of 1814-1815, an international diplomatic conference aimed at organizing the European political order after the downfall of the French Emperor Napoleon I, announced the form of cooperation that would govern the continent until 1914: the "Concert of Nations" with the European States meeting regularly to discuss issues, in particular war and trade.[8]

Intellectuals also promoted the idea of the "United States of Europe." Victor Hugo, the famous French writer, declared in 1849 during the Congress of Peace held in Paris: "A day will come when you France, you Russia, you Italy, you England, you Germany, you all, nations of the continent, without losing your distinct qualities and your glorious individuality, you will melt closely into a superior unity, and you will constitute the European fraternity." However, it took a hundred years and two World Wars to begin to build the European Union. It has been long, and it has never been easy.

It is not possible to discuss the European Union without referring to Jean Monnet, often called the "Father of Europe." He was born in Cognac, in France, into a family of cognac merchants.[9] At the age of sixteen, he abandoned his university entrance examinations. He moved to the United Kingdom, where he spent several years in London learning the cognac business with an agent of his father's company. He traveled to Scandinavia, Russia, Egypt, Canada, and the United States for the family business, Monnet Cognac. During World War I, he pushed to facilitate the cooperation between France and U.K. after meeting the French Prime minister. He was appointed deputy secretary-general of the League of Nations after the war but left to take care of the family business.

He then moved to America to accept a partnership in Blair & Co., a New York bank that merged with Bank of America in 1929. He became an international financier and was active in the economic recovery of several Central and Eastern European nations, such as Poland and Romania. In 1932, the Chinese Minister of Finance invited him to act as chairman of an east-west non-political committee in China to develop the Chinese economy. He lived in China until 1936. During World War II, Monnet had a cordial relationship with General de Gaulle but disagreed with him: he would have preferred that the General would be more open to collaboration with other French military leaders who wanted to continue the fight. As he was well-connected in the U.S., Monnet was chosen by Churchill to secure supplies from North America. He writes in his memoirs that he was sent to the U.S. and immediately became an adviser to President Roosevelt. He convinced him to launch a massive arms production program, both as an economic stimulus and to supply the Allies with military resources. He was extremely popular with the Americans and the English.

After the war, Jean Monnet was put in charge of the plan to revive the French economy as Commissioner for Planning, from December 1945 to 1952, within the American Marshall Plan loans framework. His views on Europe had been expressed in a 1943 address to de Gaulle's government in exile, in which he explained: "There will be no peace in Europe if the States are reconstituted based on national sovereignty, with all that that entails in terms of prestige politics and economic protectionism. The countries of Europe are too small to guarantee their peoples the prosperity that modern conditions make possible and consequently necessary. Prosperity for the states of Europe, and the social developments that must go with it, will only be attainable if they form a federation or a "European entity" that puts them into a common economic unit."[10]

According to Pr. Gérard Bossuat, a French historian, Jean Monnet may have taken up themes discussed during the war by John Foster Dulles, who served as United States Secretary of State under President Dwight D. Eisenhower after the war.[11] Monnet was familiar with the documents published by the "Commission to study the bases of a just and lasting peace" created by the Federal Council of the Churches of Christ chaired by John Foster Dulles. In one of the texts communicated to Monnet, Dulles proposed reorganizing continental Europe into a federated Commonwealth, to the point of saying that the re-establishment of the full sovereignty of European states would be "a political folly."[12] In all cases, Monnet was in line with the American demands for abolishing European customs duties and quota, and creating a "common economic unit."

As the French Commissioner in charge of planning, Jean Monnet worked in secret on a project to pool coal and steel, the primary sources of a possible war industry. In the spring of 1950, he presented his plan to the French Foreign Minister Robert Schuman, who secured the agreement of German Chancellor Konrad Adenauer. On the 9th of May, 1950, the European project began when French Foreign Minister Robert Schuman made public Jean Monnet's idea to unify coal and steel production in Europe under a supranational High Authority. France supported the idea because by pooling the resources needed for armaments, the Schuman plan aimed to prevent a new war between France and Germany. For West Germany, led by Konrad Adenauer, it was a way to anchor itself in the Western camp. The European Coal and Steel Community (ECSC) brought Germany, Italy, France, Belgium, the Netherlands, and Luxemburg together. It was organized with a supranational management system, which broke with the intergovernmental experiments conducted up until then.

After that, Europe moved fast. Following the energy shortage caused by the Suez crisis in 1956, France wanted Europeans to unite within an autonomous community that would lead them to energy self-sufficiency. France's partners were in favor of the creation of a common market. Two separate treaties were signed in Rome, one on the European Atomic Energy Community (Euratom), the other establishing the European Economic Community (EEC). The Common Agricultural Policy was born in 1962 after lengthy negotiations and led to the rapid modernization of European agriculture. The next step was the creation of the European Commission to manage these policies. There was also a push in 1966 toward a change in decision-making, from unanimity toward majority votes. France opposed it and maintained that countries should have the right to veto a community decision taken by majority vote if it considered that its national interests would be seriously threatened.

The European Economic Community became the European Union. The European Commission got a European budget. The powers of the European Parliament increased. At the end of the 1960s, the member states were hit by international currency disorders that undermined the functioning of the Common Market. The six founding countries agreed on a step-by-step plan to create a European economic and monetary union, which allowed after years of evolution, the creation of a common currency, the Euro.

Finally, the first enlargement of the Communities took place in 1973: after two refusals by France, the United Kingdom was officially admitted, along with Ireland and Denmark. It was only the beginning. The success of the E.U. attracted the surrounding countries: in 1995, the European Union consisted of France, Germany, Italy, Belgium, Luxembourg, the Netherlands, the United Kingdom, Ireland, Denmark, Greece, Spain, Portugal, Sweden, Finland, and Austria. These states are traditionally considered to be the old member states of the European Union. In 2004, ten more countries became E.U. members: Poland, the Czech Republic, Hungary, Slovakia, Slovenia, Latvia, Lithuania, Estonia, Malta, and Cyprus. They were joined in 2007 by Romania and Bulgaria and in 2013 by Croatia. Today, the European Union consists of twenty-seven member states, representing approximately 450 million Europeans, (after the departure of the United Kingdom on the 31st of January, 2020, following the referendum of the 23rd of June, 2016, in favor of Brexit).

In 2017, the Gross Domestic Product (GDP) of the European Union with twenty-seven member states (E.U.) represented 16 percent of world GDP, expressed in Purchasing Power Standards (PPS). China and the United States were the two largest economies, with 16.4 percent and 16.3 percent shares. But the European Union is limited by the will of its member states to keep certain activities (such as the military or health budgets) at the national level rather than to be managed at the federal level, like in the U.S.. The result is that the E.U. Budget (€164.3 billion in 2021, or $193 billion) is not comparable with the U.S. Federal budget (more than $6 trillion), Russia's expenditures (312 billion dollars), or China's (2.394 trillion dollars). Contrary to the general opinion among E.U. politicians and citizens, the E.U. is a minimal bureaucracy with limited powers to influence their lives. After all, Switzerland's Federal budget already requires 73 billion dollars for a little more than 8 million inhabitants.

The construction of Europe has been impressive, considering what has been done in seventy years through negotiation between independent member states voluntarily transferring part of their sovereignty to the Union. There was no colonization, and no invasion. The European Union's initial objective has been attained: there has been no war between E.U. member states since its formation, which is something never seen during the previous centuries. Every time the E.U. has had to face a challenge, or when disagreements appear, or there is a so-called crisis, the member states and the European Commission always find a solution.

It is undoubtedly one of the most significant achievements of the twentieth century, and, understandably, someone like Macron supports it. But it was still a challenge because of French suspicions about the European Union. The most evident reason is nationalism. It has never been easy for member states to let go of their national competencies to a supranational organism, particularly when the partners in this new body are former enemies. Such nationalist ideas have developed in France among the people on the extreme-right and some on the left, too. They are joined by people on the left and the extreme-left who oppose liberalism and suspect the E.U. to support the destruction of national social systems. These groups had been allied in 2005 when the French opposed the adoption of the European Constitution.

However, a national analysis highlights that, in 21 E.U. member states (compared with 18 in summer of 2020), a majority of respondents feel attached to the European Union.[13] In France, 57 percent of people declared that they were attached to the European Union. So, nationalism is not the only reason for the dislike of the E.U. The complexity of the E.U. is another one.

The management of the E.U. is complicated because it is not exactly a federal entity. There is no federal government with clear competencies which could manage specific domains defined in a Constitution. The European Commission, composed of Commissioners chosen by the member states and approved by the European Parliament, has the monopoly of initiative (proposing E.U. decisions, including the budget and legislation) and implements E.U. decisions. The decisions are taken either by the European Council, meaning the heads of state, alone, generally with a majority vote, but sometimes or in most cases in agreement with the European Parliament.

Such a system is an exciting puzzle for experts, who can debate about the nature of the E.U.: is it a federation or an intergovernmental body? But it is not easy to understand for the general population. In addition, countries have seldom included European history and the functioning of the E.U. institutions in children's curriculum, and the French people and their politicians are mostly ignorant on the matter. The result is that French politicians, governments included, have been able to accuse "the E.U." of being the origin of the majority of problems, even for measures voted for or proposed by France. But, as Macron's opponents realized too late, the French people, particularly young voters, know the E.U. better than their parents and are not easily abused by these tricks. Additionally, the coronavirus crisis has shown that the E.U. has been able to provide vaccines to all countries. It has been late and very bureaucratic, but the E.U. has acted consistently and seriously.

Another reproach from European citizens concerning the E.U. is that it was built without them. From 1951 to 1992, the E.U. was developed by agreements between governments ratified by the national parliaments. Later, two referendums were organized in France and in some other countries, with mixed results. The first referendum was held in September 1992. It resulted in the adoption of the Maastricht Treaty, establishing the European Union and the Economic and Monetary Union, with 51.04 percent of the vote. The second and last referendum was a failure: in May 2005, the French said no to the treaty establishing a European Constitution by 54.67 percent. The Netherlands also voted against it. France, which can be considered one of the principal founders of the European Union, curiously prevented the adoption of a European Constitution.

For European citizens, pushed by the extreme-right, the E.U. has a significant problem of illegal immigration from the Middle East and Africa, which is as sensitive politically as immigration from Mexico is in the U.S.. The first step toward a common external border management policy was taken on the 14th of June, 1985, when five of the then ten member states of the European Economic Community signed an international treaty, the so-called Schengen Agreement, to create the Schengen Area, a borderless zone. Twenty-six European countries are today part of this borderless zone, which supposes a common system to control the external borders, and a solidarity system to support the countries managing these external borders. As the E.U. does not work rapidly because of the need to negotiate agreements between the participating countries, it took time to create an adequate information system (2001) and a basic E.U. Agency to work with the member states to begin to ensure safe and well-functioning external borders providing security (FRONTEX, 2004).

After focusing on Europe during his campaign, Macron could have been satisfied with making some declarations of principle during the European Council and working mainly on national topics, as his predecessors had. Instead, on the 26th of September, 2017, he presented his initiative for a sovereign, united, and democratic Europe at Sorbonne University. Then on the 4th of March, 2019, he formulated new proposals for a "European Renaissance" by addressing all European citizens. In his speeches, there was an emphasis on principles and practical suggestions. The E.U. implemented, at least in part, the majority of his proposals. It would be tedious to list all of them, but some deserve mentioning.

After President Trump's warning that the U.S. would not systematically support the E.U. countries in case of a conflict, Macron wanted to develop a European defense. It was not successful, but he did achieve the creation of a European Defense Fund, which is now operational: the Union will invest approximately 10 billion over the period 2021-2027 in defense research projects and the industrial development of defense technologies. He pushed for the Commission to present a proposal to strengthen the European Border and Coast Guard Agency (FRONTEX) capabilities to enable it to establish a permanent corps of 10,000 E.U. border guards and reinforce its powers in the return of illegal migrants. This new E.U. legislation entered into force on the 4th of December, 2019. He pushed for the establishment of a European Climate Bank to make it possible to mobilize new public and private financing that meets the challenges of the ecological transition. This objective will be attained by the mobilization of the European Investment Bank which decided to make all of its activities fully compatible with the Paris Agreement and end the financing of projects in the fossil fuel sector as of 2021. It will increase its funding dedicated to ecological transition to 50 percent of its operations from 2025. Macron also pushed to create a carbon tax at the borders (or "carbon adjustment mechanism"), aiming at accompanying the European Union's climate ambition in the implementation of the Paris Agreement by preserving the competitiveness of European industries. On the 11th of December, 2020, the European Commission proposed introducing a border carbon tax as part of its "European Green Deal."

The most significant success of President Macron has been his ability to convince Chancellor Angela Merkel from Germany to issue E.U. joint debt on the markets to finance €500 billion in subsidies and €250 billion in loans to member states to support the E.U. recovery after the coronavirus pandemic. Based on a Franco-German initiative of the 18th of May, 2020, the Commission proposed this historic decision, approved at the E.U. level in 2020. Up to that point, Germany has always opposed the development of joint debts in the E.U.

Macron has also promoted direct democracy at the European level. The member states organized citizen consultations in 2018, and the European Commission launched an online consultation based on a questionnaire drawn up by a panel of European citizens. The European summary of these consultations was discussed at the European Council in December 2018 and helped to define the priorities of the new European Parliament and the new European Commission. Macron also proposed, along with the President of the Commission, a Conference on the Future of Europe that involved citizens' panels to reflect on the democratic functioning of the Union and on ways to strengthen Europe's sovereignty in the major policies of the Union. It should lead to concrete results for the French Presidency of the European Union in the first half of 2022.

How did he obtain these results?

Emmanuel Macron is a man who knows how to use his strengths. As already mentioned, he is extremely convincing in face-to-face meetings. He had twenty-six partners to convince, and he did something that nobody in France had done before him: he visited all the member states in the first two years of his presidency, and he generally spent more than a day in each country. He learned about the E.U. countries and their leaders.

Later, he used this knowledge to push for his candidates when prominent E.U. positions were available: he knew Ursula von der Leyen well and helped her obtain the presidency of the European Position. A French woman, Christine Lagarde, became the President of the European Central Bank. Macron also welcomed the arrival of one of his allies, the Belgian liberal Charles Michel, to head the European Council. This result would not have been possible if Macron had not visited and convinced his E.U. partners. He had an agreement with them to support his choices for these positions. His predecessors, who had been older men with more experience, behaved with arrogance toward smaller countries and failed to influence the choices. His youth and his inexperience were an asset in this particular endeavor. He had a new way of thinking and a different approach that yielded results.

Macron has also shown his power in the E.U. during Brexit, when he refused to help Boris Johnson against the demands of the E.U. for an agreement. Convinced that making Brexit too easy for the U.K. may inspire other countries to leave the E.U., he supported the Commission in its hard stance and refused to negotiate bilaterally with the U.K. Every time a conflict linked to Brexit emerges, he rejects the accommodations requested by the U.K., and the E.U. stands united behind the European Commission.

***

In an interview with the magazine *Le Grand Continent*, Macron gave the keys to his European vision. He explained that his objective is a strong political Europe. Why? He said, "Because I think that Europe does not dissolve the voice of France: France has its own conception, its own history, its own vision of international affairs, but it builds a much more useful and a stronger action if it does so through Europe. I even think this is the only way to impose our values, our common voice, to avoid the Sino-American duopoly, dislocation, and return of hostile regional powers."[14]

He has been able to push for the E.U. development, particularly in the field of defense, because his task has been facilitated by President Donald Trump, who saw Europe more as an opponent to subdue than an ally to protect. Today, President Biden's position on the alliance with the E.U. is very positive, and Macron may have to face E.U. countries preferring to stay under the American umbrella rather than developing the European Union more. Also, President Biden's diplomacy seems to prioritize the relationship with Germany, which is seen as the leading partner of the United States in Europe, and with the United Kingdom, which remains the traditional partner, even though it has left the Union. Angela Merkel was received in Washington in July, 2021, before the French leaders, the Minister of the Armed Forces, the Minister of Europe and Foreign Affairs, or President Macron.

But Macron is not always lucky: from January to June 2022, France held the rotating EU presidency, meaning that Macron was is responsible for driving forward the European Council's work on the European legislation, ensuring the continuity of the EU agenda, orderly legislative processes and cooperation among member states. It is a prestigious position, and he planned to use it to develop Europe's political and military autonomy and boost his popularity. The Russian attack on Ukraine disturbed his plans, and he had, with the European Commission, to focus on ensuring the European Union's unity to support Ukraine and adopt severe sanctions against Russia, in close coordination with the United States. It has given him in France an advantage against his competitors during the elections in April 2022, but his will to continue the dialogue with Vladimir Putin despite the Russian actions in Ukraine has not contributed to his popularity among his partners in the European Union.

Conclusion

"Avec Emmanuel, je suis tellement habituée
à ce qu'il m'arrive des choses extraordinaires
que je me demande toujours
quelle va être la prochaine aventure"
[Translation: With Emmanuel, I am so used
to extraordinary things happening to me
that I always wonder
what the next adventure will be]

— Brigitte Macron, *Elle Magazine*, 2017

If this were a novel with Emmanuel Macron as the hero, we would be in the middle of the story. We have learned about his youth, his unique love story, his marriage, and his lucky rise in the political world. We have seen his mistakes as a young president without experience and how he has recovered from his failures. We have also witnessed his successes when his youth allowed him to dare when others would have caved. We may like his young ambition and his will to change Europe and build a new world. Or we could hate it and consider it arrogance. But we would all like to know the end of the story.

The last French elections, in April for the presidential election, and in June for the parliamentary elections, have shown that French people recognize that Emmanuel Macron was the best possible candidate among those running for presidency, but they did not give him a majority in the National Assembly. It means that Macron cannot run freely the country, he needs now to find allies. He has chosen a Prime Minister, Elisabeth Borne, who was apparently a small player in the political game. Everybody thought that Macron has chosen an unobtrusive and efficient second fiddle, who would not contradict him and obey silently. In reality, Borne, who comes from the socialist party, has managed in her first months to find when necessaries allies to get a majority on her proposals in the National Assembly, and to get the respect of the French and of the political leaders on all sides. She has also made Macron change his mind about the management of the reform of the pension system by introducing a longer time than planned for negotiation. At the end of 2022, she is more popular than Emmanuel Macron among French people, who appreciate her austere and sober style, better adapted to crisis times than Macron's flamboyance.

These elections have also shown once again that Macron makes mistakes. On the second round of parliamentary election, when generally there are only 2 candidates left in a majority of the 577 single-member constituencies, Macron refused to ask his supporters to vote for the candidates on the left when they were opposed to the extreme-right, paving the way for the latter to overperform polls to win an unprecedented 89 seats and become the largest parliamentary opposition group. That caused an earthquake in France, as a majority of the population now think that Marine Le Pen's party has good chances to win the next elections at the end of Macron's second (and last) mandate.

For Macron, this was a mistake, as Macron's great fear is be succeeded by the far right. He made it possible. We have seen that Macron views himself as a character in a novel, a brilliant one and he has clearly the will to see the novel ending with his success, not by a victory of the far-right movements representing the opposite of his values. He does not want to be Barack Obama handing over the presidency to Donald Trump. That would be a slap on his face and seems to be one of his main worries, confirmed by the fact that in Italy and Sweden the populist or far-right movements won the last elections. France may be next, and Macron's image would suffer from it. He would hate it, but did not yet find the right way to prevent it.

As Macron's power seems to have reached a limit with a more independent Parliament, he seems to be concentrating mainly on international affairs and to distance himself from internal affairs, left to his Prime Minister, even if the President continues to push for his reforms. But the international landscape is difficult for Macron, who has been unsuccessful in supporting a diplomatic approach in the attack on Ukraine. He may benefit from a closer relation with President Biden, now that the disagreements following the Australia's submarines contract's conflict have been solved with some compensations for the French side. The state visit of the French President to Washington at the invitation of President Biden is the testimony of this evolution.

But Macron cannot stay away for long from France's internal politics, and there is a strong probability that he will come back with a renewed strategy. If he feels that the political negotiations block his reforms, he may decide to call for new elections, putting the blame on his opponents and asking the French to give him a full majority. But such a move is risky, and it may backfire, as it did in 1997 when President Chirac called for new elections and lost his majority in the National Assembly.

Those who know well Macron hope that he will react by finding a new and creative idea, as he did when he had his back to the wall because of the Yellow Jackets or the Benalla scandal. He tried in Autumn 2022 such a maneuver by creating a "National Council for Refoundation", vowing to carry out a "broad national consultation" on issues ranging from education and climate change to euthanasia, some of which could eventually be put up for referendum. This initiative did not work well, because it is clearly inspired from the Great Debate during the Yellow Jackets' movement, and the recommendations from the Great Debate were a deception for French people. In addition, his opponents refused the invitation of the President to discuss the future of France, seeing it as a political trap aiming at making them appear as Macron's backers. But, considering his political behavior, one can be quite sure that Macron will find another way to shake the French political world.

This ability to shapeshift, meaning this capacity to turn things around and at the same time keep in mind his initial objectives is the key element of what makes a modern political leader, living in an unstable world. His will to leave his mark on history, and not by facilitating the election of an extreme-right president, has also been a positive element for his career. His self-confidence, inherited from his protected youth, has certainly played a role in his success, and contributed to his capacity of seduction, necessary to access the highest positions. These qualities are certainly necessary for modern leaders in an unstable world facing continuously new crises.

What about the future?

With Angela Merkel's retirement, Macron is now the most experienced European leader, with an opportunity to work efficiently with other leaders, particularly with President Biden, to help the world face its environmental and political challenges. In the short term, it has helped Europe, confronted to multiple crisis (the Covid crisis, the war in Ukraine, the energy crisis) to show unity with France playing a key role due to its diplomacy and Macron's leadership. In the longer term, one can imagine that, after the next French presidential election, Emmanuel Macron may try to take one of the top European Union positions, such as the presidency of the European Commission. But his ambitions may be countered by the will of the member states to choose as usual less flamboyant politicians for these positions.

French humorist Pierre Dac, one of the first companions of de Gaulle's during his London's exile during World War II, wrote one day in the magazine *L'Os à Moëlle* that "Predictions are difficult, especially when they concern the future." It is also true for the future of the United States, the future of France, the future of Europe, the future of the world, and also certainly for the future of President Macron, considering that he has always his ways to surprise his friends, and his foes…

References

Chapter 1

[1] Editorial Team, (August 31, 2016). "Pour Emmanuel Macron, le début d'une longue course d'obstacles (Translation: For Emmanuel Macron, the Beginning of a Long Obstacle Race)". *Le Monde*.

[2] Davet, G. & Lhomme, F., (2016). *Un president ne devrait pas dire ca... les secrets d'un quinquennat* (Translation: *A President Should Not Say That... the Secrets of a Five-Year Term*), Stock.

[3] Poll, (September 2018). "Le regard des Français sur les relations franco-américaines et sur les populismes (Translation: The French View of Franco-American Relations and Populism)". *IFOP*.

[4] Echeverria, D., (2016). *Mirage in the West: A History of the French Image of American Society to 1815*. Princeton Legacy Library.

[5] Chernow, R., (2010), *Washington: A Life*, Penguin Group U.S.

[6] Echeverria, D., (1962). "L'Amérique devant l'opinion française, 1734-1870: Questions de méthode et d'interprétation (Translation: America Before French Opinion, 1734-1870: Questions of Method and Interpretation)" *Revue d'Histoire Moderne & Contemporaine*.

[7] Delorme, M.-L., (September 15, 2019). "Emmanuel Macron: "Il n'y a rien que j'aime plus que la littérature (Translation: Emmanuel Macron: "There is nothing I love more than literature")". *Le Journal du Dimanche*.

[8] Fouquet, H. (February 13, 2019)."The Moment Macron Gave Up on Trump". *Bloomberg*.

[9] Fulda, A., (2018). *Emmanuel Macron, un jeune homme si parfait* (Translation: *Emmanuel Macron, Such a Perfect Young Man*). Editions 84.

[10] Carrère, E., (October 20, 2017). "Orbiting Jupiter: My Week with Emmanuel Macron," *The Guardian*.

[11] Editorial Team, (July 14, 2020) "En marge du 14 juillet, Macron interpellé par des gilets jaunes (Translation: On the Sidelines of July 14, Macron Questioned by Yellow Vests)". *Huffington Post*.

[12] In fact, he said something like, "*I cannot even curse him,*" but the meaning in French is slightly different.

[13] Endeweld, M. (2018). *L'ambigu M. Macron* (Translation: *The Ambiguous Mr. Macron*), Points.

[14] Ibid.

[15] Fulda, A. , (2018). *Emmanuel Macron, un jeune homme si parfait* (Translation: *Emmanuel Macron, Such a Perfect Young Man*). Editions 84.

[16] Obama, B., (2006). *The Audacity of Hope: Thoughts on Reclaiming the American Dream,* Crown Publishing Group.

[17] Berretta, E., Galactéros C. & Recasens O., (June 23, 2016). "Michel Rocard: son testament politique à conserver (Translation: Michel Rocard: His Political Testament to Preserve)". *Le Point.*

[18] Ibid.

[19] Rocard, S., (2020). *C'était Michel* (Translation: *This Was Michel*). Plon.

[20] Varoufakis, Y., (2017). *Adults in the Room: My Battle with the European and American Deep Establishment.* Farrar, Straus and Giroux.

[21] Varoufakis, Y., (May 4, 2017). "Macron Came to Greece's Aid During Our Crisis. The French Left Should Back Him". *The Guardian.*

[22] Dalton, M. and Restuccia, A., (June 13, 2021). "Biden and Macron Share Affection and Worldview at G-7 Summit". *WSJ.*

Chapter 2

[1] Seunarayan, D. (2019). *Shapeshifter: How to Master the Art of Working with the Future.* Gallus Consulting Publishing.

[2] Macron's newly created political movement.

[3] From Wikipedia.

[4] Mancini, A., (March 2, 2020). "Was Courage The Cowardly Dog Based On A True Story?". *Today's Five.*
https://todaysfive.com/was-courage-the-cowardly-dog-based-on-a-true-story/

[5] To learn more about Shapeshifters in different cultures, a must read: Kachuba, J.B., (2019) *Shapeshifters: A History.* Reaktion Book.

[6] Oksman, O. (April 7, 2016). "Conspiracy Craze: Why 12 Million Americans Believe Alien Lizards Rule Us". *The Guardian.*

[7] The surge is President George W. Bush's 2007 increase in the number of American troops in Iraq.

[8] Fuligni, B., (2016). *L'art de retourner sa veste: De l'inconstance en politique* (Translation: *The Art of Flipping: Inconsistency in Politics).* La Librairie Vuibert.

[9] Emerson, R. W., (1841). *Essays, First Series.*

[10] More precisely, "about the great quarrel in the French history."

[11] It was a short sentence uttered by the Emmanuel Macron at the Elysee Palace on the evening of June 12, 2018, during an informal meeting with his advisers and published on the social network Twitter the same day.

[12] "Une petite phrase d'Emmanuel Macron sur les «milliardaires» consterne à sa gauche (Translation: Emmanuel Macron's little phrase about "billionaires" dismays his left)," Ivan Valerio, *Le Figaro,* January 7, 2015.

[13] Dupont, S., Lefebvre, E., Schaeffer, F. (January 7, 2015). "Emmanuel Macron : «Il faut des jeunes Français qui aient envie de devenir milliardaires (Translation: Emmanuel Macron: "We Need Young French People Who Want to Become Billionaires)". *Les Echos.*

[14] Endeweld, M., (2018). *L'ambigu M. Macron* (Translation: *The Ambiguous Mr. Macron).* Points.

[15] Ibid.

[16] Saward, M., (2014). "Shape-Shifting Representation". *American Political Science Review , Volume 108 , Issue 4 , November 2014 , pp. 723-736.*

[17] Seunarayan, D., (2019). *Shapeshifter: How to Master the Art of Working with the Future.* Gallus Consulting Publishing.

[18] Middleton, D., (May 16, 2016). *Are You a Shape-shifter? The Importance of Building Organizational Resilience, Daina Middleton website* , https://dainamiddleton.com/shape-shifter-importance-building-organizational-resilience/

[19] Ibid.

[20] Duhamel, A., (January 8, 2015)"Les Français adorent la nouveauté et détestent le changement (Translation: The French Love Novelty and Hate Change)". *Dernières Nouvelles d'Alsace.*

[21] Bellier, I., (1992). "Regard d'une ethnologue sur les énarques (Translation: An Ethnologist's View of the Enarques)," *L'Homme, tome 32 n°121. Anthropologie du proche. pp. 103-127.*

[22] Irish Republican Army, a name used by various paramilitary groups in Ireland throughout the twentieth and the twenty-first centuries.

[23] Euskadi Ta Askatasuna ("Basque Homeland and Liberty", an armed leftist Basque nationalist and separatist organization in the Basque Country considered as a terrorist organization by the Spanish government).

[24] *Pétanque* is a French (Provençal to be precise) outdoor game played by two opposing teams trying to throw boules (metallic spheres the size of an orange) as close as possible to a but (little wooden sphere the size of a plastic bottle cork, also called a *cochonnet*, meaning piglet).

[25] Macron E. & Fottorino E., (2017). *Macron par Macron* (Translation: *Macron by Macron*). Editions de l'Aube.

[26] Seifert, C. (2020). "The Case for Reading Fiction". *Harvard Business Review*.

[27] Comer Kidd, D. & Castano, E., (October 2013). "Reading Literary Fiction Improves Theory of Mind." *Science*.

[28] Macron, E., & Fottorino, E, (2017). "*Macron par Macron* (Translation: *Macron by Macron*)". Editions de l'Aube.

Chapter 3

[1] Amiens being a little more than 1 hour from Paris by train.

[2] There are few other ingredients for this kid-friendly recipe: eggs, honey, sugar, almond extract, and fruit in the form of jelly or compote, traditionally apple or apricot.

[3] Brigitte Macron : découvrez son interview exclusive en intégralité (Translation: Brigitte Macron: Discover Her Exclusive Interview in Full) , Elle, 2017. https://www.elle.fr/People/La-vie-des-people/News/Brigitte-Macron-decouvrez-son-interview-exclusive-en-integralite-3522842

[4] Brun, M. (2018). *Brigitte Macron l'Affranchie*. Archipoche.

[5] Macron. E., (2016). *Révolution, XO*.

[6] Besson P., (2017). *Un personnage de roman – Macron par Besson*. French and European Publications Inc.

[7] Maxime Nicole, Wikipedia, https://fr.wikipedia.org/wiki/Maxime_Nicolle

[8] Macron. E., (2016). *Révolution*, XO.

[9] Gustave Flaubert is a French author from the nineteenth century regarded as the prime representative of the realist school of French literature.

[10] "France's First Lady Brigitte Macron on Age, Falling in Love and Melania Trump," Erin Doherty and Olivia De Lamberterie, *Elle*, Nov. 27, 2017.

[11] Willsher, K., (18 August 2019). "Philippe Besson: 'I told Macron he had zero chance of becoming president'". *The Guardian*.

[12] The second one was *War Memoirs* by de Gaulle.

[13] Maclay, M., (29 October 2018). "The Modern Julien Sorel". *Standpoint*.

[14] Ibid.

[15] The information concerning the American First Ladies comes from a book by Robert P. Watson, (2014). *The Presidents' Wives: The Office of the First Lady in U.S. Politics"*. Lynne Rienner, 2nd edition.

[16] Charte de transparence relative au statut du conjoint du Chef de l'État (Translation: Transparency Charter on the Status of the Spouse of the Head of State). https://www.elysee.fr/emmanuel-macron/2017/08/21/charte-de-transparence-relative-au-statut-du-conjoint-du-chef-de-letat

[17] She called him "Sonny."

[18] Besson, P., (2017). *Un personnage de roman*. Julliard

[19] Djamshidi, A. & Schuck, N., (2019). *Madame la Présidente* (Translation: *Madame President)*. Plon.

[20] Emmanuel Macron sur RTL: "Brigitte aura un rôle, elle ne sera pas cachée," (Translation: Emmanuel Macron on RTL: "Brigitte Will Have a Role, She Will Not Be Hidden"), *RTL Radio*, Mars 3, 2017.

[21] Besson, P., (2017). *Un personnage de roman*, Julliard.

[22] Djamshidi, A. & Schuck, N. (2019). *Madame la Présidente* (Translation: *Madame President)*. Plon.

Chapter 4

[1] "Message aux Chambres (Translation: Message to the Houses)" René Coty, Président de la République, May 29, 1958.

[2] Editorial Team, (August 23, 2007). "Pour le chef de l'État, Fillon est un 'collaborateur' (Translation: For the Head of State, Fillon is a 'Collaborator')". *Le Figaro.*

[3] In 2021, the name of this conservative alliance is Les Républicains (LR).

[4] Hollande, F., (2018). *Les leçons du pouvoir.* Stock.

[5] Davet, G. & Lhomme, F. (2017). *Un président ne devrait pas dire ça...* (Translation: *A President Should Not Say That...*). Points.

[6] Vinocur, N. (January 23, 2017). "Meet the robot-taxing, marijuana-legalizing, Jeremy Corbyn of the French left". *Politico.*

[7] In English, "The Duck in Chains."

[8] Haïm L., (Jan. 19, 2017). "Oui, Emmanuel Macron est le french Obama (Translation: Yes, Emmanuel Macron is the French Obama)". *BFMTV.*

[9] Schulteis E. (April 21, 2017), "Can a French Political Upstart Ride Obama's Strategy to Victory?". *The Atlantic.*

[10] Ibid.

[11] Paul, V. (May 14, 2017). "Emmanuel Macron, un président "à l'américaine"? (Translation: Emmanuel Macron, an "American-Style" President?)". *L'Express.*

[12] Ibid.

[13] Freyssenet, E., (September 15, 2020). "Emmanuel Macron défend la 5G contre le 'modèle amish' (Translation: Emmanuel Macron Defends 5G against the 'Amish model')". *Les Echos.*

[14] The video can be watched on https://www.ina.fr/video/I04261065

[15] Gendron G., (April 24, 2017). "Dîner à la Rotonde : les macronistes ne veulent pas en faire un plat (Translation: Dinner at La Rotonde: the Macronists Don't Want to Make a Fuss)". *Libération,.*

[16] French people remembered that Macron was Minister of Economy some months before.

[17] Ardisson, T., (December 8, 2018). "Interview Marine le Pen". *Les terriens du Dimanche,* C8.

[18] Barthold, C. & Fougère, M., (March 5, 2020). "How You Can Tell Emmanuel Macron is Actually a Populist – and Why It Matters". *The Conversation.*

[19] Ibid.

20 "Réception en l'honneur des maires de France à l'occasion du congrès de l'AMF, Discours du Président de la République (Translation: Reception in Honor of the Mayors of France on the Occasion of the AMF Congress, Speech by the President of the Republic," November 21, 2018.

21 Delage, C., Macron, E. (March 19, 2017). "Présidentielle: candidats au tableau! (Translation: Presidential Election: Candidates to the Blackboard!". *C8*.

Chapter 5

1 Cooper, A. (January 6, 2019). "Alexandria Ocasio-Cortez: The Rookie Congresswoman Challenging the Democratic Establishment". *60 Minutes*, CBS News.

2 Joignot F., (April 10, 2017). "L'équipe Macron se revendique du modèle scandinave de l'Etat providence (Translation: The Macron Team Claims to Be Based on the Scandinavian Model of the Welfare State)," *Le Monde.fr*

3 Bourdu, E., (2013). *Les transformations du modèle économique suédois* (Translation: *The transformation of the Swedish economic model*). La Fabrique de l'Industrie.

4 Cooper, A. (January 6, 2019). "Alexandria Ocasio-Cortez: The Rookie Congresswoman Challenging the Democratic Establishment". *60 Minutes*, CBS News.

5 "At the same time" has been Macron's motto during the campaign, and it is still his way of thinking. Macron has been studying philosophy and he is a disciple of Hegel, the inventor of the dialectic that claims to articulate and overcome oppositions. Macron has presented the idea that he was at the same time politically of the left and of the right, for a conciliation to the generalized conflicts in French politics.

6 Marx, K., (1852). *The Eighteenth Brumaire of Louis Bonaparte*. Progress Publishers.

7 Servan-Schreiber, J.J., (1968). *The American Challenge*. Atheneum.

8 Théroux, I., (september 2014). "Vous avez dit 'social-démocrate'? (Translation: Did You Say 'Social Democrat'?". *La revue du projet*, n° 39.

9 From the 1920s to the 1970s.

10 Macke, G., (May 25, 2017). "Philippe Aghion, l'inspirateur d'Emmanuel Macron sur la croissance (Translation: Philippe Aghion, Emmanuel Macron's Inspiration on Growth)". *Challenges*.

11 Editorial Team, (April 12, 2017). "Emmanuel Macron soutenu par 40 économistes (Translation: Emmanuel Macron Supported by 40 Economists)". *Les Echos*.

[12] Kalinowski, W., (October 15, 2017). "Les réformes sociales françaises et le modèle suédois (Translation: French Social Reforms and the Swedish Model)". *Institut Veblen*.

[13] Jean Pisani-Ferry is a nonresident senior fellow at the Washington's Peterson Institute for International Economics. He holds the Tommaso Padoa-Schioppa Chair of the European University Institute in Florence and is a senior fellow at Bruegel, the European think tank.

[14] Weill, P. (December 27, 2017). "Elie Cohen et les sanctions contre les chômeurs : 'C'est le système danois de flexi sécurité' (Translation: Elie Cohen and Sanctions Against the Unemployed: 'It's the Danish Flexi Security System)". *France Inter*, Le Grand Entretien.

[15] The Veblen Institute for Economic Reforms is a French non-profit think tank promoting policies and civil society initiatives for the ecological transition.

[16] Zeballos-Roig, J., (February 3, 2020). "Bernie Sanders and AOC Support the 'Nordic Model,' which Features Robust Health and Social-Welfare Systems — One that Finland's Leader Calls 'the American Dream'". *Business Insider*.

[17] James, W., (1907). *Pragmatism, A New Name for Some Old Ways of Thinking*. Green.

[18] Special Report, (January 31, 2013). "The Secret of Their Success". *The Economist*.

[19] Bouniol, B., (May 2, 2017). "Le 'pragmatisme' d'Emmanuel Macron (Translation: The 'Pragmatism' of Emmanuel Macron)". *La Croix*.

[20] Delage, C., Macron, E. (March 19, 2017). "Présidentielle : candidats au tableau! (Translation: Presidential Election: Candidates to the Blackboard!)",*C8*.

Chapter 6

[1] Barnard, L., (Mar 21, 2020). "The Machiavelli Measure: Which Modern Leaders Fit the Definition?". *The Big Smoke*.

[2] Çavuşoğlu, M., (September 10, 2020). *Twitter*.

https://twitter.com/MevlutCavusoglu/status/1304036989524639744?s=20

[3] El-Basri, A., (September 24, 2020). "Vu du Liban. Emmanuel Macron, le Machiavel piégé (Translation: Seen from Lebanon. Emmanuel Macron, the Trapped Machiavelli". *Courrier International*.

[4] Newman, L., Vasquez, T., & Malaty, O., "Contemporary World Leaders & Their Relation to Machiavelli," *Prezi*. https://prezi.com/iszhwpvre3bu/contemporary-world-leaders-their-relation-to-machiavelli/

5 Barnard, L., (Mar 21, 2020). "The Machiavelli Measure: Which Modern Leaders Fit the Definition?". *The Big Smoke.*

6 Darragi, R., (June 21, 2014). "Book review of 'De Gaulle et Machiavel'". *Leaders.*

7 Le Bailly, D., (December 1, 2016). "Hollande, Sarkozy: la débâcle des Machiavel". *L'Obs.*

8 Machiavelli, N., (1469-1527). *The Prince.* Harmondsworth, Eng.

9 Minot, E., (February 13, 2019). "Brigitte Macron: cette autre femme de caractère sur laquelle elle peut compter à l'Elysée (Translation: Brigitte Macron: Another Woman of Character She Can Count On at the Elysée Palace)". *Gala.*

10 Vandekerkhove, C. & Coache, M., (August 22, 2018). "A l'Élysée, un nouveau projet sécurité était piloté par Alexandre Benalla (Translation: At the Elysée, a New Security Project was Led by Alexandre Benalla)". *BFMTV.*

11 Chemin, A., (July 28, 2018). "*Le Monde* identifie, sur une vidéo, un collaborateur de Macron frappant un manifestant, le 1er mai, à Paris (Translation: Le Monde Identifies, on a Video, a Macron Collaborator Hitting a Demonstrator, on May 1st, in Paris)". *Le Monde.*

12 Letter dated May 3, 2018 from Mr. Patrick STRZODA, Chief of Staff of the President of the Republic, to Mr. Alexandre BENALLA informing him of his temporary suspension (in the Senate's report).

13 Viers, A., (July 21, 2018). "Affaire Benalla: retour sur l'étrange communication de crise de Bruno Roger-Petit (Translation: Benalla Affair: Return on the Strange Crisis Communication of Bruno Roger-Petit)". *Le Parisien.*

14 Pascariello, P., Arfi, F. & Laske, K., (August 30, 2018). "Les secrets d'Alexandre Benalla sont toujours à l'abri. Et il le revendique (Translation: Alexandre Benalla's Secrets are Still Safe. And He Claims It". *Mediapart.*

15 Ibid.

16 «Affaire Benalla», Rapport d'enquête de la commission des lois du Sénat (Translation: "Benalla Case", Investigation Report of the Senate Law Committee), February 20, 2019.

17 Lisle, H., (October 9, 2018). "Quand Brigitte Macron donne une 'déculottée' à son mari Emmanuel: 'Il faut arrêter les conneries' (Translation: When Brigitte Macron Gives Her Husband Emmanuel a 'Beating': 'You Have to Stop the Bullshit'). *Femme Actuelle.*

18 Jeannin, C., (June 20, 2019). "Affaire Benalla: "On a certainement minimisé", dit Brigitte Macron sur RTL (Translation: Benalla Affair: "We Have Certainly Minimized", Says Brigitte Macron on RTL radio)". *RTL.*

[19] Crase, V., (2019). *Présumé coupable* (Translation: *Presumed Guilty*). Plon.

[20] Decugis, J.-M., Guena, P. & Leplongeon, M., (2018). *Mimi*. Grasset.

Chapter 7

[1] Lasserre, B., (February 25, 2019). "Emmanuel Macron regagne du terrain auprès des Français, les gilets jaunes en perdent (Translation: Emmanuel Macron Regains Ground with the French, the Yellow Vests Lose". *Sud Ouest*.

[2] Greene, B., (September 4, 2019). "The History of How School Buses Became Yellow". *Smithsonian Magazine*.

[3] Ibid.

[4] During the previous summer, it was disclosed that Emmanuel Macron and his wife had changed the tableware at Elysée Palace for 500,000 euros, and built a swimming pool at the fort of Bregancon, the presidents' summer residence on the French Riviera.

[5] Gérard Noiriel, G. & Truong, N., (2019). *Les gilets jaunes à la lumière de l'histoire*. Editions de l'Aube.

[6] Editorial Team, (October 19, 2020). "Éric Brunet, Héros de la droite d'argent et sarkozyste chimiquement pur (Translation: Éric Brunet, Right-Wing Silver and Chemically Pure Sarkozist". *Observatoire du journalisme*.

[7] Verner, R., (December 6, 2018). "Gilets jaunes : le profil controversé de Maxime Nicolle, alias Fly Rider (Translation: Yellow Vests: the Controversial Profile of Maxime Nicolle, Alias 'Fly Rider')". *BFMTV*.

[8] Guérard, S., (December 15, 2018). "Acte 5: témoignages de Gilets jaunes à Paris (Translation: Act 5: Testimonies of Yellow Vests in Paris)". *L'Humanité*.

[9] Collyer, R., (November 15, 2019). "A Year in the Life of Yellow Vest Protest Leader Priscillia Ludosky". *RFI International*.

[10] Wikipedia, Acte III du mouvement des Gilets jaunes (Translation: Act III of the Yellow Vests Movement).

[11] Lefèvre, T. & Guyenne, L., (November 12, 2019). "'Le 1er décembre, l'Élysée aurait pu tomber': un CRS raconte le chaos des 'gilets jaunes' l'hiver dernier" ("'On December 1, the Elysée Could Have Fallen': a CRS Recounts the Chaos of the 'Yellow Vests' Last Winter)". *France Inter radio*.

[12] Castoridis, C., (1999). *Les racines psychiques et sociales de la haine* (Translation: *The Psychic and Social Roots of Hate*). *Figures du pensable*, Éditions du Seuil.

[13] Charrel, M., (September 25, 2018). "Emmanuel Macron est-il le président des riches? (Translation: Is Emmanuel Macron the President of the Rich?)". *Le Monde*.

[14] Ruffin, F., (2019). *Ce pays que tu ne connais pas* (Translation: *This Country You Don't Know*). Les Arènes.

[15] Schiller, T. "Direct democracy". *Encyclopedia Britannica*. https://www.britannica.com/topic/direct-democracy/Countries-and-developmental-background

[16] Piper, K., (November 6, 2020) "California's Ballot Initiative System Isn't Working. How Do We Fix It?". *Vox*.

[17] In February 2021, according to a poll by CEVIPOF, only 16 percent of French people said they had confidence in political parties, which puts them far behind all other organizations, including the worst-rated ones such as social networks (17 percent), the media (28 percent) or unions (32 percent).

[18] All the statistics come from the official website of the Great Debate https://granddebat.fr/

[19] Malingre, V., (April 3, 2019). "Grand débat : le tour de France en 80 jours d'Emmanuel Macron (Translation: Great Debate: Emmanuel Macron's 80-day Tour of France". *Le Monde*.

Chapter 8

[1] This slogan was against President Sarkozy ("Sarko").

[2] "Macron! Resign!" was frequently heard during demonstrations.

[3] "When are you going to put glitter in our pensions Manu?" Manu is Emmanuel Macron nickname in France.

[4] "Elected to serve us, not to enslave us" sounds better in French.

[5] According to Wikipedia.

[6] Wilson, F.L., (Spring-Summer 1994). "Political Demonstrations in France: Protest Politics or Politics of Ritual?". *French Politics and Society, Vol. 12, No. 2/3, Berghahn Books*.

[7] French Government Publication, (October 13, 2017). "Action Publique 2022: pour une transformation du service public (Translation: Public Action 2022: for a Transformation of the Public Service)".

[8] Lichfield, J., (January 5, 2020). "Macron Was the Great Hope for Centrists. Despite His Struggles, the Hope Is Not Lost". *The Guardian.*

Chapter 9

[1] Kennedy, R.F., (2017). *Thirteen Days: A Memoir of the Cuban Missile Crisis.* Ishi Press.

[2] Kennedy, R.F., (2018). *13 jours.* Artheme Fayard-Pluriel.

[3] Kennedy, J.F., (1960). "Book Review by Senator John F. Kennedy of 'Deterrent or Defense'" by B.H. Lidell Hart, the *Saturday Review of Literature*", *The American Presidency Project.*

[4] Demaître, L. (2003) "The Art and Science of Prognostication in Early University Medicine." Luke, *Bulletin of the History of Medicine, 77, no. 4 (2003): 765-88.*

[5] Mainly the movement called OAS, organization for a secret army.

[6] Called *l'attentat de la rue des Rosiers* (Translation: Rosiers Street Terrorist Attack).

[7] La Rédaction, (8 septembre 2021). "Trente cinq ans de législation antiterroriste (Translation: Thirty-Five Years of Anti-Terrorism Legislation)", *Vie Publique.*

[8] Dispatch, (July 19, 2010). "Hundreds in Pakistan protest France's burqa ban". *Associated Press.*

[9] Editorial team ,(July 24, 2010). "Le numéro 2 d'Al Qaïda dénonce l'interdiction du voile islamique intégral en France (The Number 2 of Al Qaeda Denounces the Ban on the Full Islamic Veil in France)". *Le Point.*

[10] Planchon, R., (June 15, 2021). "Terrorisme: La France est clairement le pays d'Europe le plus touché (Translation: Terrorism: France is Clearly the Most Affected Country in Europe". *Le Figaro.*

[11] Editorial team, (June 11, 2017). "Notre-Dame Attack: Farid Ikken Appears in Paris Court". *BBC World.*

[12] Macron, E., (January 4, 2018). "Transcription du discours des vœux du Président de la République aux autorités religieuses (Translation: Transcript of the Speech of the President of the Republic to the Religious Authorities)". *French Presidency.*

[13] Roy, O., (November 23, 2015). "Le djihadisme est une révolte générationnelle et nihiliste (Jihadism Is a Generational and Nihilistic Revolt)". *Le Monde.fr.*

[14] Poll, (November 2, 2020). "Le rapport à la laïcité à l'heure de la lutte contre l'islamisme et le projet de loi contre les séparatismes (Translation: The Relationship to Secularism at the Time of the Fight against Islamism and the Bill against Separatism)". *IFOP.*

[15] Faye, O. & Lemarié, A. (October 2, 2020). "Emmanuel Macron présente son plan contre 'le séparatisme islamique' (Translation: Emmanuel Macron Presents His Plan against 'Islamic Separatism'". *Le Monde.*

[16] Bill to strengthen the respect of the principles of the Republic, Parliament, July 27th 2021 version.

[17] First cases of coronavirus disease 2019 (COVID-19) in France: surveillance, investigations and control measures, January, 2020.

[18] All statistics from Health Statistics, OECD, 2020.

[19] https://en-marche.fr/emmanuel-macron/le-programme/sante

[20] https://www.worldometers.info/coronavirus/, June 19, 2021

[21] Boone, L., Moulin, A.-M., Briet, R. & Parneix, P., (May 18, 2021). "Rapport final de la mission indépendante nationale sur l'évaluation de la gestion de la crise Covid-19 et sur l'anticipation des risques pandémiques (Translation: Final Report of the National Independent Mission on the Evaluation of the Management of the Covid-19 Crisis and on the Anticipation of Pandemic Risks)". *Vie Publique.*

[22] She left the government on February 20, 2020.

[23] Lachassze, J., (March 7, 2020). "Emmanuel et Brigitte Macron au théâtre pour inciter les Français à sortir malgré le coronavirus (Translation: Emmanuel and Brigitte Macron at the Theater to Encourage the French to Go Out Despite the Coronavirus)". *BFMTV-AFP.*

[24] Salvi, H., (April 5, 2020). "L'étonnant départ de la conseillère santé d'Emmanuel Macron (Translation: The Surprising Departure of Emmanuel Macron's Health Advisor)". *Mediapart.*

[25] In French, Haute Autorité de Santé.

[26] Ibid.

[27] Service sciences, (26 mars 2020). "Qui compose le conseil scientifique Covid-19, créé pour aider le gouvernement face à la crise ? (Translation: Who Is on the Covid-19 Scientific Council, Created to Help the Government Deal with the Crisis?) ". *Le Monde.*

[28] On 15 June 2021.

[29] Presidential address, March 12, 2021,

[30] Lemarié, A., (March 30, 2021). "Comment l'entourage d'Emmanuel Macron met en scène un président qui serait devenu épidémiologiste (Translation: How Emmanuel Macron's Entourage Portrays a President who has Become an Epidemiologist)". *Le Monde*.

[31] Ibid.

[32] Gatinois, C., (April 20, 2021). "Pour Emmanuel Macron, plus que la gestion de l'épidémie, c'est la sortie de crise qui pourrait être déterminante (Translation: For Emmanuel Macron, More than the Management of the Epidemic, it is the End of the Crisis that Could be Decisive)". *Le Monde*.

Chapter 10

[1] Interview by Michel Droit, ORTF, December 14, 1965.

[2] Introduction of all Asterix comic books popular in France and in the world, whose hero is Asterix the Gaul.

[3] Gauls or Gallics were a group of Celtic peoples of Continental Europe in the Iron Age and the Roman period (roughly from the 5th century BC to the 5th century AD).

[4] The following development is inspired by Zede, C., (2018). *Les Gaulois dans les manuels de sixième issus de la réforme des collège* (Translation: *The Gauls in the Sixth Grade Textbooks Resulting from the College Reform*) (2015-2016). *Education*. 2018. hal-02370985.

[5] Thierry, A. (1828). *Histoire des Gaulois, depuis les temps les plus reculés jusqu'à l'entière soumission de la Gaule à la domination romaine* (Translation: *History of the Gauls, from the Most Remote Times until the Complete Submission of Gaul to Roman Domination*). Sautelet et Cie.

[6] This is an extract from a children's history textbook: *Histoire de France – Cours élémentaire* (Translation: *History of France – Elementary School*) by Ernest Lavisse, Armand Colin, 1913.

[7] Malrain, F. & Poux, M., (2011). *Qui étaient les Gaulois* (Translation: *Who Were the Gauls*. La Martinière.

[8] https://www.insee.fr/fr/statistiques/3633212

[9] Batalova, J., Hanna, M. & Christopher Levesque, (2021). *Frequently Requested Statistics on Immigrants and Immigration in the United States*. Migration Policy Institute.

[10] Misandeau, A., (September 20, 2016). "Nos ancêtres les Gaulois, un vieux credo de Nicolas Sarkozy (Translation: Our Ancestors the Gauls, an Old Credo of Nicolas Sarkozy)". *Le Figaro.*

[11] Flexicurity is a strategy for enhancing, at the same time, flexibility and security in the labor market. It attempts to reconcile employers' need for a flexible workforce with workers' need for security – confidence that they will not face long periods of unemployment. It has been promoted by the Nordic countries.

[12] https://www.globalfirepower.com/countries-listing-nato-members.php

[13] https://www.defense.gouv.fr/var/dicod/storage/images/base-de-medias/images/ operations/autres-operations/carte-deploiement-ops/190805_emacom_deploiements opearmeesfrancaises_rvb_vf/9733385-1-fre-FR/190805_emacom_deploiements opearmeesfrancaises_rvb_vf.jpg

[14] If the Prime Minister can speak abroad on behalf of France during an official trip, he will always do so within a framework defined, by mutual agreement, with the President.

[15] North Atlantic Treaty Organization.

[16] Vaïsse, M. & Sebag, C., (2009). "France and NATO: A History". *Politique Etrangère, 2009/5 (Hors série), pages 139-150.*

[17] Decision of the French German Summit, La Rochelle, May 22, 1992.

[18] Directorate General for External Security (DGSE), sometimes referred to simply as External Security (ES).

[19] Thiboud, E., (June 2, 2017). "Du gaullisme au néo-conservatisme, comment la diplomatie française est devenue atlantiste (Translation: From Gaullism to Neo-Conservatism, How French Diplomacy Became Atlanticist)". *Figarovox.*

[20] Schmidt, P., (2008) *A Hybrid Relationship: Transatlantic Security Cooperation Beyond NATO.* Peter Lang Publishing.

[21] Rieth, B., (April 21, 2017). "Sans surprise, Dominique de Villepin sort du bois pour soutenir Macron (Translation: Not Surprisingly, Dominique de Villepin Sticks His Head above the Parapet to Support Macron)". *Marianne.*

[22] Editorial team, (June 27, 2018). "Les doutes de Villepin sur la méthode Macron (Translation: Villepin's Doubts about Macron's Method)". *Paris Match.*

[23] Interviews with *Le Soir, Le Temps, The Guardian, Corriere della Sera, El Pais, Süddeutsche Zeitung, Gazeta Wyborcza* on June 21, 2021.

[24] Editorial team, (November 7, 2019). "Emmanuel Macron Warns Europe: NATO Is Becoming Brain-Dead". *The Economist*.

[25] A bringing up to date, a modernization, a change.

[26] Speech by the President of the Republic at the Ambassadors' Conference, August 27, 2018.

[27] Semo, M., (26 August 2019). "En plein G7, le chef de la diplomatie iranienne a effectué une visite surprise à Biarritz (Translation: In the Middle of the G7, the Head of Iranian Diplomacy Made a Surprise Visit to Biarritz)". *Le Monde*.

[28] Fassihi, F. & Gladstone, R. (Sept. 30, 2019). "How Iran's President Left Trump Hanging, and Macron in the Hall". *The New York Times*.

[29] Kaval, A. & Smolar, P., (December 21, 2019). "Nucléaire iranien: l'échec de la médiation française entre les Etats-Unis et l'Iran (Translation: Iranian Nuclear Program: the Failure of French Mediation between the United States and Iran)". *Le Monde*.

[30] Lasserre, I., (June 21, 2017). "Emmanuel Macron au *Figaro*: 'L'Europe n'est pas un supermarché' (Translation: Emmanuel Macron to Le Figaro: 'Europe is not a supermarket')". *Le Figaro*.

[31] Ibid.

[32] Article 42(7) of the Treaty on European Union.

[33] Herreros, R., (August 13, 2020). "Pourquoi Macron renforce la présence militaire de la France en Méditerranée (Translation: Why Macron is Strengthening France's Military Presence in the Mediterranean)". *Huffpost*.

[34] Press Conference by General De Gaulle, President of the Republic, Palais de l'Elysée (Paris), January 31, 1964.

[35] Editorial Team, (March 11, 2021). "Pour rattraper son retard, Macron pousse le business français en Arabie saoudite (Translation: To Catch Up, Macron Pushes French Business in Saudi Arabia)". *Challenges*.

[36] Verner, R., (July 16, 2017). "'Cher Bibi': Macron et Netanyahu affichent leur proximité (Translation: 'Dear Bibi': Macron and Netanyahu Show How Close They Are)". *BFMTV*.

[37] Editorial Team, (July 2, 2020). "La CEDH condamne la France pour les 'conditions d'existence inhumaines' de demandeurs d'asile (Translation: The European Court of Human Rights Condemns France for 'Inhumane Living Conditions' of Asylum Seekers)" *Le Monde and AFP*.

[38] Andreani, G., (June 21, 2017). "Macron et l'international: le sens d'une victoire (Translation: Macron and International Affairs: the Meaning of a Victory)". *Telos*.

[39] Leali, G., (June 7, 2021). "Foreign Investors (Slightly) Prefer France to UK, Study Finds". *Politico.eu*.

[40] Editorial Team, (Decembre 4, 2020). "Erdogan Expresses Hope that France Will 'Get Rid of Macron' as Soon as Possible". *France 24*.

Chapter 11

[1] Lhaïk, C., (September 22, 2017). "La voie étroite de Macron l'Européen (Translation: The Narrow Path of Macron the European)". *L'Express.fr*.

[2] Cautres, B., Chopin, T., Rivière, E, (2020). *Les Francais et l'Europe: entre defiance et ambivalence* (Translation: *The French and Europe: Between Defiance and Ambivalence*). Institut Jacques Delors, Report 119.

[3] The U.K. left the E.U. in 2021.

[4] Directorate-General for Communication, (2019), *Standard Eurobarometer 92*, European Commission.

[5] Debate between Emmanuel Macron and Marine Le Pen before the last round of the presidential election, May 3, 2017.

[6] The Great Debate with 10 candidates, French television, April 4, 2017.

[7] Kortunov, A., (February 18, 2016). "How Would You Call a Grown Up 'Political Dwarf'?". *Russian International Affairs Council website*.

[8] The Concert of Nations is a set of political beliefs that emerged in the nineteenth century at the Congress of Vienna but continue to be influential for international relations even up to the present day. It is used to describe international relations which are not based on war as the main tool.

[9] His memoirs, which inspired this text, were published in French by Fayard publisher in 1976, and in English by Doubleday in 1978.

[10] Veneziani, L., (May 5, 2018). "The Day of Europe". *Vocal Europe*,.

[11] Bossuat, G., (1997). *L'Europe des Francais, 1943-1959, La IVème République aux sources de l'Europe communautaire* (Translation: *The Europe of the French, 1943-1959, The Fourth Republic at the Source of the European Community*). Publications de la Sorbonne.

[12] Long Range Peace Objectives, Federal Council of the Churches of Christ , September 18, 1941.

[13] Directorate-General for Communication, (Winter 2020-2021). *Standard Eurobarometer 94, European Citizenship Survey.* European Commission.

[14] Editorial Team, (November 16, 2020). "La doctrine Macron: une conversation avec le Président français (Translation: The Macron Doctrine: a Conversation with the French President)". *Le Grand Continent.*

https://legrandcontinent.eu/fr/2020/11/16/macron/